SEX
STUPIDITY
AND
GREED

Copyright © 1997 by Ian Grey
ISBN: 0-9651042-7-3

Library of Congress Cataloging-in-Publication Data
A catalog record for this book is available from the Library of Congress

Bookstore Distribution
US: Consortium, 1045 Westgate Drive, St. Paul, MN 55114-1065, orders 1-800-283-3572, tel.
    612-221-9035, fax 612-221-0124;
UK & Europe: Airlift Book Co., 8 The Arena, Mollison Avenue, Enfield Middlesex, England
    EN3-7NJ, tel. 181-804-0400, fax 181-804-0044.

Non-Bookstore Distribution
Last Gasp, 777 Florida Street, San Francisco, CA 94110, tel. 415-864-6636, fax 415-824-1836

For a catalog, send SASE to: JUNO BOOKS, 180 Varick Street, 10th Floor, New York, NY
    10014;   tel.   212-807-7300,   fax   212-807-7355,   toll   free   1-800-758-5238,
    email junobook@interport.net. Or visit us online at www.junobooks.com.

Printed in Germany

10 9 8 7 6 5 4 3 2 1

SEX
STUPIDITY
AND
GREED

INSIDE THE
AMERICAN MOVIE INDUSTRY

BY IAN GREY

New York City

Acknowledgments

Special thanks to Kit Messick, my tireless researcher.

For ideas, info, graciously answering weird questions and speaking up:
Kim Bernstein, Paula Bernstein, Peter Bowen, Susan Brownmiller, Angela Cappetta, Elizabeth
    Cornell, Lisa Churgin, Irene Conneley, Franklin Davis, "Debbie", Roger Devine, Deborah
    Drier, "E", Harlan Ellison, John Fasano, Andy Fierberg, *Fangoria, Filmmaker Magazine,*
    Michael Gingold, Paula Guran, Dona Hall, Warren Hamilton, Dian Hanson, Bob Harris,
    Amy Hobby, Clint Howard, Andrew Johnston, "T.K.", Kim Kaufman, Marcia Kirkley, Jeff
    Kisseloff, Michael Lehmann, Ulli Lommel, Tim Lucas, Angus Macdonald, Karol Martesko,
    Victoria Maxwell, Scott McCauly, Terry McGerry, Dr. Robert McMullen, Terri Mabrey,
    Kristin Mirenda, "ND", Dr. Ruth Ochroch, Danelle Perry, Dan Persons, Julie Plec, John
    Scoleri, David J. Schow, Adrienne Shelley, David J. Skal, Some Guy at the Screen Actor's
    Guild, Jill Stempel, Leslie Sternbergh, Julie Strain, Anthony Timpone, Janet Tingey, "T",
    Ian Toll, Peter Trachtenberg, Gail Vachon, Christine Vachon, Mark Voelpel, Stacey Wacknov,
    John Waters, Sarah Maupin Wenk, *Wetbones,* Jeff Whittington and Sean Young.

Special Secret Thanks to various people at Miramax, New Line, MCA, Fox, and ICM who were
    kind enough to speak, so I won't list them.
Special Life Support Systems: Karen Backus, Belinda Gray
Continuity and Language Consultant: "The Laser"
Sanity Support Systems by Richard Holtz
Thanks to Erin Clermont and Jonathan Hayes for allowing me to use Echo's M/TV conference
    as a one-stop networking/emergency-info-query/idea-try-out-space, and to Stacy Horn
    for access.

Above and beyond the call of duty thanks to Andrea Juno.
Special Thanks to: Simone Katz, one incredibly cool, efficient and patient Managing Editor, and
    Jon Keith, without Whom...

Editor-in-Chief: Andrea Juno, Managing Editor: Simone Katz, Book Designer: Katharine Gates,
    Front Cover Designer: Kayley LeFaiver, Proofreader: Irene Connelly. Thanks to Susanna
    Deines, Stacey St. Onge, and special thanks to Ken Werner.

Table of Contents

INTRODUCTION

After I watched over a thousand movies in one year, I knew something was rotten.

I had this job as one of those invisible people who do capsule reviews for video guides. For a guy with an obsessive love of the movies, this was great—I was getting *paid* to see them.

Unfortunately, the movies I was getting paid to see were from the years 1994 and 1995, a period jam-packed with aspiring blockbusters like *Waterworld*, *Assassins*, *Blown Away* and (inconceivable as it may seem) worse.

I found that, in some diabolical way, the movies seemed to have interchangeable plot and character components; one stupid action movie was essentially the same as any number of other stupid action movies. I marvelled at the outright arrogance and contempt these movies exhibited toward their audiences; annoyed at the shameless pop song soundtracks played at maxed-out volume, and dizzied by the spastic, low-attention span camera techniques. And downright pissed off when products stopped being merely placed in the movies and became integral parts of the actors' on-screen dialogue! I routinely found myself leaving the multiplex in a rotten mood, with this dazed and confused expression on my face as I wondered, "What the hell was *that*?"

The job ended, but it was too late for me. I was disgusted. I knew that the majority of Hollywood movies—whatever the period—have always been awful, and that we just tend to glorify the few good ones. But the scores of films I'd just seen were different: they sucked with a *purpose*.

• • • • • • •

In my teens, I was a musician. I played in two rock groups which released major-label albums. (This was the early '80s, when huge corporations started to buy up both music and movie companies, thereby blurring the social lines between both.) As a struggling musician, I was granted wallflower status by the rich and famous and got invited to a lot of fancy Hollywood parties. Between nibbles from astronomically-priced buffets, I watched the depravity and hysteria bubbling up under the glitz.

When my band's record tanked, I got a new agent. She believed that *all* forms of entertainment would soon merge, and so she took me to even more parties, premieres and shifty after-hours joints. Finally, my career going nowhere, I tired of the desperation and vapidity of the music business in favor of the desperation and neurosis of the publishing business, and moved to New York (where I continued to work for a while in music, as a producer). Looking back at Hollywood from the safety of Manhattan, I was now able to sort out the various—dumb, sad, strange or sordid—events I endured.

But enough about me.

• • • • • • •

The people interviewed for this book have worked inside and outside the industry. Sometimes their connection with the movies may seem to be a stretch. So it's interesting how many of these disparate views converge, as when media critic Mark Crispin Miller and horror director Wes Craven independently say the same things about insidious new forms of information control. Or when B-movie sex goddess Julie Strain, culture critic David J. Skal, media-mauled actress Sean Young, and even my own shrink, Dr. Ruth Ochroch, reveal an inadvertent unity of vision regarding everything from surgical breast enhancement to media-influenced sexual politics. They create a chorus of accusation: the movies have gone wrong in some terrible way, and more importantly, they mirror what's going on around us.

• • • • • • •

Recently, I passed a multiplex. 14 screens. Seven were playing *Jurassic Park 2: The Lost World*, a movie crammed full of product tie-ins. The other seven were playing this month's explosion-porn feature, *Con-Air*. And this is in New York, supposedly Cultureville, USA, where there are only three theaters that show "independent films." It's ironic that, with the aid of new technology, it's cheaper and easier than ever to make films, but because of a lack of venues and distribution, there's nowhere to show them.

One of the reasons for that began back in the '80s, when the Reagan administration commenced its systematic obliteration of anti-trust laws, and steamrolled the feeding-frenzy of the merger and acquisition business. The process continued with the Telecommunications Act of 1994. This Congressional legislation was, in short, supposed to make mergers even easier, and also somehow revitalize competition. And yes, that sounds like a bunch of crap to me too.

Now, a small clutch of corporations that include Time Warner, Viacom, Sony, Disney/CapCities and newspaper magnate Rupert Murdoch's News Corporation, [see chart on pages 230-231] have absorbed and controlled—not unlike *The Blob*—everything you see on a multiplex screen, hear on non-college radio, rent at a video chain, or read in a national publication or major-city newspaper. Each constitutes a vast monopoly resulting in a tight "information loop." Whether manifested as a movie, a fashion article, or a piece on international policy, all information goes through the same corporate information processor for maximum, broad-based profit.

The loop starts with the major studios (what we don't see are the larger corporate owners and stockholders of these studios). It then extends downward to assorted agents. As well as securing work for their clients and keeping stalkers at bay, agents also make certain their clients do not interface with any aspect of media that is not pre-approved, whether tacitly or directly, by the studios/corporations. A caste of publicists, employed by the studios/corporations, close the loop. They are the masters of spin control, the cutting-edge art form at the close of the century. Between the corporations, studios, assorted agencies and publicists, a veritable "Wall" against inquiry is created.

When one of the interviewees in this book suddenly and mysteriously stops talking, it's the incredible, free-floating power of the "Wall" at work, resulting in a reality-based paranoia with an unspoken but well understood mantra, that one doesn't divulge negative inside information about the industry because one's career could end *just like that* if the wrong word is uttered.

The ultimate effect of corporate monopolization of information is that you get a system that is not only invested in the dumbing-down of movies, but of the entire culture. Anything that rises an inch above the mediocrity-line and exposes the usual crap to be just that, crap, is either sound-bited into moronic levels or, worse, not covered at all by the press. This hastens the atrophying of intelligent conversation about reported events and the mutation of news gathering into simply another forum for the fine art of spin doctoring.

In lemming-like fashion, we strive to emulate the advertisements the movies have become. We struggle to acquire the perfect bodies, computers, and other fine products of a media-invented "life." Inevitably, we find ourselves wanting. Meanwhile, "adult discourse" is systematically squelched in favor of "entertainment," which is considered sacrosanct, as well as being this country's second largest export (just behind military hardware). In this process of cultural erosion, the ability to examine, critique or even take an extended look at any part of real life is worn away by the steady profusion of mediated idiocy.

Not to be depressing or anything.

WATERWORLD

So it went like this.

Somebody got the idea that remaking *Mad Max* in a world that's become one huge ocean would make a neat movie.

Quickly, it was ascertained that in order for the movie to be a megahit, a megastar was needed. So it was decided that Kevin Costner, cold on the heels of not one (*Wyatt Earp*), but two (*Robin Hood*) stratospherically budgeted flops, would be the ideal star in this tale of a maverick sailor with webbed hands and gills who drinks his own urine (this *is* the future).

The script (still under construction) set most of the action on two sets: a huge retrofitted City-on-the-Sea and an equally immense Slave's Quarters (to be filled with hundreds of slaves, or rather, actors). At the behest of actor (and now producer) Costner, an army of filmdom's finest art directors, special effects people, and architectural designers spent about six expensive months on the massive designing task. Finally, sets were constructed in Hawaii's Kawaihae Harbor, ignoring the location's infamous reputation for, as a *Waterworld* diving consultant put it in *GQ Magazine* (August 1995), local winds which "blow like the Devil's ass." And he wasn't even mentioning the area's tendency of being periodically demolished by raging tsunamis.

Still, the finished sets were indeed grand things, complete with docks, livable "apartments," various cranes, lifts, giant spearguns and rivets galore.

Shooting was about to begin, when, one fateful night, the production ignored tsunami warnings blaring from sirens everywhere.

The next morning, it was discovered that the Slave Quarters set, down to the last rivet, had sunk twenty thousand leagues under the sea (or more accurately, 160 feet).

See, the set was made of steel.

So what we have here is literally hundreds of techs, stars and executives acting in either some weird conspiratorial economic plot or else the biggest imaginable act of combined denial and stupidity against a rather well-known fact: If one puts a very heavy piece of *anything* (in this case something largely made of *steel*, and weighing nearly 1,000 tons) in a body of water, there is a really good chance it will, well, sink.

And so it did.

Brain-dead they may have been, but this setback was stoically accepted and the Slave City was raised from the briny depths at a cost of about half a million dollars. It was also never used again for filming. According to reports, the film's producers seriously discussed re-sinking the Slave Quarters and the City-on-the-Sea sets when filming was done. This was nixed at the last moment when someone noted that the set's toxic paints would kill every sea-dwelling creature in the bay.

Despite the multimillions spent here, the final film is a truly horrid thing to behold. Even Costner's gills look cheap and fake. Rumor has it that he *did* produce and ingest his own urine, while providing in the process a fine metaphor for the eccentric, but not especially smart, star's ego. Or maybe there was some Hindu reference we missed.

But back to those sinking Slave Quarters: Its mindless construction is a starting point for an examination of a Hollywood that, in this case, has lost all touch (literally) with reality.

Leaving out for a minute the possibility that some Wall Street tycoon urged this on because he *knew* the thing would sink, and so shorted all his shares in US Steel (far-fetched, but what *isn't* in this story?), or that the film was designed, for obscure reasons, to dump a Third World country's GNP, we are still faced with some pungent realities, or rather, their wholesale denial.

Waterworld's magnificent gaffe provides one of the more amazing pre-millennial acts of a culture and economy at the end of its wits: A world so dazzled and dazed with information overload and last-ditch greed that one could easily present it as a harbinger for a spectacular decline.

To wit: If the exporters of this nation's second biggest commodity (entertainment) can't suss out that really big steel cities do not float, or worse, if they don't give a fuck as long as they turn some quick greenbacks, then we're all in trouble.

Waterworld vs. Real World

Waterworld Budget:

(*Variety* 3/25/96)

Production:	$172 million
Advertising:	$ 60 million
Prints:	$ 6 million
	TOTAL: $238 million

Other Annual Budgets:

U.S.A. Cities:

Little Rock, Arkansas	$96.9 million
Kennebunkport, Maine	$6.9 million
Fargo, North Dakota	$25.9 million

Other Countries:

Grenada	$126.7 million
Falkland Islands	$28.5 million
Equatorial Guinea	$35.9 million
Tonga	$86.0 million

OSCAR NIGHT, 1981

Had my original plans worked out, I'd now be having pleasant memories of a fine evening spent with my agent Diane and her friend Britt. Over steak and wine, I would perhaps have asked Ms. Ekland about her experiences with, say, director William Friedkin (as she had once starred in Friedkin's *The Night They Raided Minsky's*).

What actually happens is another story.

After opening for British techno-popsters Ultravox at the Whiskey, I retire to my dingy dressing room, mulling over the show's various failures. Like any sleazy rock club, the place is hot in a gamy sort of way. After struggling with the dressing room door, which tends to freeze on ancient hinges before suddenly snapping shut with repressed inertial force, I make my way to the bathroom (to get cleaned up for the meet with Diane and her old pal, the still luminous Ms. Ekland). I walk right into a shuffling male with his hair cut into what looks like a fourteenth-century monk's tonsure, his body obscured by a thick fur coat that seems of some obscure Eskimo design. He does not sweat.

"Excuse me, excuse me," Peter Gabriel says.

"Sure."

Mr. Gabriel shuffles on.

Back to the dressing room, and after a brief confrontation with the querulous door, I'm suddenly surrounded by the members of Queen (in town to promote the soundtrack of *Flash Gordon*, which they had just scored). Their sexually ambiguous lead singer, Freddie Mercury, is noticeable by his absence.

The three Brit rockers are very polite, and chat with my agent Diane, saying she looks good, which is true (Diane just turned fifty). Queen guitarist

Brian May engages me in a conversation about the use of exotic guitar picks, while I keep an eye out for the glamorous Ms. Ekland. "I quite fancy a six pence instead of your usual pick, but in the States, there's only quarters," May opines. "But your quarters—no offense—they lack a certain resonance."

Diane disappears and reappears in a snap, now armed with a Cheshire grin. "Britt's here, she's shy. Don't fuck up. Be polite, she's my friend."

At that very moment, there's a delicate knock at the door. A roadie scuttles over, swings the heavy metal door open, and there, bathed in gritty half-light, is Ms. Ekland.

She looks as if she's dressed for a premiere instead of drinks at some okay bistro: sleek bolero jacket, very short Carnaby mini (well, it looks mod to me), glowing Nordic complexion. Old style movie star glamour. She reaches out a delicate hand, smiles gingerly. "Hello, hello. I'm Britt; you must be—"

But I'm already on my feet, trying to make my mouth form the word *"No!"*

I'm too late. Simultaneously, Britt's eyes widen in confusion and the door loses its precarious balance. It makes an ominous creak, Britt tries to move, face filled with sudden horror, but she's frozen. Everyone watches as the door suddenly springs shut, battering Ms. Ekland directly in the face and catapulting her backwards. Despondent, I listen as she lets out a yelp and tumbles down some stairs.

Diane, horror-stricken, shouts: "Damn! Wait here. I'm sure she's devastated."

I want to help, but apparently my efforts would only redouble Ms. Ekland's mortification at such an inelegant exit. The door opens, and there's Peter Gabriel again. He excuses himself and leaves, still not sweating. An ICM lackey, Rob Kahane (an obsequious social-climber) appears and, as a matter of course, starts gushing in slurred Hollywood-speak about how *fabulous* I am. Unable to look beyond his meticulously manicured beard and his nose, powdered ever-so-decadently with forgotten blow, I manage to control myself and not slug him on general principles (Mr. Kahane now manages Madonna).

Wolfgang Puck is beaming. "So you see, zees is the new pizza."

"Marvelous!" enthuses Diane.

We've left the Whiskey and are now sitting in a new West Hollywood eatery called Spago, presided over by chef Wolfgang Puck, a nice guy in meticulous chef's whites. Diane and I are alone at our table, as Britt, suffering no serious injuries from her fall except perhaps to her pride, gracefully declined to come with us.

Mr. Puck explains about something called *nouvelle cuisine* to me and Diane in charmingly halting English. On my plate is a small triangle of pizza surrounded by a lot of plate. The restaurant itself is nice, sort of art gallery–white with matching bad art. We're there for the Oscar party, which Diane thought would be a swell place to meet people who could kick-start my musical career into overdrive.

"Donald Sutherland is coming," Diane announces, sipping at a Rammaloosa. As a musician in the early '80s, still riding the nihilistic power crest of punk, it escapes me what a chat with a tall, Canadian ex-anti-establishment icon such as Sutherland could do for my career (such as it was). "Get that look off your face," Diane says. "Donald is sweet. Everybody likes him. And you never know who everybody may turn out to be."

I nod, being young and at the mercy of Diane's rolling upper-class Brit accent which always makes everything sound reasonable. Mr. Puck bends over and whispers in my ear, "The mushroom ees, of course, best." A swarthy Eurotrash sort of guy named Marcel appears and sits with us. After exchanging non-English pleasantries with Diane, he admits in mischievous tones that he's just in from Haiti.

"The boys, Diane! *C'est magnifique!*"

"Oh, Marcel, you are *irrepressible!*"

"Well, a man must follow his muse." He glances Ian-wards. "And this is your new talent?"

Later, I learn that Haiti possesses some sort of carnal status symbol value because of the easy access of its famously attractive indigenous boys. It's a somewhat exotic correlation, I guess, to straight males procuring possible trophy wives from the endless starlet pool. Marcel, like many of the Europeans Diane intro's me to, seems to do nothing, professionally.

Marcel confides that, until the Oscar show starts in earnest, this will be a pretty dull place. "But Ian Copeland (manager of the Police and owner of IRS Records and Filmworks) has just bought a mansion in the hills! The party—it is exclusive, ah, but not for *Diane*—" a smile to me—"or, of course, Diane's clients."

And so with that we say goodnight to Marcel.

At the door, we run into another of Diane's clients, the very pretty Colleen Camp (wearing a classy Audrey Hepburn–like crinoline number), who has just starred in Peter Bogdanovich's *They All Laughed*. Colleen, a fine actress, tolerates an odd sort of fame arising from her cameo in *Apocalypse Now*, wherein she played one of three strippers airlifted into 'Nam. (Ms. Camp would later be typecast into playing a sort of EveryMom in features like *Wayne's World*).

Colleen seems quite agitated, and pulls Diane off for a quick conference. When they're done, Colleen is crying, and runs to the bathroom.

I ask "What?" (I knew she was having a torrid affair with some famed, but somewhat screw-loose, actor.)

Diane answers, "Pacino. He's rented a single room in Hell's Kitchen for a film. He hasn't left his room for months."

"Why?"

"It's a long story. Some Beckett sort of thing. Actors, eh?"

At Ian Copeland's new mansion, Dom De Luise has managed to entangle himself in the ornate Victorian grillwork of the gate, creating a sort of impromptu self-crucifixion pose while sobbing all over his tuxedo.

Soon he is crying into Diane's shoulders. After a time, he cheers up, tells a couple of ribald jokes, and de-crucifies himself. We then wander off to the party proper, which is taking place on the mansion's vast lawn (complete with Hawaiian Tiki decor). We pass a bush in which two people are coupling halfheartedly.

"Poor Dom," Diane says after Dom goes for a drink decorated with multiple plastic monkeys. I'd like to ask what was wrong with De Luise, but decide it wise to just let it pass. We walk by groups of men in suits (execs) and starlets in tans, none of which seem to notice our existence.

Later, after a brief chat with Ian Copeland, (who wore multiple scarves, talked annoyingly fast, and was, I thought, a total dickhead) we leave. In the car,

Diane says, "You should have been nicer to Ian, Ian. He's starting a film division soon."

"He's a dickhead."

"That's your problem," Diane replies rather portentously.

At the sight of a red-haired thin man, Diane corners me, saying "This is Mr._____." He's a real record executive, currently producing a Bette Midler album, and apparently in dire need of songs. For once I feel I have reason to be where I am.

We sit in a secluded area with Mr._____. He admits the Midler album is in trouble, what with her wanting to do "the hard rock thing." Beneath the wood table, Diane gives me a discreet kick.

"What sort of hard rock?" I ask.

"Well, there's the problem; Bette really isn't that good a hard rock singer. We've recorded more than two hundred songs, but still, I don't know."

I'm stunned. Recording two hundred songs at the going rate would bring the record to at least half a million dollars.

I ask which of the two hundred songs they are going to use.

"Well, to be honest"— Mr._____ shifts uncomfortably—"none of them."

Mouth agape, I say, "You recorded *two hundred* songs and not one—"

Diane's more forceful kick silences me.

"Well, tonight she's working on a Stones tune, 'Beast of Burden.'"

I try to imagine the impressive stupidity of people who, after two hundred tries, decide that having a superior Borscht Belt piano lounge singer/comedian cover "Beast of Burden" would be some sort of artistic answer. I say as much without much finesse. Mr._____ glares at me.

Near Doheny, another party, some weird apartment. Looks like a leftover set from *The Lady From Shanghai*, all faux-Asian appointments. Village People on the stereo. A frightening-looking man in battle fatigues waves a bottle of Benedictine, hurling an invective of gibberish at a young girl trying to look unfazed. A few feet away is an exotic-looking and highly animated Latina with four strapping consorts in tow. Because of their garish attire (pimp-esque suits for the men, an anatomically revealing slip-thing for the woman) I mistake all of them for high-priced hired sexual help. The Latina, I'll later be told, is Maria Conchita Alonso, who is starring in a film with Robin Williams. The four consorts will remain mysterious and speak no English. I'm intro'ed by some actor-friend of Diane's to a distinguished-looking fellow, British director Peter Medak. I'm thrilled, as Medak's *The Ruling Class* is one of my all-time favorite films.

Determined not to continue in the spirit of the Midler fiasco, I tell him right off that I loved *The Ruling Class*. He thanks me, but then says it tanked at the box office. Looking grim, he adds that he's working on a horror film now (*The Changeling*) as though it's all over for him as far as quality cinema is concerned (a sentiment echoed by the film biz at the time).

Being a big horror fan myself, I innocently worsen things by enthusing, "Hey, that's great, Peter!"

"It's all the work I can get," he says with defeat, then with a slight smile. "Thanks about *The Ruling Class*, though."

On the way to the bathroom I spot Britt Ekland, who smiles forgivingly at me (but keeps her distance). Then I encounter Samantha Eggar, whose work I found very impressive.

In *The Collector*, Ms. Eggar plays a plucky and pretty Brit who fights against a loony Terrence Stamp who is imprisoning her for sexually suspect reasons. In David Cronenberg's *The Brood*, Ms. Eggar plays an insane mother whose pathological anger causes her to give birth to mutant "children of rage," and who spends a lot of time eating the placenta off her gruesome spawn. I had seen that film at least three times, impressed by its startling juxtaposition of hardcore gore and quiet thoughtfulness.

I gush my (sincere) appreciation about her work in that film.

I notice Ms. Eggar's shocking appearance; just ten years ago a spirited ingenue, she now looks like all that fine English breeding is barely hanging from bones exhausted by God knows what, her face layered with peeling foundation. Ms. Eggar proves quite polite and pleasant, but on mention of *The Brood,* her eyes light with what I swear is madness as she literally *screams,* "That fucking film! *Disgusting! I hated it!* Just the *memory* of it makes me sick,

I tell you, sick!"

After excusing herself. Diane returns with some nascent screenwriter in tow. "So how are we doing, eh?"

Back at Spago. It's a fuckin' madhouse.

I immediately discern a sort of hierarchy: at the top, seated in the best seats overlooking the glitter of the nighttime LA cityscape, are studio execs in conservative garb, and their glittery concubines. Mainly they keep to themselves, buffeted from the hoi polloi by some unseen power.

Noticeably down in the food chain, and sitting in markedly less fabulous locations, are the evening's favored stars. I think I can see Ben Cross, male lead of the favored *Chariots of Fire* chatting with Wolfgang (no doubt about small pizzas). The room is redolent of rampant celebrity, equal parts calculated sex appeal and type-A careerist musk. Faces and names blur, while everyone is dressed in either Oscar Chic (Bob Mackie or faux Mackie for the less famous) or going for the Steve Spielberg-Casual look (ratty jeans, t-shirt, baseball cap). The females tend towards frosted blond hair, eerily perma-tanned skin and the aforementioned sequined dresses that will probably rate a mention tomorrow in Mr. Blackwell's "Worst Dressed" column. Various up-and-comers hold up the small, cramped bar, eyes beady with designs and too much cut cocaine. At this point, I just want badly to go see Sparks, a favorite band of mine, who are doing a special gig somewhere up the street.

(Sparks were a quirky band whose trademarks were hyperactive, cabaret style melodies sung by what sounded like anxious castrati against styles that ranged from hard rock to electro-disco. After years of floundering in the US, they achieved a great deal of fame in England and were considered an important influence on such wide-ranging bands as Depeche Mode, Siouxsie & The Banshees, Oasis and Jello Biafra.)

Coming from somewhere in the vicinity of the bathroom, I hear a terrible screeching noise, apparently the result of human lungs. Curious, I get up to see what the unholy caterwauling is about, and am promptly collared by some overdressed fellow whom Diane had earlier told me had "a project."

"It's Goldie," whispers the Man With A Project with a hateful sort of glee. "She's trashed. She wants more blow, but someone won't let her into the bathroom."

The terrible yelling continues, now accompanied by frenzied pounding. I disengage myself from the Project Guy, and return to my seat just in time to see the approach of a very tall man, swathed in Armani, his hair blow-dried to creepy perfection, the inevitable mustache obscuring the upper member of a pair of thick lips. In a questionable Teutonic accent, he says, "Diane! You look lovely! May I join you?"

He imperiously takes a chair and leans back as though the world is his garden party. He turns out to be Giorgio Moroder, composer of *Midnight Express*'s Oscar-winning score, producer of synth-driven techno hits with Donna Summer, Blondie and currently lining something up with David Bowie. He oozes testosterone, money and attitude.

Suddenly and without warning, Giorgio's head swivels mechanically and I am caught, in deer-in-headlights fashion, by his distressingly macho gaze. "So! Diane has told me all about you." He chuckles at this. I glance at Diane, who looks pleased. Trying to be pleasant, and seeing here a subject on which we might be simpatico, I say, "So I hear you're producing Sparks."

Giorgio smiles, orders some complex drink from a terrified-looking waitress—her first night, I guess. There's some hubbub as a person, a dead ringer for Veronica Lake, right down to the peek-a-boo blond hair and snappy blue-sequined wrap, makes a grand entrance.

Diane laughs affectionately. "I understand that's Tommy Lasorda's son."

"Lasorda as in the Dodgers' manager?"

Diane regales me and Giorgio with tales of the chubby baseball manager's efforts to distance himself from his flamboyant offspring. Then Giorgio's head does that swivel thing again. "Sparks, you say?" Another insinuating smile, showing rows and rows of perfect, and vaguely feral-looking, teeth.

"Um, yeah. I'd heard you were going to produce them."

"*Produce* them?"

He laughs. A big, swallowing sort of laugh. "*Produce* them? You must be joking! I don't *produce* anyone—I *own* them!"

Diane titters nervously. I wish Donald Sutherland would fucking show up.

After all this, I did make it to the Sparks show. They were really cool, and, more important, *real*. Real guitars, real loud. If Giorgio did own them, he was rather blasé with his product, as I did not see him there.

Later that evening, and back at Spago. Donald Sutherland finally does show up. He's very nice, and asks me if anything's wrong. We have a nice talk, nothing about movies.

Chariots of Fire wins best picture. I hadn't liked the film that much, but mine is obviously the minority opinion as almost hysterical applause breaks out in the packed restaurant. Wolfgang, beaming his high-wattage smile, unveils a special pizza to commemorate the event.

POSTSCRIPT:

Britt Ekland: In 1981, Ms. Ekland was working on the hilariously campy Jacqueline Susann's *Valley of the Dolls* (1981). Sadly, her career quickly skidded downhill, as advancing age (in Hollywood terms) had her showing up in really awful genre and "erotic" films such as *Love Scenes* (1984), *Fraternity Vacation* (1985) and *Beverly Hills Vamp* (1988).

William Friedkin: After directing Ms. Ekland in *The Night They Raided Minsky's* (1968), Friedkin scored with *The French Connection* (1971) and *The Exorcist* (1973). A gifted director, Friedkin has since been relegated to work-for-hire crap shoots such as *Blue Chips* (1994) and *Jade* (1995). He tried to recapture his *Exorcist* clout with the supernatural *The Guardian* (1988), but it was a no-go. He makes a nice living, though.

Peter Gabriel: Traumatized by his extended affair with the somewhat unusual Rosanna Arquette (*Crash*, *Desperately Seeking Susan*), singer/musician Gabriel recorded his seventh solo album, *Us*, featuring the hit "Digging in the Dirt." As of this writing, Gabriel has added music to the white-guy-out-of-water comedy, *Jungle 2 Jungle* (1996).

Nouvelle cuisine: In a rare example of things getting better, people started noticing that there wasn't much cuisine in this nouvelle style of cooking. More belly-filling food modes such as Cajun and Northern Italian cooking are currently in vogue.

Cocaine: After somebody figured that cutting and compressing it with baking soda turned mere cocaine into crack, and after crack became the drug of choice in the ghetto, cocaine became passé. Also, the late '80s recovery phase made admitting to drug use out, and having babies in.

Undaunted, an entire new generation of idiots have now embraced the far more dangerous heroin as the drug of chic choice. This was championed for the first time in the movies via Quentin Tarantino's glamorous portrayal of said narcotic in *Pulp Fiction*.

AIDS: AIDS was first recognized as being an independent disease in 1981, when members of the gay community, needle-sharing addicts and Haitians came down with deadly, unexplained symptoms.

Marcel: Died of complications from AIDS in 1989.

Queen and Freddie Mercury: Queen, as of this writing, has released one last record featuring their signature heavy metal-kitsch style since the sad demise of lead singer/writer Freddie Mercury, dead of AIDS at age 45, on November 24, 1991.

Wolfgang Puck: Still runs Spago, sells his recipes on the Web, and has a line of frozen pizzas available at a supermarket near you.

Donald Sutherland: Still a nice guy. Sutherland continues to work steadily, mainly as a character actor, and has now appeared in over 40 theatrical films.

Dom De Luise: Like many a '70s icon, De Luise has seen hard times of late, appearing mainly in low-budget films of every stripe, doing quickies in Europe, and in general, making a living. Currently, he's perhaps best known for his voice, heard to amusing effect in *An American Tail* (1986) and *All Dogs Go to Heaven* (1989).

Giorgio Moroder: After peaking with his obnoxious score for the obnoxious *Top Gun* (1986), Mr. Moroder seems, from all appearances, to have exited the film scene.

Mr._____: After his dog days dealing with Bette, Mr._____ has ascended to the highest realms of the recording industry. With all of my name-dropping in this book, this is the one person I'm too afraid of to use his real name.

Peter Medak: Years of toiling as a journeyman TV and film director in the '80s paid off when the immensely talented Medak hit his stride with smart crime thrillers such as *The Krays* (1990) and *Romeo Is Bleeding* (1993).

Samantha Eggar: I didn't know it at the time, but one reason for Ms. Eggar's frayed spirits when I met her may have been her career. She had already appeared in *Demonoid* (1981), an awful Mexican horror film which featured dialogue such as, "Cut off my hand or I'll kill you!" Sadly, this would be followed by more grade-

Z screen fodder. A comeback was hoped for in the big-budgeted *Batman* knock-off, *The Phantom* (1995). Unfortunately for the talented Ms. Eggar, the film tanked at the box office.

Diane: In a fit of sanity, Diane left the film business entirely, and lives in a former monastery in Australia. She is very happy now.

Dave and Raquel and Tahnee and Wonderbra™

An interesting bit of dysfunctional theater, sexual innuendo and general meta-familial weirdness was performed live on the stages of *Late Night with David Letterman* on July 19, 1985.

The occasion was the ritualistic plugging of a new film by one of its main participants. In this case, the film in question was the gratingly perky, aliens-love-us film *Cocoon* (1985), the plugee Tahnee Welch, daughter of Raquel, and, of course, the mediator at the electronic altar, Dave (and isn't it funny the way we're on a first-name-familiar basis with our late-night surrogate-somethings).

Anyway, in the film to be plugged, Ms. Welch plays a comely alien who, for reasons that place the film firmly in the science fiction genre, falls in love with Steve Guttenberg. As ritual has it, her only job with Dave was to say how swell the film was, how the cast and crew had become a family positively full of mutual adoration, and then view a film clip and maybe offer an amusing tale or two.

What we got was an obviously uncomfortable, although fetching, Tahnee, who showed a remarkable disdain for the entire ceremony, causing Dave to shift uncomfortably, and not just because of Tahnee's breaking of TV film-plug tradition. In comparison, things would get even odder when mother Raquel (*Kansas City Bomber*), came on the show in low-cut leotards to chide her uppity offspring.

But we get ahead of ourselves.

First, Dave tries to break the ice with:

Dave: You all right? Not nervous?

Tahnee: Yes.

Dave: Why do you think you're nervous?

Tahnee: Because of you.

Tahnee then relates a dream about herself and Dave that she had the prior evening, something about driving around, that ended with Tahnee getting a headache. The audience roars with taboo carnal joviality, while Dave shifts uncomfortably in the frank young female's presence, finally saying:

Dave: People have dreams like that all the time—

Tahnee: With *you* in them?
            (More titters from the audience.)

Getting himself on firmer, less sexually agitated grounds, Dave retreats to the safety of the plug for her new film.

Dave: Is this your first film?

Tahnee: No.

Dave: Your first feature film?

Tahnee: No.

The star offspring refuses to bite. Dave says this is a big film, it's directed by *Ron Howard*. The ritual is going to shit and Dave knows it. Tahnee looks, more than anything, like a hip high-schooler whose dumb Dad keeps showing her report card to strangers.

Note: Before all this, Dave derided Raquel for not being on the show, calling her a "deadbeat." Tahnee shrugged.

But back to Tahnee and *Cocoon:* Avoiding an appraisal of the film's merits, she instead reveals to Dave that dolphins (used extensively in *Cocoon*) tend to "get horny" around cast members, that "you can see it when they jump out of the water—"

Dave: Ha. Yeah.
             (Audience cracks up)

Then, finally, after some hard pressing from Dave, we get Tahnee's assessment of *Cocoon*, admitting that "well, ah, *some* people like it," and basically imparting that it was, in her young opinion, like, really stupid.

For a millisecond, silence breaks out on the set of *Late Night with David Letterman* and, one assumes, across America, as the ritual of the plug bit the dirt courtesy of this insouciant young female. I'd like to note that this bit of *verité* melodrama, however tatty and sordid, was real, live and unmediated stuff. For a moment, through corporate oversight, we were allowed to peek behind the facades of all concerned to see the not-so-pretty humans beneath.

Trying to save the day, Dave utters some of his patented smirky half-sentences, raises his eyebrows, and mugs for the camera in a manner suggesting a paucity of future *Letterman* appearances for Ms. Welch. Tahnee giggles, shrugs, and then lapses into what would now be termed a "slackeresque" repose of extreme disinterest.

As the show breaks up for a merciful commercial, a technician slips up, allowing us a momentary view of the elder Dave and the teen Tahnee caught on the set looking like tourists from warring countries.

A year later, the "deadbeat" Raquel finally *does* show up, her face made to appear a few years younger than her daughter's, a spicy outfit painted on, while flirting like crazy with Dave and plugging her new exercise book. No sooner has the applause died, then the two older folks embark on a vigorous appraisal of daughter Tahnee's appearance (a *year* earlier, as we noted). After admitting that Tahnee was indeed pretty and smart, Raquel makes vague reference to the problems inherent in mother-daughter relationships.

Dave: Do you have a kind of ongoing thing that irritates you that she does?

Raquel: No—actually, nothing in *particular* that she does…it's just that as a
             mother, you tell 'em things you know that'll help, and they don't lis-
             ten to you.

After this, Mom proceeds to:

1) Show photos from her exercise book of herself in a revealing body stocking doing various "splits." The camera moves in on an assortment of gymnastic crotch shots. The audience goes wild, while Dave offers wisecracking support.

2) Talk about her upcoming stint in Atlantic City.

3) Flirt some more with Dave.

4) Boast of her ability to do Elvis impressions.

After some more good-natured jesting, the two part company. Raquel shows up on the show in 1993 wearing yet another outfit not unlike those worn by Miss Kitty on *Gunsmoke*, and plugs her latest ventures. Dave's fondness of Ms. Welch is quite obvious, as he repeatedly sneaks glances at her hourglass perma-body, his mien devolving to that of a hormone-addled teen. References are made by Letterman about the two of them "getting married," and being—a glance at Welch's upper body—"a good pair." The audience loves it, firmly in Dave's implication-heavy, libidinous thrall. Raquel makes glancing reference to her lovely, lovely children.

POSTSCRIPT:

The elder Welch went on to star that same year in *Tainted Blood*, playing a writer doing research on children who inherit homicidal tendencies from their parents.

Tahnee has recently been seen playing Viva in *I Shot Andy Warhol*.

Dave is, of course, a national institution.

While compiling interviews for this book, I ran a gauntlet of management, public relations flacks, personal handlers and twitchy assistants that made my job seem like *The Sweet Smell of Success* as penned by Franz Kafka. I encountered an almost palpable sense of bubbling-under paranoia while talking to people in most every strata of mainstream and "indie" film that went far beyond mere fears of unemployment. I mean, Hollywood has always been a tiny town that plays it close to the vest, but this free-floating anxiety was, in a word, *weird*.

Still, some celebrities *would* talk, although almost all would, at some juncture, ask me very politely not to quote them when anything of interest was uttered. Often I was advised that my entire career could be obliterated just like *that* were I to reveal even the teensiest morsel of select inside-movie info.

I mean, jeez.

I also learned that fascinating spectacles such the Dave-Tahnee imbroglio are mainly a thing of the past. Sexual hijinks like those seen on *Letterman* are one thing (the impromptu Drew Barrymore striptease comes to mind), and can be seen taken to full dehumanizing effect on *Geraldo* any day.

But Tahnee Welch committed the one unpardonable sin of post-corporate Hollywood: *She dissed the Product* (in this case, *Cocoon*).

Lip service is still paid to "star power," but with market research and focus groups run by megacorporations for better control of the markets they create, "stardom" is a thing often subject to corporate interpretations of public whims, and, in general, nothing to bank on (consider the up-and-down careers of Linda Hamilton, David Caruso, Mickey Rourke or, for that matter, Raquel Welch). The person bestowed with fame is but a small cog integrated into the movie machine, a replaceable, and by nature not very long-lived cog at that. I myself had an illuminating, if rather humiliating, experience with information and the movie machine while doing one interview for this book.

I had managed to secure an interview with an MTV Networks production executive who had also been a PR person for such artists as Michael Jackson, Whitney Houston, Jonathan Demme, Barbara Streisand and U2. Excited that I'd finally found someone near the top of the (mis)information pyramid, I conducted the interview for juicy scoops and gossip.

This person requested anonymity. I was anxiously anticipating being thrilled, mainly because it was coming from a genuine Person in the Know.

Things started out well:

IG: When you have a company like MTV that's owned by a company that owns magazines and other media outlets, well, it's kinda incestuous.

A: It *is* incestuous. But now the new word for it is "synergy." [chuckles ironically] Twenty years ago, the whole thing that's going on with Viacom [the fact that Viacom owns MTV Networks, Paramount and Blockbuster] would be called "conflict of interest."

But then "conflict of interest" turned into "cross-collateralization," and now it's being spun as "synergy." So Viacom owns Paramount Pictures which produces *Entertainment Tonight*. So obviously, any Paramount pictures are going to get a lot of "presence" on *Entertainment Tonight*. *ET* will be the show that'll get the "exclusive" behind-the-scenes stuff. You have all these department heads all basically reporting to the same head honcho, and the order just trickles down from above: "*ET will like this Paramount picture!*"

[Sounding authentically disgusted] There's no place for *smallness* anymore [in movies]. Everything has to be *grand*. It's *insane* greed.

So many companies have vested interests in entertainment now and there's so much stuff [in the programming] that *doesn't belong* there. Sometimes I think maybe it's their purpose to keep you confused, in a state of *perpetual dissonance*.

IG: And there's never been an FCC antitrust action—I mean, this *is* a monopoly kind of thing—

A: Nope! Never. My guess is there hasn't been antitrust litigation because people don't complain.

As far as any salacious tidbits of gossip it was pretty much downhill from there: I was then told the same rumors about various stars' sexual preferences that I'm sure the reader has heard ad nauseam. I was told that Barbara Streisand was a "control freak," that Liza Minelli was sweet but kinda fucked up, that Dean Martin drank heavily and that Michael Jackson had had sex with a child and was probably a homosexual of some sort.

To say the least, none of this was exactly banner news. But this was, after all, a professional PR person doing their job and in retrospect, what Anonymous said about the industry was revealing. The fact that I craved gossip so eagerly was humbling, showing that, no matter how cynical at heart one can be, deep inside is an *Entertainment Tonight* viewer waiting to get out.

• • • • • • •

Still, if only as an accidental side effect of my efforts, I *did* experience some bracing encounters with authentically strange celebrity.

In response to a query for an interview with the once-fabulous Karen Black, I received an oddly-worded e-mail from some Unknown Party asking me what I was up to anyway (leaking state secrets, I was tempted to reply). I then got a call from a representative of Ms. Black's for further non-e-mail interrogation, which I politely declined.

Finally, after I'd thought the trail had gone cold, Ms. Black called me and demanded, in a breathless voice, to know what I wanted with her. An interview, I said. Then she started talking about documentaries, Francis Ford Coppola's wife, and her confusion about where she was supposed to be at various times that week. At one particularly fascinating juncture, Ms. Black demanded I divulge my age (the dark side of my 30s at the time). Confused, I relayed this information, resulting in Ms. Black uttering a cryptic, "Hmmm well. Okay."

Whatever. And to be fair to Ms. Black, her reaction to the idea of a book published outside (and not controlled by) the *Entertainment Weekly*/Lee Solters Agency/Viacom loop was no less off-the-wall than those of other talent I spoke with.

Via her agent, I "spoke" with Linda Blair. After about six phone calls and three letters—most of which were concerned with explaining the seemingly outrageous idea of writing a book on Hollywood for an independent publisher—I was finally informed that Ms. Blair was adamant I focus my piece with her on the mistreatment of cats and dogs on Earth. A fine cause, but apparently not one for which I evinced enough fervor, as I was finally turned down.

Another star whose light had dimmed somewhat, a male this time, responded to me via his wife, who managed his affairs. I was inches from convincing her to get her husband to commit to an interview when, in the middle of a pleasant chat, and apropos of absolutely nothing, she simply began screaming incomprehensible stuff at me. And I'm a polite sort of person.

Celebrity today is not only strange, it's become downright scary: most of all to those who are famous, or are in anyway connected with celebrity (one inside source was almost fired from their job at a major agency for e-mailing me the names of two major stars *represented* by the agency—this information is a matter of public record). With all this, I began to understand this ambient anxiety: When the company that reports the news is often owned by the company who makes the films which are cast and represented by a scant few agencies who are snugly under the covers with *all* of the above, one must be almost pathologically circumspect.

A digression:

I had occasion to visit a Wonderbra™ runway show (don't ask). In an atmosphere of corporate self-congratulation and hubris gone surreal via the strutting of fifty nearly nude Wonderbra™-ettes striding down a runway surrounded by hundreds of stuffed shirts trying to look blasé, I managed, with effort, to look past the flesh and see the Real Business here.

We were all given a glitzy promotional bag, largish in size and colored a vibrant yellow and sleek black. Stuffed with fluffy wads of what looked like excited yellow toilet paper, the bag seemed bursting with the promise of fabulous gifts. Upon opening it, I found it was instead filled with advertisements for the full Wonderbra™ line. (Oh, there was a little Wonderbra™ hat. Didn't fit.)

Otherwise, the bag was empty. Talk about easy-access metaphors.

Anyway, the ad copy waxed rhapsodic about the bras on runway display with evocative names such as "Matte About You,"™ "Racer-Back Lift"™, "Lace Innocence"™ and "Boy Leg Brief"™. Furthermore, the copy touted the archetype of the Wonderbra™ Woman: a free-spirited person whose open arms signify that she has "just broken all her (ex's) records," (*records?*) and that despite this breakup, she "isn't exactly mourning," a state of being, one supposes, best enacted by wearing a Wonderbra™.

So perpetual dissonance invades the lingerie biz—okay. But on closer examination of the models and their chosen bras, one realizes how savvy Wonderbra™ is, for it is really selling the same thing Hollywood is selling, and it isn't sex (although "sex" is the transmission system).

What Wonderbra™ is selling is a set of corporate-designed Identities-To-Go. These seem to have included:

Corporate Woman with Dangerous Breasts (bra: padded, sculpted for twin bullet effect—the female version of a Power Tie, I suppose)

Power Gamine (a concession to less genetically "blessed" humans. The model in question was relatively short of stature. Her implants made up for it. The bra was pretty anonymous)

Gen X "What bra?" (plain cups, stretchy straps with model wearing it making it clear via anorexic body that eating, sleeping and being conscious are not integral parts of being cool)

Over 30, Might As Well Give Up (a "structured" affair with a highly exaggerated cup, with the model's breasts sitting glumly in these extended shelves. The model really was, I guess, over 30. Well, maybe 25)

Basically, Wonderbra™ was setting up a sort of undergarment Central Casting, with corporate headquarters deciding the roles of the American woman via this tiny garment. And that the choices available to you, The Wonderbra™ Woman, were as limited as the choices one has when viewing female roles on the screen. They were (and are) as much a part of commerce-control systems as the ready-to-emulate slip-on personas of a Julia Roberts, Cameron Diaz, or Alicia Silverstone, and just as subject to pre-designed obsolescence and are, perhaps, a reason for *consumer*-induced neurosis.

What Wonderbra™ and Hollywood are saying via this truncated line of Possible Human Personas is akin to the famous *Saturday Night Live* routine: "I'm Chevy Chase—and you're not." It imagines a corporate world of Brand Name girls buying Brand Name Products and Services (like, say, movies). It reinforces the corporate ideal that we, and not just Hollywood stars, are replaceable cogs in a big, invisible machine only made visible via the instructions of advertising. Which implies that we have no value beyond what is designed for us with each season. In Hollywood, stereotyping has always been a problem, but now tens of millions of dollars ride on your stereotype. Pressure to conform to a constantly changing, corporate-designed aesthetic is always around, on the screen or in everyday life.

So if you have smallish breasts, more than .02% body fat or any features outside currently prevailing corporate definitions, you just don't exist in the Wonderbra™ or movie world and better get with the Program (implants still available). If you are a businesswoman who does not want to be a power-suited, torpedo-chested creature *à la* Demi Moore in *Disclosure*, then forget it—how could a man ever take you seriously?

"Consume, implant or die" seems to be the message. And so it goes, all down the line.

Alias Alan Smithee

About two minutes into the network premiere of David Lynch's *Dune*, a weird thing happened.

The film, set in a remote future, treats us to an astonishing opening montage of exotic planetary systems, rococo spacecraft and a veiled woman saying intriguing things about a rare spice that warps reality.

So far, so interesting.

Then, the movie just *stops*, and is replaced by this awful, static drawing, looking like something out of a fourth-grade history book and depicting battling gladiators stuck in some sort of medieval Arizona. A stentorian voice-over explains, *real slowly*, what we are going to see, with an assumption that we, the audience, share an intelligence level that matches the drawing.

Over the next several hours, the action is continually ground to a halt by more drawings and growingly desperate explanations of *Dune*'s admittedly incoherent story line. Not helping any was the network's decision to cut about half an hour from the film, which was originally trimmed down for its theatrical release from seven hours to three. The sum effect is a viewing experience that comes off like *Blue Velvet in Space: The Classics Illustrated Version*.

And another film was so massacred its own creator opted for the only escape clause allowed by the Director's Guild:

Lynch had his name dropped from the credits, replaced with that of "Alan Smithee," and another entry was made to the filmography of the nonexistent auteur.

"Alan Smithee" (an anagram for "The Alias Men") is, in short, a means of maintaining director anonymity while simultaneously thumbing one's nose at the studio that helped destroy one's film in the first place. It was first used in 1968 by director Jud Taylor on *Fade-In*. Master film director Don Siegel (*Invasion of the Body Snatchers, The Beguiled*) became the second to resort to Smithee when his film *Death of a Gunfighter* (1969) ran into studio interference. The breaking point came when the studio demanded that veteran Siegel co-direct his film with inexperienced director Robert Totten. Both directors were so displeased with the situation and resultant film that they gave it over (credit-wise) to Smithee. Today, using the pseudonym is an accepted practice.

With these two examples in mind, it becomes understandable how one "director" could be responsible for everything from the provocatively titled Z-budget gore-film *Bloodsucking Pharaohs in Pittsburgh* (1991) to the somber '80s 'Nam character study, *Let's Get Harry* (1986). Or be able to spackle "his" awful films with prestige names like Robert Duvall, Dennis Hopper, Sean Young and Christopher Plummer, stalwart check-seekers like Broderick Crawford, James Whitmore and Darren McGavin, or a sad parade of aging, poorly-agented or just plain on-the-skids lesser lights like Peggy Lipton, Mako, Chelsea Field, Gary Busey, Lyle Waggoner and even professional letter pointer Vanna White.

As for the films themselves, they run from just plain bad to a level of almost Olympian awfulness. Examples include the Down-Under comedy *Shrimp on the Barbie* (1990), detailing the travails of a Mexican chef (ex-pro stoned guy, Cheech Marin) lost in the wilds of Australia for no apparent reason. Or *Backtrack* (1989), a cut 'n paste mess that conjures up the narrative and editing quirks of Antonioni's immortal *Blow Up* (the similarities end there) as it tells of English-accented, lingerie-clad political artist (Jodie Foster) being tracked by jazz-loving if maniacal hit man (Dennis Hopper). Eventually, the two shuck it all to fall in love and buy a nice boat, the better to take a impromptu final trip to New Zealand. The film is listed at video stores as a mystery.

As becomes obvious, the ways a film joins the Smithee canon are as varied as its entries are terrible. A particularly vivid example is the baffling case of the fourth entry in director/writer Clive Barker's immensely profitable *Hellraiser* series.

First off, Barker hasn't had much to do with the *Hellraiser* series since its first sequel, *Hellraiser II: Hellbound*. Still, the fourth installment, eventually titled *Hellraiser: Bloodline*, seemed promising.

The movie would take Pinhead, the titular Demon from EveryHell, and follow his bloody exploits through seventeenth-century France, present-day America and finally into a deep space future. In "high concept" terms (a truly Smithee-ian formulation), we would have had a combination of *Dangerous Liaisons*, *Fatal Attraction* and *Star Wars* gone *Grand Guignol*.

What we got was a mess. And a mess that took *two years* to complete.

The assigned director was special makeup effects expert, Kevin Yeagher, who approached his debut with great enthusiasm. Unfortunately, what Yeagher was enthusiastic about was the original, century-spanning idea, which was dropped *after* filming began and replaced with a confusing present-day monster story with bonus past and future sequences. At some point, a wily executive noticed that all this "imagination" run amok was going to cost *money*. The budget was then set at six million, hardly enough for a regular drama, to say nothing of a film set to span three centuries and a couple planets.

Despite constant front-office interference, a morphing script (ambiguously credited to "an idea by Clive Barker") and the pitiable budget, Yeagher finished the film and handed in his cut.

Yeager's cut was then *re-cut* by the studio into a number of configurations and running times. Original scripter Peter Atkins was replaced during post-production re-writes, while the studio hired Joe Chappelle (who had directed a *Halloween* sequel) to shoot *more* footage, which was then incorporated into the film. The final movie, as Anthony Ferrante put it in *Fangoria* magazine (April 1996) "begins in the future, goes to the past, ends up in the present and then concludes back in the future…"

As predictably abysmal and incoherent as it turned out, *Hellraiser: Bloodline* was still treated to an expensive theatrical release. It flopped, but is doing well on video. Yeagher gave his credit to Alan Smithee and is back at work as a special effects makeup person. Happily.

Still, *Hellraiser: Bloodline* is hardly an aberration. That accomplished directors like David Lynch and Don Siegel are forced to resort to Smithee is a phenomenon indigenous to the entire management-heavy, corporate machine of modern Hollywood. Disaster seems preordained in a system that dictates that an endless queue of executives give copious illiterate notes to hapless directors in a system that truly does seem, so to speak, Hellbound.

POSTSCRIPT:

LOS ANGELES—First, it was reported in *Variety* that Harvey Weinstein, the Co-Chairman of Miramax Pictures, would play tough-guy detective Sam Rizzo in *An Alan Smithee Film*, written by Joe (Highest Paid Screenwriter in History) Eszterhas and directed by the notoriously mediocre Arthur Hiller (*Love Story, Silver Streak, Miracle of the White Stallions*).

Reportedly, the film would concern the efforts to locate the print of an action film starring Sylvester Stallone, Whoopi Goldberg, and Jackie Chan. The film-in-a-film's director, Alan Smithee, was being put to the test by Eric Idle.

As of this writing, it has been announced that Hiller (who is also president of the Academy of Motion Picture Arts and Sciences), supposedly suffered "creative differences" with writer Eszterhas. The result is that Hiller is choosing to have his name left off the film, and yes, having it replaced with "Alan Smithee."

Island of Dr. Moreau

"There's anxiety everywhere...There's a palpable tension.
Everything has to succeed—or else. I'm telling you, it's viral."
—Steven Spielberg, 1989, on the "blockbuster mentality."
Nancy Griffin and Kim Masters, *Hit & Run: How Jon*
Peters and Peter Guber Took Sony for a Ride in Hollywood

Back in 1931, one of the great horror films of all time, indeed, one of the finer films of its period, *Island of Lost Souls*, was filmed. Based on a novel by H.G. Wells, it starred Charles Laughton as an obese, whip-wielding mad scientist (Moreau) engaged in the business of fusing human and animal genes on a remote island, creating a half-human, mutant race of wretched creatures. Moreau keeps his underclass of dark-skinned mutants in line with promises of surgically-created, complete humanity. If these promises don't keep the mutants in their proper place, there's always the threat of the whip or a visit to Moreau's jail-like vivisection room, "The House of Pain."

A young man is stranded on Moreau's island, and falls for a "panther-woman" named Lota. The mutants finally overthrow their tyrant creator, while the young man leaves the island before having a chance to consummate his near-inter-species relationship with Lota. The movie sent many a shiver down audience spines—especially in a scene where the mutants tear Laughton to pieces with his own instruments.

The film is clearly a case study in class warfare and "taboo" inter-species sexuality. It's also a great basic premise for a scary movie. And since it worked in '31, they figured it would work again.

In 1977, the film was remade in TV-tone color. A spry and athletic Burt Lancaster was cast as the mad Moreau, apparently by someone with a learning disorder. Another baffling casting choice was that of Richard Baseheart, best known as a submarine captain on TV's *Voyage to the Bottom of the Sea*. Here, Baseheart was assigned a role played in the original film by Bela Lugosi, the half-dog character who leads the mutants to rebellion. For reasons unknown, the film's title was changed back to Wells' original, *The Island of Doctor Moreau*.

Result: Audiences stayed away in droves.

So why the remake? A simple reason: FX master John Chambers had won an Oscar for his work on *The Planet of the Apes* where, via new technology, he had created believable human-apes. One can imagine the executives' shouts ringing around corporate HQs Hollywood-wide: "Get us a script that has animal people in it!"

So somebody secured the *Island* script. The first thing they did in *this* version was make the new film's mutants—now called "Manimals"—cute and rather cuddly (this was after *Star Wars* made irresistible the limitless fiscal benefits of spin-off toys and action figures.) In the interest of broader appeal, the class/race angle was jettisoned. The topic of taboo inter-species romance—a creepy but essential element of the tale—was toned down to almost nothing.

Unsurprisingly, the resulting film was a supreme bore, but the Manimal effects were superb. When the movie tanked at the box office, executives shrugged a collective shoulder, erroneously figuring that America was simply "off" horror flicks. Today, the idea of what the public thinks isn't perceived as being as much of a problem. When a media behemoth like Time Warner— which owns cable networks like HBO, CNN, entertainment "news" networks like E! and studios like Castle Rock and New Line Cinema—decides on making a new project, it simply marshals its manifold resources, and does massive market research. Based on these statistics, the new film product is streamlined to appeal to the targeted demographic. Pre-release saturation advertising via corporate-owned media further lessens the possibility of failure. Not that it always works.

Speaking of New Line Cinema: In 1995, the studio launched another remake of *Island*. Although Hollywood had changed, had become a "content provider" for conglomerates such as Rupert Murdoch's News Corporation, Viacom and Disney/CapCities, it was still determined to make the same mistakes it did in 1977, albeit on a grander scale. It would even endeavor to add a few new blunders.

At first, the remake seemed promising, starring would-be super-hunk Val Kilmer and a more-eccentric-than-ever Marlon Brando. A grand budget was promised, with the enterprise to be directed by Richard Stanley, a South African who had made two excellent low budget films—*Hardware* and *Dust Devil* (both of which were, for reasons unknown, cut to ribbons on their stateside release). All his life, though, Stanley had dreamed of creating the ultimate *Island of Doctor Moreau*. But that dream quickly devolved into a surreal nightmare.

After a mere three days of filming, Stanley left the production. At first, recalls film historian Ian Toll, Stanley's sudden exit was reported to be due to the director becoming "so disgusted at the amount of studio interference that he dropped out of filmmaking altogether and joined some bizarre Tasmanian cult called 'the ferals.'"

Extreme, perhaps, but understandable. Were it only the truth.

Allegedly, Stanley was thrown off-Island by an egomaniacal Kilmer (A.K.A. "the most hated man in Hollywood"—*New York Daily News*). The studio interference was no illusion. Again, the race/class/sexual angles—the entire point of *Moreau*—were blunted. Resulting holes in narrative logic were filled with computer-generated special effects. And the story gaps were plentiful, as Stanley's original script was still being retooled to studio specifications during filming.

The finished product, *The Island of Doctor Moreau*, baffled critics. When faced with its singular brand of stupidity, most couldn't even suss out just *how* to properly pan the monstrosity.

Still, the viewing public dropped $9 million on *Moreau*'s first weekend outside of captivity. This on a film that took mere stupidity to levels of unintentional surrealism not seen since the heydays of Ed Wood, Jr. After all, it isn't every day that one gets to see a fearsomely corpulent Brando dressed in saris while motoring about in a makeshift Pope-mobile, or to watch Mr. Kilmer (as the star insisted the crew address him) make out with mutant pigs, kill bunnies for kicks, shoot up strange drugs, or do his *own* Brando impression, complete with pillows under his shirt to approximate his better's girth. By the time the feline-esque love interest Fairuza Balk is strung up by a dog-man, it is incontestable that one is in the presence of a very *special* film. When a veteran industry insider (who requested anonymity) was queried as to what sort of thinking was behind the release of *Moreau* madness, she promptly replied, "You're asking the wrong question. What makes you think they think at all?"

Then she added, "Furthermore, you *never, ever*, unless you're seriously on the inside of these things, have any idea what really happened."

Soon after *Moreau's* big opening weekend, box office tallies withered. New Line figured out that they had a very weird sort of dog on their hands, and instead of just yanking it from distribution (a pricey act, with over a thousand prints in circulation), decided instead to go with a daring, "it's-so-bad-it's-good!" campaign. Ads that one day were touting *Moreau* as a riveting, sci-fi thriller were suddenly gushing blurbs like "Campy, creepy and cool!" The film's troubled production history—usually a thing closed out to the media—became part of "the sell" as tantalizing bits were "leaked out" to the press.

We were *now* told that original director Stanley, instead of scooting to Tasmania, had been fired and replaced by a reportedly sodden John Frankenheimer (*The Manchurian Candidate*). Even more bizarre, and sad, considering that this had started as Stanley's dream project, were reports that after being kicked off the production, the director did not just go home.

Now it was revealed that Stanley convinced a sympathetic makeup crew to do their magic on him, resulting in the ex-director appearing in many scenes (unbeknownst to Frankenheimer and company) as just another mutant. I can only guess what it felt like for Stanley to be playing an unknown monster in a movie he had, in essence, created.

Further reports about the general disarray of the production (the general subhuman behavior of *Mr.* Kilmer and the bizarre antics of the always-interesting Brando) became part of the revisionist sell. Based on box office tallies, it seems to have worked: Americans went in droves to see a total mess, perhaps to participate in their own interactive version of TV's *Mystery Science Theater 3000*, wherein a guy and some robots trade quips over various B movie turkeys.

Besides being an example of a Hollywood that, among many things, seemed determined to ignore its own history, there was something even more revealing to be found in this strange tale.

The Island of Doctor Moreau, despite being addled, absurd, plotless, and acted by its principals as if they were not only all appearing in several different movies, but several different movies filmed on several different *planets*—despite all this—*The Island of Doctor Moreau* is, without question, the most amusing, interesting and, to say the least, unique film to wing its way out of Hollywood in years.

In other words: Only by fucking up on a monumental scale has corporate-style Hollywood moviemaking created a film that brazenly destroys formula, contributing images hellbound to stay in the viewers' minds for years to come, a film imbued, because of the very human foibles of its deranged creators, with a strange sense of humanity that, were it the work of a person possessed of a Gallic last name, would be called "visionary."

Yes, it's gotten that pitiful.

Bernard Weintraub, writing in the *New York Times*, takes note of the fact—and I paraphrase—that films have become so volcanically rotten that in 1996, Hollywood was in a state of extreme anxiety trying to find *any* movie worthy of an Oscar nod. As one not-to-be-quoted "executive" commented in the same article, the fact that, out of the 190 films released that year, none were deemed Oscar-worthy, was downright "pathetic."

The *Times* is known for its understatement.

Going on, the piece notes that execs at Tri-Star, Disney and other major junk providers are baffled over the financial failures of such high-hopes as *Fled* (an unaccredited remake of *The Defiant Ones*), *Flipper* (the continuing saga of many a Baby Boomer's favorite TV *delphinidae*) and the revealingly titled *The Stupids*.

Still, the 69th Annual Academy Awards were held. Necessity truly became the mother of invention as the glut of big-studio garbage was handily ignored as 1996 was spin-doctored into The Year of the Independent Film (with its associative images of brave new visions, techniques, topics and what have you).

What we got in this Year of the (Seemingly) Independent Film was:

The English Patient, a film in the classically protracted mode of the nostalgically overrated David Lean. Promoted as "independent," the film starred such actors as Ralph Fiennes and Kristen Scott Thomas, was shot on exotic locations from Rome to Tunisia, and cost $31 million. The film was released by Miramax, which is owned by Disney. It won a lot of gold statues, including Best Picture.

Another Best Picture nominee was *Shine*, a TV Disease-of-the-Week weepy. It was produced by Fine Line, a division of Ted Turner's media empire.

Then there was *Jerry Maguire*, starring Tom Cruise. Produced by Tri-Star Pictures, it was the only openly studio-produced film nominated for Best Picture. I suppose this seemed "indie" because it had dialogue that lasted for long stretches of its running time.

One actual, no-kidding independent feature, Mike Leigh's unique and intelligent *Secrets & Lies* (October Pictures), was nominated for Best Picture. It lost.

While Hollywood was congratulating itself on TV for its contributions to quality film, it continued its real raison d'être: making really expensive visual junk food.

New, big-budget versions of TV's *The Mod Squad* and *The Avengers* were being prepped, while down in Mexico, James Cameron was busy at work at his epic re-enactment of the sinking of the *Titanic*, the budget of which has been estimated to clock in at $200-280 million dollars. *Titanic* will have to make more money than any film in history just to break even.

But this is a business where there is no future beyond the current season's projected earnings, run by corporations that have no concern for anything beyond what last year's market research indicated. And so, nobody figures that having a movie, *any* movie, named after the greatest oceangoing disaster in history might be, well, kind of a bad idea.

Undaunted, the *Times* reported major producer Arnold Kopelson (*The Fugitive*) as having said, "From my standpoint, event programming [mega-budgeted, star- and effects-driven movies] is the way to go now... I'd rather spend

$70 million on a movie than $40 million because then I could go to the stars and get the kind of big action scenes that get people out of their homes…"

Apparently, it hasn't occurred to Mr. Kopelson that a cheaper way of getting people out of their homes is to make less crappy films.

Meanwhile, Fox's celebration of the end of the world, the vapid '50s throwback *Independence Day*, is well on its way to becoming the most profitable "event film" in world history, which makes a person wonder just what, beneath its can-do facade, America really wants of the new millennium.

Writing in *The New Yorker*, critic John Weir speculated that *Independence Day* indeed gives its audience what it craves: "spectacular nothing."

For once, Hollywood was able and happy to deliver.

DEVOLUTION OF A FRANCHISE

- **1989 *Batman*. Directed by Tim Burton. 126 minutes.**
  Quirky auteur Burton creates a brutally expressionist Gotham City, inspired to a great extent by cartoonist Frank Miller's revisionist take on Batman, The Dark Knight. The shadow-packed cityscape is a-crawl with crime and maniacs of every stripe (including Jack Nicholson's literally scarred arch-lunatic, The Joker). The caped crusader—by day, reluctant industrialist Bruce Wayne—is portrayed by Michael Keaton as a deeply disturbed man, forever twisted by the childhood trauma of seeing his parents murdered, and dismissive of his vast inherited wealth. Although he triumphs against the bad guys, he does not get the girl, as he is, after all, a severe headcase. The film is a singular vision.

- **1991 *Batman Returns*. Directed by Tim Burton. 126 minutes.**
  Along with Batman's continuing bouts of neurosis, we meet The Penguin (who became a criminal because of parental neglect and abuse), and a villainous developer (played à la Donald Trump by Christopher Walken). Gotham is more corrupt than ever; it's winter, people are haggard-looking and Batman's love interest turns out to be the emotionally shattered Michelle Pffeifer, who, after nearly being killed by Walken, metamorphoses into Cat Woman. Sadly, neither Bat nor Cat is emotionally up to consummating their seemingly fated romance, due to their internal demons. Danny Elfman's brooding orchestral score is a brilliant counterpart to the film's dark world view. This and the original *Batman* are perhaps the most interesting and "individual" of studio-financed, big-budget films.

• **1995** *Batman Forever*. **Directed by Joel Schumacher. 131 minutes.**
In veteran hack Schumacher's (*Flatliners, St. Elmo's Fire*) *Batman,* the troubled hero is
played by Val Kilmer in a manner that suggests he is not so much plagued by inner
demons as just slightly distracted. He almost gets The Girl (Nicole Kidman) and
Robin is introduced to the series to 1) keep our mournful hero company; 2) add
some trendy ambi-sexual fireworks to the proceedings; and 3) lend some Gen-X sizzle
to the franchise. Gotham is still dark, but more in the mode of a somewhat taciturn
Billy Joel video, and when things get too interesting, Jim Carrey mugs it up while
garbed in colorful Ziggy Stardust threads as the impressively unthreatening villain, The
Riddler. Lots of neon signs announce lots of products, along with a wide assortment
of "alternative" rock songs for the soundtrack album. An aggressively bad movie.

• **1997** *Batman and Robin*. **Directed by Joel Schumacher. 136 minutes.**
For about five minutes, it's amusing to watch *Batman & Robin*'s speedy melange of
Hong Kong action films, retro-psychedelic color schemes and endless Toys-R-Us-™
friendly Bat paraphernalia. But after almost an hour with no story in sight, the effect
is merely soporific.

Eventually, we meet Arnold as "Mr. Freeze," a guy in a blue *Robocop* suit who,
well, likes to freeze people. Uma Thurman appears as an insane environmentalist
who, via a fall into some genetically-superior ivy, becomes arch-villainess "Poison
Ivy." The wit stays at this level for the film's running time. Alicia Silverstone, because
she can ride a motorcycle and is Batman's servant's relative, becomes Batgirl.
Eventually, Arnold decides to freeze the world. He fails. The End.

Gone completely are Gotham's grim expressionistic flourishes. The new look is
Blade Runner lite, with all the ambiance of an old Lava Lamp. Everybody has lots of
money, except for two scenes in which poor people are shown to be dirty, psychopathic criminals. The soundtrack/CD songs now include techno, alternative rock
and country and western; something to please every market segment.

Most changed of all is Batman/Bruce Wayne—a constantly smiling, going-to-
gray-but-still-hunky George Clooney.

He now owns a *fleet* of Batmobiles, has a busty WASP trophy fiancée, and isn't
above making tit and dick jokes. Whereas he was once scornful of his inherited
wealth, he is now proud of the ascendance of his multinational corporation (most
every item in the film bears the Wayne Industries imprint). At several points,
Clooney scolds Robin and Batgirl for not being "team players," and constantly refers
to his ensemble of superheroes (and the people who love them) as "family."

To not be a team player and to disrespect family are the only things in this
movie that manage to wipe the ever-present grin off Clooney's face. Basically, the
new Batman is an idealized Michael Eisner with a Hugh Hefner gloss.

• • • • • • •

As an inspection of the above film's running times shows, movies are not only getting crappier, they're getting longer.

Until the late '80s, movies ran an average of 90 to 94 minutes, with longer running times reserved for globe-spanning epics such as 1960's *Exodus* (139 minutes).

A random sampling of recent hits shows increasingly longer running times to be the norm, regardless of genre. *Scent of a Woman* (1992), *The Bodyguard* (1992), *Clear and Present Danger* (1994) and *Speed 2: Cruise Control* (1997) all clock in at well over 120 minutes. The rough average length of current blockbusters is about 110 minutes. Yet screenplays have grown no lengthier—they are still 90 to 92 pages long, with the idea that each page works out to about one minute of screen time still the screenwriter's rule of thumb.

Then it hit me: scenes lingering on various product placements, tie-in pop music interludes and extended special effect sequences—all this takes time. So movies are still 90 minutes long, plus commercials and effects.

Too Many Writers Spoil The Script: Screenwriter John Fasano

"Everybody in Hollywood hates to think about writing. It's so uncompromisable in a sense. There's no easy way to improve it...You can't make it better with a deal."

—Tom Wolfe, quoted in *The Devil's Candy* by Julie Salamon

PARTIAL FILMOGRAPHY

As director

The Edge of Hell	(1987)
Rock 'N Roll Nightmare	(1987)
Black Roses	(1988)
The Jitters	(1989)

As writer and/or producer

Another 48 Hours	(1990)
Alien 3 (uncredited)	(1992)
Rapid Fire	(1992)
Tombstone	(1993)
Judge Dredd	(1995)
The Hunchback	(1997)

It's one thing to have a person screaming about what a mess things are. It's another (and much more disturbing) matter when a person says that the sky is indeed falling, and then calmly explains how and why it is doing so.

John Fasano is that calm man. Over six feet tall, with the build and expression of a taciturn miner, and the mind and manner of an economics professor,

Mr. Fasano has been turning a good profit writing screenplays for such block-buster-mentality features as *Another 48 Hours, Alien 3* ("I wrote the shooting draft of *Alien 3* and got no credit in the arbitration"), *Tombstone* and others, shrugging his pragmatic way through the dumb labyrinth that passes for modern filmmaking.

In response to my questions about the tumultuous production history of *Alien 3* (directed by David Fincher), Fasano held no grudge, but simply explained:

> JF: Vincent Ward was the original director of *Alien 3*.
>
> They'd gone through about 8 writers...and they said "We're going to hire you to write *Alien 4*, but it's *really* going to be *Alien 3*, because we just hired Vincent Ward and he's going to direct *Alien 3* and we'll take [screenwriter] David Twohy's script and make *that Alien 4*.
>
> He had this idea about monks in space.
>
> IG: Um...Monks in—who had this idea?
>
> JF: Vincent had this idea.
>
> IG: Oh.

Years before, sci-fi author William Gibson wrote a screenplay of *Alien 3* for a healthy figure. From this, only an idea about bar code tattoos remains in the film. After Gibson's version was worked over by several writers, Fasano was hired to write his own. He envisioned an off-world colony of sequestered Luddite monks. The theme of the film would be religion.

This theme was kept by Vincent Ward, a New Zealand director known for the fascinating fantasy film *The Navigator* (1989). More writers and their drafts came and went. Then Ward was dumped from the project, and replaced by David Fincher, who would go on to do superior work with *Seven* (1995), but before *Alien 3* had only shot music videos and commercials.

Fincher convinced producer Sigourney Weaver he was the man for *Alien 3* when he told her the first thing he would do was shave her head. The next thing Fincher did was turn the movie into a sort of prison film (requiring more rewrites), albeit with religious trappings. Just how deep these trappings ran is today a mystery. In a conversation with *Alien 3*'s composer Elliot Goldenthal, I was told that most all religious symbolism was cut from the film just prior to release by 20th Century Fox (a division of News Corporation).

This last-minute editing, along with the endless parade of contributors, helped explain my reaction to initially seeing the film. The first two thirds of *Alien 3* are an incomprehensible hash (if a beautifully-shot one), while the last "act" is quite stirring. But after so many hands had been in the *Alien* soup, it was deemed that Fasano not be given credit in the Writer's Guild of America arbitration. He takes it in stride, though, seeing it as business-as-usual, and explains:

JF: I was in the hands of 12 gods.

IG: 12...Do you mean 12 *people* worked on this? 12 *writers*?

JF: Yeah. And I was the 11th of 12 writers on *Judge Dredd* also.

IG: But this whole thing of having 12 writers...Sigourney Weaver produced *Alien 3*—wasn't she in control?

JF: The first eight or nine guys were writing different kinds of stories in the hope that when they were done, they'd get to Sigourney.

She'd just had her baby and I went with her to The Four Seasons restaurant and met with her. Her biggest concern was she wanted to die at the end. She felt—and I think she was right—that she'd beat this thing once, then she beat it again, and it was getting ridiculous! She fought the Mother Alien hand-to-hand and if she came back again, it was like she failed. A hollow victory.

But the studio said, "We can't kill Sigourney, we can't kill 'Ripley,'" so I had the lead priest, that was her friend, give her the Heimlich Maneuver, and pulls the alien out of her throat into his own, and *he* jumps into the fire. And he dies and she lives and he turns out to be a robot. The whole Third Act is how I wrote it...

They fired Vincent because he wouldn't move at the pace the studio wanted...he'd spent 2 years working on *The Navigator*, and the studio concept is: If we're ready to shoot, it doesn't matter what state the script is in, you start, you go.

Anyway, it seems to me there's three kinds of films:

There's films written by one guy for twenty years who's fought and fought for it and found an actor that wanted to be attached to it so it got made.

And then there's films where they bought a concept, kept rewriting with whoever was hot that week, and kept rewriting it with 13 writers until it got made, like *Judge Dredd*.

And then there's films where they buy a script, whether it's good or not, but *Arnold* wants to do it...they go right into production and fix it while they're doing it.

Still confused over the expensive and, it seems to me, redundant multiple-writer approach to films, I ask Fasano how this came about.

JF: See, TV shows were written for years by teams, by pools of writers. *The Dick Van Dyke Show* had four or five guys per show. And when Michael Eisner and Jeff Katzenberg [studio kingpins] went to Paramount, they took that [TV] structure to Paramount, and made all those movies like the first *48 Hours*, *Flashdance*—all those movies they had in the early '80s that made all that money and everyone said "Oh! That's what it is. It's loads of writers!"

In the old days, before a television mentality took over films—in the early '70s at Warner Bros.—think about all those great movies—what would they do?

They'd pitch the story, a guy like ['70s producer] Sid Beckerman would say it was good or bad, and he'd gone to Harvard and he really gave good notes—and say "Yeah! Let's sell this movie."

Now, you go and you pitch to someone who's just out of school—business school or film school—and they're like 25-year-old junior executives and they have to go to their boss and get it covered. It then goes to *his* boss and then to *his* boss who goes to the head of the studio.

IG: Do you think the "blockbuster" school of filmmaking—started with *Star Wars*, *Close Encounters* and other effect-driven, fun park movies—ended the age of the single-author film? Has the very quality of writing atrophied due to studio interference?

JF: Well, there's still good writers, but you're not getting one guy writing a movie anymore. Even if you see the credit that says that, the studio system *demands* that lots of people work on these movies.

IG: Okay, but what I'm trying to see are ways a writer gets some autonomy over his or her vision. Can you become producer as well as writer, and wrest some control that way?

JF: They resist that *a lot*.

This isn't a slam on directors—I don't want this to come off like that at all—but basically, I'm sitting in a room, I come up with an idea, I write it.

Like Charles Pogue—he did *Dragonheart* which he worked on for years—and then they go to make the movie, and they don't want him around. Because once the movie physically starts to be shot, it belongs to the *director*, and if he had to keep looking over his shoulder at the writer for approval, he'll look weak in front of the crew.

But on every film, there's an 800-pound gorilla, and the 800-pound gorilla gets to sit anywhere he wants. When you're doing *Another 48 Hours*, Eddie Murphy's the 800-pound gorilla. When you're doing *Alien 3*, Sigourney Weaver's the 800-pound gorilla.

IG: Okay. On another tack:

It seems to me that the experience of going to the movies is one of audience manipulation. Before the movie starts, you're urged to buy tubs of popcorn and soda which are covered with ads for upcoming films. The concession stand sells T-shirts with movie logos, and other promotional tie-ins. Then you sit through five or six trailers for coming attractions, plus various wide-screen ads. By the time you sit through all this advertising, the actual movie often seems like an afterthought to the entire experience. So everything that comes before the movie is there to pummel the audience member into a malleable, unquestioning mood. It becomes a selling environment as opposed to a place to see movies.

JF: *Star Wars* started that. Merchandising didn't exist before *Star Wars*.

IG: But now it's escalated to where the merchandising is actually in the movie!

JF: Well, *Jurassic Park* had the plush toys and lunch boxes in the movie so you could see them, and there was a book about the making of Jurassic Park. And it's seen in the movie, the book you can go buy.

I don't have a problem with that...I don't have a problem with *Judge Dredd* and *Demolition Man* and *Waterworld* toys. Nobody bought them, right? So if people didn't like the movie, they're not going to run to buy the merchandising.

IG: But you still have 13 writers for a movie that has 50 associated toys and you don't even know if anyone's going to see the damned thing!

JF: Well, I've been told the reason there's, say, 13 writers, is because they can't make up their minds, they can't pull the trigger.

There are people, like [producer/studio execs] Joe Roth, Sid Sheinberg, and Geffen—they have that capability, but it's not in their hands anymore. [David] Selznick didn't have 200 vice presidents and junior vice-presidents, and senior vice-presidents underneath him.

I fall silent. The idea of having to run a gauntlet of 200 vice presidents in order to get script approved and a movie in gear is so stupifyingly redundant that all I can muster up in the way of a question is:

IG: Um—why is it set up in such a, well, redundant manner?

JF: [Takes a big breath] Okay.
      It used to be that government's responsibility was just to protect our borders and oversee the army. Now, you go to Washington and you'll find all of these...[trails off] It's big business, the money is there.
      So they spend it.

IG: So even if someone as powerful as David Geffen gets real hot on a project he still has to go through this immense bureaucracy.

JF: No—that's not true. But—it's either gotten to him personally, or it's worked its way *through* the bureaucracy. In other words, if you're at a cocktail party with Stallone and he says "I want to do this," it could be shooting within a month. But if someone brought a script they thought would be good *for* Stallone, it would have to survive that whole process.
      A good example: this guy had the rights to *The Fantastic Four* [a comic strip]. They had a five-year option on it—I don't know exactly—from Marvel Comics. For five years they wrote scripts. *None* of which they liked. Which is *impossible*.
      They get to a point where if they don't make a movie in three months, they're going to lose the option. But if they make a movie—any movie!—they keep the character rights and they can resell them to somebody else.
      So, they have Roger Corman make a movie of *The Fantastic Four* for like $180,000 that's just dreadful. I've seen it...
      Anyway, they made it, said "Thank you," put it on the shelf and then they went to Fox with the characters. [Now] Chris Columbus is going to do a huge *Fantastic Four* at Fox! But the original guy is *still* involved in it because they have the rights by making the Corman movie.
      Well. When I wrote *The Three Musketeers* for Columbia, they had me do 15 drafts of it. At the same time, Disney was doing one, Tri-Star was doing one. And people wanted to direct my movie: Roger Donaldson [*No Way Out*] wanted to direct it, Sam Raimi [*Evil Dead*] wanted to direct it, Johnny Depp wanted to be *in* it and Columbia could not pull the trigger.

IG: Ah...why?

JF: I don't know. I have no idea what it was. But Disney, whose script was nowhere as good a shape as ours, was in a race with us and they started production because *they knew* the people at Columbia kept going in and out of their jobs, so nobody wanted to push any project unless it was a quote-end-quote "surefire" hit. Like *The Last Action Hero* [starring Arnold Schwarzenegger], which was directed by John McTiernan, had all these actors—

IG: But that was a bomb!

JF: —yeah, but what I'm saying is that on *paper*, it was a surefire hit. In other words—no one got fired over *The Last Action Hero*. And similarly, nobody got fired for losing the race to Disney after paying me a half million dollars to write a script for *The Three Musketeers* that they never made.

I find myself almost in awe of something so impeccably deranged: this idea of making a movie you never plan to release so you can retain the rights to a script to make a movie that may never be produced. All this so that *maybe* you'll score in some highly speculative manner several years down the line. But Fasano shrugs off the *Fantastic Four* maneuvers with:

JF: The deal with Marvel is, if you actually start principal photography before the end of your option period, then you keep the rights to the characters, let's say, for another three years. So you can do *sequels*. So they needed to make *a* film of *The Fantastic Four* so they can hold onto the rights and then sell them to Fox.

I have a tape of it [the Corman film] here at my house. They sell it at science fiction conventions as an oddity. I mean, they shot it, somebody directed it, people acted in it, they made this movie and just—put it aside. To me, it's the total extension of what you told me about your friend [a person who prefers to remain anonymous who lives off un-produced scripts] and with me—I mean, most of the money I live off is from turnaround scripts. That's what every writer is living off of!

Think about this:

If you have 200 executives at each studio—even if you have 50—each one of those executives has to justify his position by showing he has stuff going across his desk, by getting scripts developed, giving writers notes. I've had meetings with people with *nothing* going on, but they needed to show they were having meetings every day. They need it to show they're doing *something*.

IG: Would it be accurate then to say that movies are made and scripts are written to keep people in jobs?

JF: Sure.

Fasano then speaks of common 1980s business practices that led to the near-hobbling of the US economy such as constructing office buildings in markets that had no need for new office buildings. Most of these ventures tanked, resulting in many urban centers being filled with useless construction and falsely inflated local economies. Meanwhile, the Savings and Loans had, via this scam, become fatally overextended.

JF: It's the same thing as anything. It's why we pay our farmers to grow less corn, you know? It's what happened in business in America.

And I'll give you a great example:

When I was in college, I was hired to be the film librarian by Time/Life, and they were going to do a knock-off of *TV Guide*. They hired me to write a capsule review of every movie that had ever been made. But, they never intended this magazine to come out. I have five or six issues here, they test-marketed it, ultimately the editor said this was all to burn up some excess profit.

I find I need this explained, this idea of a need to "burn up some excess profit"—especially in a business that constantly claims that its preference for lowest-common-denominator crap is based on how hard it is to *create* profits.

JF: [Assuming a tone that suggests everybody knows this] Well, they'd have to pay taxes on it.

Like, for example, *Another 48 Hours*, where I worked very closely with the line producer: It cost $38 million in "cash"—when I got my first statement. As a writer you get a profit statement, if you have profit-participation.

The first statement said "Negative cost of the movie: $58 million."

["Negative cost" is the price of making a film—not including printing, distributing and marketing—subtracted from the actual gross.]

That's because, every time you shoot on a lot, there's 35% overhead, and some of these buildings at Columbia were built in the 'Teens, you know? And paid for by *millions* of films. And everyone is shooting at the same 35% overhead.

IG: But they still charge you for that.

JF: Right.

IG: So that's part of their profit.

JF: Right.

So, in other words, when someone says they spent $60 million on the movie, and they lost money—on any movie, not that particular one—they didn't! Because as they were shooting the movie, they put $12 million in their pocket over the course of the production of the film. They were already into profit.

IG: So you're paying for production facilities that cost nothing. It's pure profit.

JF: Right.

There's a pause as I realize the enormity of what he's just said: That, if what he says is true, then *everything* one reads about budgets high and low, about battles fought between directors and corporations for funds, about most fucking *everything* that has *anything* to do with the reportage of how much movies cost to make, and therefore, how much they earn, is, in a word, bullshit.

But just in case I'm off-base here, I say:

IG: Okay. So therefore, it's really hard for a movie to lose money. Um—did I get that right?

JF: Yeah.
       [But] on *paper, every* movie that's ever been made has lost money.

CEO Search

Thinking about those two hundred vice-presidents, I decided that I'd call the CEO in charge of such an egregious corporate redundancy. At random, I decided on Warner Bros. President Terry Semel. I found that the results of my executive search would strangely echo another effort to pierce the simultaneously mystifying and dunder-headed veil of corporate information control.

A month earlier, I'd engaged in a fruitless quest to find out who owned the rights to the popular film *Heathers* (I had a photo from the film that I wanted clearance for).

The film's director, Michael Lehmann, did not know who owned *Heathers*. Nor did the film's producer. So I called New World Pictures, who had distributed *Heathers*.

Someone at New World told me they were out of business. But...if that was so, who was I talking to?

"I sit in a room and answer questions like yours, mainly," the guy on the other end said, as I imagined a cinematic Maytag™ repairman. He then suggested a call to Transworld Pictures, who were also belly-up. I was ready to deep-six the entire thing, when the New World Maytag™ guy called.

"Call this number," he said, "and ask for Richard."

Richard (whoever he was) said it was highly unlikely I'd get clearance on the photo (which I was now growing to despise), and told me to call this guy named Greg.

Some on-hold Muzak, and Greg picked up. Yes, he knew about *Heathers*.

"When New World went bankrupt, their library was sold along with their other assets, and we bought *Heathers* at that time. By we, I mean Fox Pictures.

The people I work for."

Fox Pictures is owned by Rupurt Murdoch's News Corporation. Which also owns Fox TV, on which *Heathers* had been playing all that week.

Greg, a nice guy, switched me to a higher-up in P.R. who did Fox Pictures' "clearance and permissions."

"*Heathers?*" the young voice asked.

"Yeah."

"Gee, I don't know anything about that movie. Hmm..." Nails clicked on an unseen desk. "Wait! Wasn't Winona Ryder in that?"

Sigh. "Yes."

"Cool! That was on TV this week, wasn't it?"

So only via unexpected dumb luck was I able to negotiate the labyrinth of corporate Hollywood and find out who the hell owned a popular, fairly recent film. After weeks of effort, they quoted an obscenely high price to reproduce the photo. I decided I could live without it.

While I didn't hold out high hopes of actually getting through to Warner Bros. Terry Semel, I figured they'd at least be better organized.

Miraculously, my first call got me into Semel's office. But that was quickly corrected when the secretary, upon hearing me describe myself as "a writer," switched me to publicity. An upbeat young woman named Cherry told me that Mr. Semel was having a meeting the next morning. I started to feel lucky again.

That momentary lapse of naïveté evaporated the next morning when Cherry said, "I'm sorry, but you'll have to talk to Charlotte—

"—Who is—"

"—head of P.R. What magazine did you say you're from?"

Uh-oh. "Um...I'm not from a magazine. I'm writing a book. On the movies."

A sudden pause in the bubbling conversation. "A *book?*"

"Yes. A book."

Cherry made the audio equivalent of a frown, then brightened. "Oh! Then you want to talk to *corporate* P.R.! Let me switch you!"

While I was being switched, I thought about how Cherry seemed to have no problem connecting me into the pipeline of publicity *if I worked for a magazine*. It didn't escape me that Time Warner owns *Entertainment Weekly*, *People*, and a slew of other low-attention-span, pop culture publications where inflammatory info like Charlie Sheen beating up on his girlfriend is sandwiched, willy-nilly, in with the latest on Mira Sorvino's love life, then forgotten by the next profile on the Sheens of the industry. Not to get all *X-Files* about this, but the truth is out there, it's just hidden in plain sight. I guess the editorial boards of these magazines assume the audience has a memory no longer than the shelf-life of cultured yogurt.

But books tend to last a bit longer and don't get shredded at week's end. So I ended up speaking with Barbara Brogliatti, head of Warner's corporate publicity. Or rather, her assistant, an amiable woman named Catherine, who said that Ms. Brogliatti would not be in all day, nor would Mr. Semel (who, according to Cherry over in *non*-corporate P.R., was, at that very moment, in his office).

Whatever. I asked Catherine if she could she tell me the established protocol for setting up an interview with Mr. Semel.

"What book company did you say you work for?"

I said that it was a small, independent press.

"Cool! Hold on!"

Holding on, I felt reverberations of my quest for *Heathers*, as yet another cheerful soul kept me an inch from the keys of the information kingdom. Access to information, whether absurdly small or scary-huge, seemed to be a matter of smiley-faced red tape perpetuated by well-intentioned corporate underlings. No big conspiracy theory at play.

Catherine was back on the line. "I'm sorry, Barbara's not in, and what was the name of your company again?"

After a few more calls to Warner, Barbara Brogliatti called *me* back. I gave her a quick run-through about how I was working on a book about film for an independent publisher. She explained how busy Mr. Semel was, what with running a major studio and all that entails. I assured her I only wanted to ask a few questions and be on my way. I asked my standard question: "What's the protocol for this sort of thing?"

Barbara paused a long time, sighed, and finally said, "Well, actually, it's just impossible."

Breathlessly, lest I miss the moment, I dove in for a last-ditch "Just five questions, Barbara? I could e-mail them. He could answer at his leisure...."

Barbara's voice chilled and was replaced by a crisp business brush-off. "Well, I guess you can send me a fax. I'd need you to list *all* the industry people you've interviewed," (I was willing to do this but it made me feel like I would be naming names to the House Committee on Un-American Activities) "the aim of your book," ("aim" seemed like a rather sinister choice of words) "and something about your publisher. And then, well... I can't promise you anything, you know?"

I said I knew. Months went by. She was right—it was impossible.

Censorship: The MPAA

In November of 1968, the Motion Picture Association of America (MPAA) introduced the first standardized censorship system in reaction to the changing nature of films in the 1960s.

Echoing the cultural tumult of that decade, films and their makers became more bold when addressing sex, violence and previously "taboo" subject matter. With no across-the-board means of controlling this "new breed" of film—from which major studios were now making considerable money—the MPAA, under the leadership of Jack Valenti, created the ratings system.

According to Valenti, these ratings would aid parents in protecting their children from movies depicting what he bemoaned as dealing with "insurrection on the campus, riots in the streets, rise in women's liberation, protest of the young, doubts about the institution of marriage, abandonment of old guiding slogans, and the crumbling of social traditions." (All quotes, unless otherwise listed, are from the MPAA's Web page: http://www.mpaa.org/mpaa.html)

It was two films in particular that stirred Valenti and the MPAA into action: *Who's Afraid of Virginia Wolf* (1966) because of the use of the words "screw" and "hump the hostess" (Warner Bros., the film's producer, dumped the "screw" but kept the "hostess" bit), and Antonioni's *Blow Up* (1967) which featured extended nude scenes. The final catalyzing event came in April, 1968, when the U.S. Supreme Court upheld "the constitutional power of states and cities to prevent the exposure of children to books and films which could not be denied to adults."

Valenti, an ex-bomber pilot, adman and consultant to President Johnson, met with the major studios, and with representatives for theater chains and movie distributors. Soon after, the entire industry adapted the ratings, placing them on all movie advertising materials, prefacing the movies themselves and the trailers that advertised them. Even the trailers were rated.

Newspapers—then the main avenue of advertising for films—adopted the ratings system instantly. It gave them a ready-made reference as to which film was and wasn't obscene, and so guided them in their choice of what movie ads to run. At this point, *all* film advertising materials now carried the MPAA brand.

It is significant to note that no moviemaking group, such as the Director's Guild, was included in these groundbreaking arbitrations. Although Valenti and the MPAA insist to this day that having a film rated is voluntary, it has always been integral to this system that if a film was not submitted to the ratings board, newspapers would not advertise the film. For the first time, two forms of media—film and print—would conspire to control how we perceive information (in this case, movies).

The initial rating system was, at first glance, disarmingly simple: G for "General audiences," M for "Mature," R for "Restricted," with nobody under 16 (a few months later, 17) years old admitted without an adult or parental guardian. This cut-off age varies to this day, depending on the jurisdiction. The last rating was X: "Nobody under 17 allowed."

In 1969, the M category was changed to GP ("General audiences. Parental suggestion advised"), and later to PG ("Parental guidance suggested"). Two amendments were made to the original ratings. There was, in 1984, the addition of the PG-13 category for films: "PARENTS STRONGLY CAUTIONED. Some material may be inappropriate for children under 13." According to the MPAA, this helps indicate "a higher level of intensity" than a PG, while the X was replaced with the more euphemistic NC-17: "No Children Under 17 Admitted."

One reason the NC-17 was created was because pornography producers of the time latched onto the taboo status the MPAA's X provided, and slapped it on ad materials for their films. Valenti retaliated with the creation of NC-17, and made all his ratings registered trademarks of the MPAA. This insured that *his* system would not be usurped by others. It also distanced the ratings system from the world of porn. As an incidental sop to filmmakers, NC-17 was to impart the perception that the film with this rating was truly "adult," and one with "artistic content."

But no matter. The end effect of an X *or* an NC-17 is the same: The majority of newspapers, magazines, television and radio stations will not accept the advertising of a stigmatized film. This can effectively condemn a film to death.

The MPAA itself is made up of Valenti and a board of 17 vice-presidents and functionaries, plus representatives from all the major studios (who are all charter members of the MPAA). There is no representation by independent filmmakers or directors.

Under MPAA guidelines, films are rated by "a Board of...8-11 members...who serve terms of varying length [and] work for the Classification and Rating Administration." The only qualifications for these people is that they "must have a shared parenthood experience, must be possessed of an intelligent maturity, and most of all, have the capacity to put themselves in the role of most American parents so they can view a film and apply a rating that most parents would find suitable and helpful in aiding their decisions about their children's moviegoing." There is another panel of 14-18 people who also possess no special knowledge of film who come into play if a film's producer wants to appeal a rating.

So, according to the MPAA, the reason for its existence is to save our children from disturbing images and ideas, and to help parents do the same for their kids, but both points fall apart in reality. All this talk about children, in terms of procedure, is really secondary. The first person to be affected—usually to his or her detriment—is the filmmaker, who runs a severe fiscal risk with an NC-17 and its attendant media and advertising blackout. Also, many theaters are wary of booking films with the NC-17 brand. While Valenti may claim that the ratings board saves films from government tampering, it only institutionalizes that tampering by having one group (his MPAA) do the tampering, via a set of constantly shifting "moral" guidelines. And while holding out the carrot of creative freedom, it also makes clear the limits on that freedom, and the punishment waiting should those limits be transgressed.

The first two X ratings were given to, respectively, *The Killing of Sister George* (1968), because it was about lesbians, and *Midnight Cowboy* (1968) because its title character, a hustler, has gay encounters. Also, at the time, the words "fuck" or "shit" or the depiction of *any* drug use automatically gave the film an R rating (until the 1976 anti-blacklist film, *The Front*, made MPAA history by allowing Woody Allen to say "fuck" and get a GP rating).

Both *Sister* and *Midnight* are now out on video with an R rating. Like pornographers of the time, the producers of these films found that the X brand on their films added a certain "nasty" glamour that actually boosted ticket sales. Other films also exploited this cache of the forbidden—usually "exploitation" or genre efforts—and one saw the irony of an X actually drumming up interest for films that might have slipped by unnoticed. But with the replacement of the NC-17, this has changed.

The reason for the disparity of the ratings over the years—the changing of *Sister* and *Midnight's* damning X in '69 to its current, accessible R—is due, according to Valenti, to the changing nature of what society finds upsetting in terms of content (or, more accurately, what *the board* finds disturbing). That a film can become less "X"-ish over time is of small condolence to a filmmaker whose movie has either been cut to incomprehensible ribbons or rated into obscurity because of the perceived morals present at the time of its rating.

Because the ratings board claims it rates all films on a "by case" basis and holds no prejudice regarding any type of film, it's significant to note that— especially in the last 15 years—NC-17's are almost always given to independent films either produced or released by companies that are not MPAA signatories. These films include the critically praised *The Cook, The Thief, His Wife & Her Lover* (1989, Peter Greenaway, Palace/Miramax), *Santa Sangre* (1989 Alexandro Jodorowsky, Intersound), *Tie Me Up! Tie Me Down!* (1990, Pedro Almodovar, Laurenfilm, S.A.) and *Poison* (1991, Todd Haynes, Zeitgeist Films).

In the opinion of independent filmmaker Ulli Lommel, "I think the MPAA was created by the major studios to protect themselves against independents. In the 80s, most of the independent distributors died. What happened is, the majors produced exploitation movies with big budgets like *Lethal Weapon*, which in the end are much less fun, and took the independent market away. And if you still wanted to make a movie that was pushing the envelope, they'd just give you an X rating. But if it had been a studio film, you could get away with much more."

As of this writing, only two NC-17's have ever been given to major studio releases: Russ Meyer's hilarious sex satire, *Beyond the Valley of the Dolls* (20th Century Fox, 1970), and Paul Verhoeven's inadvertently hilarious strip-joint exposé *Showgirls* (United Artists, 1995).

Going all the way back to *Midnight Cowboy*, *Killing of Sister George* and *Blow Out*, the predominant cause for an NC-17 is a sexual one (*all* of the above-listed films were sexually "problematic"). Bodies may be shredded (*Die Hard II*—20th Century Fox, R), ice-picked (*Basic Instinct*—Tri-Star, R) or shot to ribbons (any big-budget action movie) but God forbid we should see naked bodies making love. Nakedness itself is subjected to a hypocritical, unspoken code, with nudity allowed for women, but male nakedness usually limited to chests and fleeting glimpses of buttocks, with the showing of an actual penis out of the question. (And what sort of message does this give children?)

With all this in mind, Valenti's claim—"contrary to popular notion, violence is not treated more leniently than any of the other material"— is simply not true.

Although it changes through the years, the MPAA *does* have a moral agenda. It is one that, if only by default, promotes mindless, consequence-free violence in major studio films, and negates any serious depiction or "discussion" of adult themes or sexuality. And the key word here is "adult," because, even in less "permissive" times, a soft-core, frat-boy annoyance like *Porky's* (1984, 20th Century Fox) and its slew of imitators had no trouble getting an R (one *Porky's* "highlight" had Kim Cattrall driven into a psycho-sexual frenzy after sniffing some boys' socks and jockstraps, while some other boys peeked from afar and made leering remarks). So it seems sex is okay as long as the film is a major studio effort, the people in the film morons and the sex straight off the scribbling in a junior high school lavatory.

Things become even more insidious, in terms of ultimate censorship, when one takes into account the policies of major video outlets such as Blockbuster Video and Wal-Mart.

For years, theatrical release revenues have been on a downslide, to the point where a theatrical release becomes, to a great degree, a form of advertising for multi-media incarnations such as video, laserdisc, DVD, HDTV and future "delivery systems," where the real money is. Both Blockbuster and Wal-Mart have made it policy to ban *any* title with an NC-17 rating. It has also been reported that they will send NC-17's back to their producers and then back to the MPAA for special R-rated Blockbuster Video editions.

The MPAA maintains it is free of any commercial considerations. In its statement of purpose, it claims that it bases ratings on "theme, violence, language, nudity, sensuality, drug abuse, and other elements." Good wording there, as it allows the Ratings Board free reign to curb anyone's creative freedom and just say it was an "other element" situation.

In reality, it's more likely these objectionable "themes" and "other elements" are usually parts of a movie that in some way are critical of consumer culture, or the corporations that encourage it. Although *Passenger 57* (1992), *On Deadly Ground* (1994), *Outbreak* (1995) and hundreds of other action films routinely present us with "corporate bad guys"—usually with all the believability of a Saturday morning cartoon "heavy"—in the end, it's another set of "good" corporate types who help save the day. In fact, the juxtaposition of "good" corporate types vanquishing bad is seen in innumerable action films, and so strengthens the idea of the Company as a stable, self-servicing entity that, in the end, will take care of things to the customer's satisfaction. A movie that honestly cuts close to the corporate bone like George Romero's *Dawn of the Dead* (1979), with its perfect metaphor of mall shoppers as the living dead, is another matter entirely, and would probably have trouble garnering even an NC-17 if released today. In Greenaway's *The Cook, The Thief, His Wife & Her Lover*, it would *seem* that the film got its NC-17 because it dealt with cannibalism and showed—for about two seconds—a dead man's penis. But what Greenaway's film is really about is the absurdity of mindless acquisition, a bad choice for a movie released at the peak of the Reagan/Bush era.

So what would happen if the MPAA were somehow abolished, if there were no censors?

Probably nothing. Or at least not the things pro-MPAA people would have you think.

The issue of our children being saved from dangerous ideas and images in movies is only an issue if you could also remove children from a culture and mediascape infinitely more dangerous than any movie (here in reality, rape, incest, murder, you name it—are, well, for real).

If parents performed the job of parenting (something people tacitly hand over to the MPAA, TV censors—and now the V-chip—with increasing regularity, creating a new form of absentee parenting), this issue would become negligible. Minus ratings and their technological supports, parents might spend the scant time needed to figure out for themselves that certain films are for adults and deal with it from there. And perhaps parents would stop their kids from gorging on TV (where there's an average of five acts of simulated violence every prime time night, and 20-25 violent acts on Saturday morning children's TV). In short, there's nothing awful under the sun a kid today hasn't seen simulated or talked about on TV, in magazines, or on the 7 o'clock news.

If there were no censors, filmmakers could pursue with impunity whatever topics and visions they liked. But, by and large, they don't. Years of fighting the constantly shifting content "guidelines" of the rating system have made experienced filmmakers weary of anything that will incur the MPAA's disapproval, while a new generation of film careerists don't even bother to challenge the ratings system and its artistically limiting restrictions.

But we *do* have censors. With the MPAA on the job, what we really lose is the chance to see movies truly geared for adults, whether in terms of content and/or imagery.

POSTSCRIPT

According to a piece written by Neil Strauss, "family retailers such as Kmart and Blockbuster Video are, as a matter of policy, recutting movies, removing scenes and changing video boxes, often without the director's consent, so that Blockbuster, the huge video chain, will put them on its shelves."

Director Oliver Stone (whose "director's cut" of *Natural Born Killers* (1994) was banned by Blockbuster, Kmart *and* Wal-Mart) describes Blockbuster's and the studios' compliance as "a new form of censorship. . . Studios like Warner Bros. won't even release a film rated NC-17. People don't understand how much power these corporations have."

Recent examples of Blockbuster-edited films run the gamut from the critically acclaimed *Wide Sargasso Sea* (1993) to the trashy-fun B movie *Sgt. Kabukiman* (1995).

According to Chuck Warn, a spokesman for the Directors Guild of America, "Often times, editing changes are made without the filmmaker's knowledge. It can be very damaging to someone's career."

As of December 9, 1996, Blockbuster had 4,500 outlets nationwide, and rented out as much as 30% of all videos rented that year. It is expected to double that market share over the next year.

In the Belly of the Beast: Director Michael Lehmann

PARTIAL FILMOGRAPHY:

Heathers	1987
Meet the Applegates	1989
Hudson Hawk	1991
Airheads	1994
Ed Wood (assoc. producer)	1994
The Truth about Cats and Dogs	1995
My Giant	1998
Stormy Weather	199—?

In 1987, a film sneaked into the theaters of America, a brilliantly misanthropic take on a perennial movie set-up: high school as rite of passage. It was a nasty, pathological, closed world populated by cliques, racism, and idiotic teachers, with a bomb-wielding psycho as the primary love interest. A world where blowing up the school was an "up" moment, where the depressed and alienated heroine (a then-unknown Winona Ryder) could mutter: "My teen angst bullshit just got a body count."

All this at the peak of the Reagan Years.

The film, *Heathers*, did nicely at the box office, and became a cult favorite. Its director was Michael Lehmann.

So it came as a crushing blow when this sparkling, obnoxiously satirical director's next film (after the ambitious, but flawed, *Meet the Applegates*) should turn out to be the bloated "action" flop *Hudson Hawk*, complete with legendary troubled production, and packed to the gills with stars (Bruce Willis, Andie MacDowell, James Coburn).

Lehmann is a soft-spoken and well-meaning person but also sometimes maddeningly careful with his remarks about the business he is in.

The strangest (and perhaps most revealing) thing about our conversation was that when we spoke about "They," we always knew "who" we were talking about (mainly, the corporate types who thwart Lehmann's every other move).

I also got a palpable sense of Faustian tragedy when talking with Lehmann: Here's a man who's working in the belly of the Beast, but who *also* wants to and occasionally can speak the truth, although every word may wake that Beast that allows him to make films.

And sometimes doesn't.

IG: Was there ever a moment when you were making *Hudson Hawk* that you thought about *Heathers* and your work at film school and wondered "What am I *doing* here?"

ML: Yeeeaaahhh. Well. You mean what am I doing making bad movies?

IG: Well, not so much bad as big-budgeted, packed with stars, tons of foreign locations, zillions of dollars. Like that. My first reaction to hearing you'd directed this after *Heathers* was, *excuse me?*

ML: Yeah, well, there was a perverse desire on my part to take a genre that is ruled by convention and...try to pervert it...So people always ask me, "Why did you do *Hudson Hawk?*" and I say: Because I thought I could do something very unusual in a very usual genre.

I ask about Bruce Willis's reported ego problems and sundry studio interferences. Lehmann seems reluctant to take these particular bulls by the horn— he *does* have to work with these people—but still offers:

ML: You know, when you make a movie of that scale, *a lot* of people have a stake in making it something that fits *their* needs. At any point, there's more forces at play than when you make a small film and it's just the director.

[Its failure] was very difficult for me personally, because my experience was really in making more personal films. I thought I could get away with working the same way on a larger picture. It just does not happen.

You can say, "How *naïve* were you?" I mean, I'm sure James Cameron, who's very successful at these big films, thinks they're personal films, but you need to get a success at that level first. Before you can use that kind of power with the kind of people who make those movies.

"(Bruce) Willis had great expectations for *Hudson Hawk*. The star called all the creative shots...imposing his will on director Michael Lehmann...Willis was told that the cost of the film had passed $50 million. 'I don't give a shit,' he reportedly answered...an insider says, 'They didn't ever stop him. They let him go totally insane.'"

—Nancy Griffin and Kim Masters, *Hit & Run: How Jon Peters and Peter Guber Took Sony for a Ride in Hollywood*

IG: I read an interview with John Schlesinger where he says he no longer makes films like *Midnight Cowboy, Sunday, Bloody Sunday*—all these great films. Now he's making awful suspense and action movies. And he said something like, "Well, I like to keep working, number one, and two, They wouldn't *allow* me to make a movie like *Midnight Cowboy* today."
Do you think that's true?

ML: ...For one thing, I wouldn't say I'm not *allowed*, it's that I can't get anybody to *pay* to make those films. It does come down to simple economics. If the studios thought that a movie like *Midnight Cowboy* was going to be successful right now—at this point, you've got to look at the kind of movies that make money.

At this answer, I have to wonder: How can you claim studios "allow" films to be made, while saying at the same time that they only pay for—meaning "allow"—movies that are perceived to be moneymakers? The two ideas are self-canceling. So:

IG: Then what you're talking about, essentially, is sequels without original films.

ML: The glib answer which you hear from a lot of people, and I think has a lot of truth to it, is that over the years, the science of marketing product has become more sophisticated.
You get people being trained in business schools, and as people with that kind of background get involved in the decision making positions, then you find them operating according to the science of marketing, which is sell people a product that's familiar, right?
If you're trying to sell people on something they aren't familiar with, it's a crapshoot. And because the decisions that make a movie happen a year before a movie hits a theater, you start to see why conserva-

tive marketing people will look at it and say, "Well, we're into a product
that'll cost anywhere from $15 to $150 million by the time the advertising
is paid for—how do we sell enough tickets to get our money back and
more?" So, when you're one of those people, you don't think about *content*,
you think about what *elements* you can use to sell a movie to audiences.

IG: But *Heathers* got released, and it was definitely this oddball, spunky little
movie. Why couldn't you do another film in that vain?

ML: One of the things that happens—and for this I have no excuse—if you
want to make really unusual movies, you have to make them on a really
low budget.

    Heathers cost somewhere under $3 million. You *can* make movies
cheaply. But everybody involved can't get paid very much. In fact, you
can't get known actors—*Heathers* had teenagers; none of them were
known very much at the time. It does happen. *Pulp Fiction* is a good
example, where you get pretty well-known actors—including Bruce
Willis—to take far less money than they normally would. It's because
they think it's cool material or something, and you get the movie made.

    You can do what Todd Haynes or Hal Hartley do, make low budget
films outside Hollywood. Or you can do what the Coen brothers do and
put together a company and do their own financing. *Hudsucker Proxy* was
probably a bit like *Hudson Hawk*, in the sense that it was a big movie
that, for the marketplace, was *too* big for the kind of sensibility that was
behind it.

IG: You mention Todd Haynes and Hal Hartley. After *Heathers*, why did you
even *want* big stars and bigger budgets? They (Haynes and Hartley) seem
to get along pretty well without them.

ML: They get along okay. I've asked myself the question...

    To me, the idea of working in an artistically conservative field that
was polluted by marketing...if I could somehow get in there and do
really odd, really good work in that context—it would kind of be the
right niche for me to carve out, you know what I mean?

    I would love to be able to do that, but I've realized I've been less
successful at it than I'd hoped. And I'm also realizing after years that it's a
game that's very tough to win—

IG: —that it's making a deal with the Devil, once you get those stars, those
budgets—

ML: Yeah—it's hard to do what you want to do.

    And then you start making little changes [to placate studio people]
and you think, "Well, okay, I can do this a little differently," and pretty
soon you've ruined your movie.

Ultimately, you are either a fully independent filmmaker, or you can work in the system. To try to be in-between—which I tried to do and will keep trying to do, because I think I'm figuring out how to do it—

IG: —you mean, how to fool Them?

ML: I used to think that, but I've realized that the people who run the entertainment business are too smart to be fooled that way. People don't just part with sums of money this high, are much more *involved* and much more *nervous* about losing their money.

So, anything that's risky or unusual—forget it.

IG: How do you run this gauntlet? How do you inject satiric or subversive aspects into the work?

ML: You push really hard all over the place. Even to make a movie like *The Truth about Cats and Dogs*, which I think is a very mainstream movie, and then have it star Janeane Garofalo—you can't *imagine*.

IG: Why? Was there a problem because she's not blond, blue-eyed, not—aw, hell, let's face it: she's *ethnic*.

ML: Yeah!

And I think the reason I was able to get it together is that people think Janeane is really *funny*.

I got involved partly because I saw it as a great vehicle for Janeane. There was no question about her talent, it was more—"How do we sell this to a mainstream, large audience as a movie with Janeane Garofalo, when nobody knows who she is in the world that pays for movie tickets?" And I said, "Well, you make a really good movie and people will come." Getting Uma Thurman involved was helpful because of [her success in] *Pulp Fiction*.

These guys do *research* to see who audiences will pay money to see! *But you can never predict who's going to want to see somebody they've never seen before.*

When you try to tell them marketing *isn't* a science, they show statistics. What I found, and this is interesting and it absolutely disgusted me to find out is: These people are not evil! I wish they were!

IG: I talked to another director, and he thought the worst thing was that they were indifferent. That indifference was worse than if they were monsters, because if they were monsters, then you could just get a stake and a hammer and—

ML: —I don't agree with that. If they were indifferent, it would be easier for me because then I could call them indifferent monsters.

The real problem is that the people who get into business positions in the movies—I think they could be off selling shoes, or oil or something,

but they've made choices to get into the entertainment field because somehow they find it glamorous or interesting. They think that on some level
they're involved in the creation of, if not art, then popular culture.

Probably what makes some of the more difficult movie executives—
for *me* difficult—what makes them *scary*, is that they're *not* indifferent, that
they really care and they really have horrible taste! They're not monsters—but they don't think like artists or creative people. They're dealing
in another realm. They want to make good *product*.

IG: With the blockbuster mentality in mind, why does every movie a) have
to cost so much, and b) why, even if it somehow doesn't cost much, are
the returns expected to be so high?

ML: You're asking the wrong guy! I was delighted *The Truth about Cats and
Dogs* cost very little by studio standards and made a moderate amount. As
far as I'm concerned, it's a big success.

But you compare it to the summer blockbusters and it's a joke. *The
Cable Guy*, which is ludicrously considered a disappointment, made more
money in two weeks than Cats and Dogs made in ten weeks.

I ask about another one of Lehmann's films that was full of good inten-
tions and came out less than satisfying—his rock 'n roll comedy, *Airheads*.

ML: I wanted to make a rock 'n roll picture. It was a rock 'n roll movie and I
was obligated to make it a PG-13. Which meant we couldn't even use
the word "fuck" in the movie. So right off the top, well—it was not clear
to me...I just didn't realize what I was getting into [about the rating]. I
also didn't realize the studio would say this is a youth-oriented movie,
and they [kids] can't get into an R-rated movie, and I said "Bullshit, I
went to R-rated movies all the time." They said, "Oh no; it's changed,
things are more conservative. Kids can't get into those movies."

I had the same problem with *Cats and Dogs*, where I had to make *big*
changes to make it PG-13. Ultimately, I appealed the ratings board until I
got a cut I could stand behind.

IG: Do you have to pay for those ratings appeals to the MPAA yourself?

ML: Well—you mean the studio has to pay for them. Usually what happens
is you appeal and they say No. Plain and simple. They don't change
very often...

But I want to get back to what I said about *taste*. In *Airheads*, I'd cast
Steve Buscemi, who I think is a great actor and I think he was good in
it, and I had to fight *really hard* to get him approved.

In the first week of shooting I had a confrontation with one of the executives at Fox, who said "We're not making *Reservoir Dogs* here!" They were worried the movie would be too hip!

I really felt like saying "You guys would be *lucky* if you had anything *close* to a *Reservoir Dogs* on your hands!" It was all about having people like Steve in the movie. I'd make it too hard-edged, and I said I *can't* make it hard-edged with this PG-13 stranglehold and because essentially they would have shut the movie down and [it would have] been the end of my career as a director in Hollywood.

IG: For doing *what*?

ML: For not making it into a nice, clean, funny teen movie.

Then after *Airheads* came out, the studio's going "We need to make more movies like *Pulp Fiction*!" The *same guys* who'd threatened to shut down the movie for being too much like *Reservoir Dogs*!

IG: How do you deal with this?

ML: You realize that the reason they said it is because they saw *Pulp Fiction* could make money.

IG: So you're dealing with a business environment where the people who decide what kind of films you make are always trying to second-guess the impossible.

ML: *Ab-so-lutely*! And the reason independent movies are and always will be more interesting, more varied, more *intelligent* is that they're creatively driven by the artist.

IG: Do you ever just get exhausted by it all, and just go, "Screw it, I want to make another weird movie?"

ML: Yes. All the time. Part of my problem is the weird projects I get involved in are all set up in the studios. So they're living a slow, painful death. You can't get them out of the hands of studios when they get there. For me to go back to really independent stuff, I'd need to find a way to extricate myself from the studios altogether. Then you're talking two to three years to get together a project.

It's hard for me to do that, because, like John Schlesinger said, I love to work. I'm in the studio world and I can make movies and it's hard to leave. Hard to get out—the temptation is always so strong. The temptation that you'll be able to make an interesting film that'll be released by a major studio and seen around the world by everybody and become part of the popular culture: that's a strong temptation.

IG: So is that the dangling carrot—that you can make a film a lot of people will see, as opposed to something that just shows in a few "art" houses?

ML: I really do think so. There's a lot of great filmmakers who don't seem to care about that. They're driven by a personal vision and happy to have their work seen by 20,000 people and get nice reviews in the smarter publications.

        I actually really admire that, but once you get bitten, so to speak, by Hollywood, it's hard to turn away from it. You're always thinking you'll be able to make that great film—

IG: —that sneaks through the cracks in the wall—

ML: Yeah. I like to think that I started off making films that were fairly sub-versive, and that's what I'd like to be doing, but there's the question of how do you get those things through? *Pulp Fiction*, by the way, is probably the only case.

IG: So if you even vary an inch from formula, it's "avant garde" in their eyes.

ML: That's true.

With that depressing thought in mind, I bring up a concept I'd cobbled together while grocery shopping.

The idea is: in the real world, you have, say, Skippy™ peanut butter. It's never going to go above a certain level sales-wise, but it does sell at a steady clip. In Hollywood, before the Blockbuster began eating everything else in sight, you had certain films—"B" films, if you like—that came out without the expectation of making a mint, just turning a steady, reliable profit—the Skippy™ of film. That seems to be the basis of a functioning capitalistic economy. But if you have an industry where Lehmann's modestly-budgeted *Truth about Cats and Dogs*, or even more irrationally, Jim Carrey's *The Cable Guy*, which "only" earned a measly 80 mil or so, can be considered *failures* (or worse, "negligible" earners)—isn't the entire system headed for a serious fall?

Although Lehmann insists that somebody at Fox was pleased to have a modest success like *Cats and Dogs*, I press on, saying I'm talking more metaphorically—that it's just the idea of everything having to have these inflated budgets, this general sense of hugeness. It just seems like a setup for a scary crash.

ML: I think you might just be getting millennial.

IG: [Laughs—but thinks, So?] But these films *do* suck away at the talent pool. And everything starts looking the same, feeling the same as the same people keep churning out basically the same movie. I saw *Eraser*—a very competent thing with all the pieces in the usual places—with a very "normal," suburban crowd, and when it was over, everybody just had this dulled, glazed look to them.

ML: But once again, that movie made lots of money for the people who made it.

IG: So we're in for more of the same.

ML: Yes.

IG: So your vision of the future is that they will keep pumping out this stuff, and guys like you will keep struggling to sneak stuff in the back door.

ML: Yeah. Yeah. I think the making of big pictures will continue because as home systems become more sophisticated, you're going to have to find ways—and this is part of what's going on—of getting people out of their house.

The *bad* news is that the easiest way to distinguish theatrical entertainment from home entertainment is just the level of *spectacle.*

You get to see on a big screen a tornado throw a cow around.

While I'm always game to make remarks about *Twister*'s acclaimed flying cow effect, I'm also thinking that Lehmann has it all backwards here. That with videos, CD-ROMs, DVDs and all the rest, what "They" want is to *keep* you home. Or at The Mall, fervently shopping for the latest videos, CD-ROMs, DVDs and all the rest. Either way, it seems a rather bleak scenario.

ML: I think the only thing that will save us from that bleak scenario is that people will leave home to see a smaller, smarter film if somehow they figure out it's worth their while.

IG: On what screens, I wonder?

ML: I'm still hoping. But it's still product to them, they're talking "product." Art in the early 20th century tradition of being driven by an individual— well, there's never been much room for that in Hollywood. But yes, people like me are going to try to sneak it in there.

POSTSCRIPT:

I spoke with Lehmann months later. He was, once again, trying to convince those people with horrible taste to do something not horrible.

He was desperately trying to bring an adaptation of Carl Hiaasen's *Stormy Weather* to the screen minus the grisly fate met by the imbecilic adaptation of Hiaasen's other fine book, *Striptease*.

Possibly one of America's finest working popular satirists, Hiaasen tells in *Stormy Weather* a tale of Florida *after* a hurricane. It's a character-driven thing, focusing on the foibles of an arrestingly offbeat cast of characters. The execs—hearing only the hurricane and not the story—say something like, "Oh! Cool! So it'll be like *Twister*, but with laughs, right?"

POST-POSTSCRIPT:

A couple months after this, I called Lehmann again. Graciously, he talked to me from the set of his new film, which I learned was not *Stormy Weather*, but rather, the new Billy Crystal sports comedy, *My Giant*.

Sexual Awakenings

Beginning in the '60s, movies became increasingly direct in addressing sexual matters and images. Many of these films were aimed at the burgeoning "youth culture" of the time, and were often financed by small companies and individuals given more creative latitude due to the breakup of the "studio system." Just a few examples are Francis Ford Coppola's *You're a Big Boy Now* (1966), a psychedelic boy-coming-of-age-with-a-stripper film, John Huston's depressing look at a closeted military man in *Reflections in a Golden Eye* (1967), and Jim McBride's all-nude stroll through a post-apocalyptic world in *Glen and Randa* (1969).

The big sex breakthrough came in 1969 with the popularity of *I Am Curious:Yellow*, a pretty terrible film from Denmark that had a few very explicit sex scenes. Because of its popularity, *Yellow* cued Hollywood to a frank, more "European" expression of sex and nudity. America was finally ready.

The majority of these '60s movies were either naïve or dated in terms of technique and attitude, but this is mitigated by the fact that this was the first time people were trying to deal in a vaguely adult way with sex in American film. Compared to the way sex is presented in movies today, these films were virtual paragons of audacity and insight. Now, on-screen sex, like plot and character, has become nothing more than a bit of information, ready for pruning via what one might call the word processor mode of filmmaking. That is, cut, paste and, most often for a Blockbuster Video release, delete.

The '70s came and Hollywood cinema, for the first time, engaged in a very brief period of sexual frankness, maturity and intelligence. A period that began somewhere at the tail end of the '60s, and ended around the time of the Reagan '80s reign of unfettered deregulation, greed, and corporate control. For the only time in the history of American movies, one could actually listen to an actor say something like "I do nudity, but only if it's part of the story" and not burst out laughing.

For evidence, witness the examples of these fine-to-classic films:

Dog Day Afternoon (1975). Al Pacino robs a New York bank to pay for his boyfriend's sex change operation.

Coming Home (1978). A soldier returns from 'Nam not only crippled, but unable to get his Little Fella working. A game Jane Fonda tries to help.

Last Tango in Paris (1972). Okay, it was directed by a Euro-guy (Bertolucci) and shot in Europe, but for all intents and purposes, is basically an ode to American male menopause, featuring a pre-whale-shaped Marlon Brando cynically summing up male/female relationships with the immortal line "Let's just say we're talking a flying fuck on a rolling donut." And despite the notorious butter/sodomy scene, which *is* fairly explicit, what is *not* explicit is the brand of butter used for this famed rear entry. Something product-placement-happy, modern cinema would never slip up on.

Now, can you imagine any current major star playing a gay bank robber, an impotent wreck, or a chubby sodomist (or being allowed to do so by his studio)?

I can't. And I thought about it a long time.

Porn Queenpin:
Pornographer Dian Hanson

Dian Hanson is an extremely successful businesswoman. Tall, attractive and highly literate, she is able to expound with great wit and grace on most any subject.

Her business is that of soft-core pornography, her empire built mainly around fetish magazines such as *Leg Show* ("catering to foot fetishists, people who like old fashioned glamour photography, all manner of odd and out-dated lingerie"), *Juggs* ("the sideshow of tit mags") and *Bust Out* ("totally unnatural, heavily modified women").

So what, one may ask, is a woman of such a specific pedigree doing in a book dealing, one way or another, with film?

Well, what is film but an endless parade of bodies captured in silver nitrate for our viewing pleasure? And what are our deep-seated, unspoken motives when we gaze at these objects of our celluloid desire? And why the hell does Demi Moore keep getting her body redone?

Ms. Hanson seems uniquely suited, being a woman who traffics in bodies and desires, to attempt answers to these vitally important questions. Especially the last one.

IG: Is there any essential difference between your magazines and their audience and what we get in high-ticket films like *Striptease* [featuring Demi Moore's newly-augmented décolletage]?

DH: Yes. Pornography is successful. This flurry of strip movies are bombs.

IG: Why?

DH: Because they don't deliver anything. For the same reason upscale porn has always failed: there isn't enough to masturbate to. Pornography is about the promotion of masturbation, and men have different triggers. In hardcore, they're getting off on the spectacle of sex.

IG: So these erotic, made-for-cable movies—

DH: —there's just not enough there. I read a really good review that said most of the movers and shakers in Hollywood are wealthy middle-aged men who get a kick out of seeing Demi Moore's boobs, while the majority of the masturbators could care less about Demi Moore and her boobs. I mean, really: *who cares?* The appeal in my magazines...it's like seeing a neighbor with her boobs out. They're never going to get to have Demi Moore, she really isn't doing enough and she just isn't sexy enough. It's more stimulating to see a *real* dancer. And of course *Showgirls* [mega-flop about strippers written by revered hack Joe Eszterhaus] was heinous. As all the girls pointed out, they don't have big enough tits.

IG: Well then, what's the allure of nude movie star magazines?

DH: Those magazines seem to be more popular with women then with men. What I like about them—and they're one of the few magazines with a crossover audience—is the pleasure of comparison, like, Ha! Look at her! I look better than *her!* We had an issue of *Celebrity Sleuth* here in the office, and the women went for it faster than the men.

IG: Do you think there's a female version of pornography?

DH: Sure. Romance novels. Soap operas. Women's fantasy needs are different from men's. Men fantasize heavily about raw sex. Women, the majority, fantasize romance, because they're getting plenty of sex in their lives. Men are not getting enough sex: men with their greater levels of testosterone, and their role as *sperminators*. The male role is to eject their sperm into as many orifices as possible. It's a biological imperative. Women's biological imperative is to *select* the proper one. And kick the rejects out.

IG: Bodies. We were on the topic of Demi Moore and her morphing breasts, but then there's Melanie Griffith, Cher and, of course, Jane Fonda. I wonder if it's all a trickle-down effect from porn.

DH: You mean with tit jobs?

IG: Well, surgery in general. It seems there are really no women in mainstream films who are unmodified. With real breasts. For starters.

DH: There aren't in *America.*
    One of the problems in the sex industry is that by the time a girl's 18, she's already had her boob job. *Playboy* had an issue out with girls who

are "hardbodies": all muscle, and every one of them has a tit job. This is a new level—100% tit-job. *And these women are not even professional models!*

We are in a country where the first thing a women does when entering an appearance field is get a tit job. We are a computer-generated nation. I lay it all at the feet of Barbie™. She's to blame for all of this. There's a stripper out there who has the Mattel logo tattooed on her lower back! Just like Barbie™. Barbie™ is the ideal—a generation's ideal.

IG: Which would make Pamela Sue Anderson—

DH: Oh! I love her! She is Barbie™ incarnate!

She is computer-designed to appeal to men. She is *exactly everything* men desire biologically—a delicate chin, big wide-set eyes, abnormally large lips—of course, she's also got more Dynel™ coming out her head than any Barbie™ doll ever did. She should be made our National Bimbo.

IG: Then what's behind this desire for huge-breasted, Barbie women?

DH: We're a competitive nation. We're a nation of rejects and criminals. Aggressive people, people who left their homelands because they either had the drive, or they had to get out really fast! We figure out what sells best, we're capitalistic, and we perfect a product. And when women are the product, *the women perfect themselves.* Blond hair sells best. Lots of blond hair sells better. Little noses sell, big lips sell, big breasts sell. Tight high buttocks. They've figured it out and nobody wants to be left behind.

It's like agriculture—they figured out the perfect chicken, they've found what American livestock is ideal chicken for biggest breast yield, the ideal cow for pounds of meat for pound of bone, so they said, "Okay, we have the best—we won't have any other kind." They keep breeding and of course they end up *inbreeding* and the whole system is starting to collapse—

IG: —in porn, or in culture in general?

DH: It's just in porn. Right now, at least.

But it trickles down into the movies and television. TV and the movies are following *after* pornography.

IG: Can you think of a mainstream film you found erotic at all?

DH: A-ha! *Spartacus!* I *love* that there was a suggestion that *people had sex.* In *Spartacus* you had men toiling around in these minimal things, and there was that wonderful scene where the women come around to pick the men for the gladiator contest or whatever. And the women go down the line and are obviously seeing them as sex objects. They're talking about their qualities, *whispering* about the black man. And they pick this one and say, "Oh! And have them wear as *little* as is necessary!"

Of course, I also like a man with brains, which is my own duality, and men have a problem with duality.

IG: So that could be why women are portrayed in movies as either virgins or whores?

DH: I think it's because they're written by Joe Eszterhas. That poor, pathetic creature. Good Lord.

Selected Works of Joe Eszterhas, America's Highest-Paid Writer:

Fatal Attraction (1985) A married man's life is torn asunder by a quickie affair with a libidinous, insane, rabbit-killing book editor, played by Glenn Close.

Basic Instinct (1992) A cop seduced by a lunatic, ice-pick wielding, bisexual female (Sharon Stone).

Sliver (1993) An unduly sexual woman (Sharon Stone) moves into a high-rise condo and is quickly stalked by a psychopath, notably inhibiting her libidinous tendencies.

Showgirls (1995) The lives of strippers. A lunatic attacks one. She fights back, moves to LA.

DH: My complaint is that they're all so predictable. I just went to see *Independence Day*, and I was thrilled that they would *dare* to be so cliché! They put every single American movie cliché into a computer. One more cliché and the whole thing would just fall apart.

IG: The women in that. Amazing. A stripper, of course. And the competent Secretary of State—

DH: —who wears high heels—

IG: —in the middle of the apocalypse—

DH: —and it's the middle of the night, and she's checking on her ex-husband who we know she's going to be reunited with, because that's another American movie cliché. She never thinks to kick those things off!

IG: Going back to something you touched on—about how sex in mainstream films is inherently unsatisfying because they don't deliver the goods. If that's true, why are they there? All those obligatory love-making scenes.

DH: Because movie guys want to see chicks! And if you look at the biggest-grossing movies of all time? There's *no sex in them.*

The Ten Biggest Grossing Movies of All Time

Movie	Release Year	Total Gross	Adjusted Gross
1. Gone With the Wind	1939	$193.6	$863.3
2. Star Wars	1977	$322.8	$632.5
3. E.T	1982	$399.8	$594.3
4. The Ten Commandments	1956	$65.5	$572.5
5. The Sound of Music	1965	$163.2	$570.6
6. Jaws	1975	$260.0	$559.7
7. Doctor Zhivago	1965	$111.7	$542.5
8. The Jungle Book	1967	$135.5	$485.3
9. Snow White and the Seven Dwarfs	1937	$184.9	$476.3
10. Ben-Hur	1959	$70.0	$470.6

[Yep, not much sex.]

IG: Okay. I was wondering if there were any current stars you think are truly sexy.

DH: Well, if you really want to know about one I don't get *at all*, that would be Bridget Fonda. She is the blandest human being on the face of the Earth. She looks like an alien that came out of the mothership in *Close Encounters.* And yet guys love her [makes a baffled sound].

B-Girl of the Gods:
Actress Julie Strain

PARTIAL FILMOGRAPHY

Film	Year	Role
Double Impact	1991	Student
Sunset Heat	1991	Party Statuette
Kuffs	1992	Kane's girl
Psycho Cop 2	1992	Stephanie
Unnamable II	1992	Creature
Witchcraft IV: Virgin Heart	1992	Belladonna
Enemy Gold	1993	Jewel Panther
Fit to Kill	1993	Blue Steele
Future Shock	1993	Female Dancer
Love Bites	1993	Female Jogger
Beverly Hills Cop III	1994	Annihilator Girl
Sorceress	1994	Erica
Naked Gun 33 1/3:	1994	Dominatrix
Dallas Connection, The	1995	Black Widow
Married People, Single Sex II	1995	S&M woman
Midnight Confessions	1995	Mariana
Heavy Metal II	(in production)	

BOOKS

It's Only Art if It's Well Hung	(1996, Heavy Metal Publishing)
Sex Symbol Dynasty	(1996, Heavy Metal Publishing)

CD-ROM

Penthouse Interactive Virtual Photo Shoot, Disc 1
Johnny Mnemonic
Heidi's House

* Voted Worst Dressed of 1995 by *Star Magazine*
* Voted "Queen of B Movies" by *Premiere Magazine*

On the shelves of garishly-packaged direct-to-video action, sci-fi, horror and erotic thrillers, is a fascinating cinematic sexual ghetto.

The films are off-Hollywood, low-budget affairs, but are filled with a crackling, vibrant energy evident in even the cheapest production. They have titles like *Hollywood Chainsaw Hookers* (1988), *Witchcraft IV: Virgin Heart* (1992), and *Final Impact* (1991), and no pretensions to being "art" or to anything else except delivering what the titles promise. Often, directors and stars pitch in to pay for their films.

Here, B movie starlets and their admirers have found an alternative to the stultifying sameness and impersonal sexual presentation of corporate-managed movie sexuality. The lives of these films' glamorously down-scale stars—the trailer-park kung-fu queen, Cynthia Rothrock, no-nonsense fatale Michelle Bauer and blue-collar tough guy Martin Kove—are regularly chronicled with obsessive, affectionate detail in magazines like *Femme Fatale* and *Scream Queens*, in an endless assortment of 'zines, and via web-pages often frequented by the stars themselves.

It's an eccentric netherworld of film nerds, college students, and people tired of cookie-cutter effects/plots/bullshit. True filmmaking independence and a real sense of connectivity between "stars" and "fans" is the rule (as evidenced, for example, by personal star appearances at conventions and "alternative culture" stores).

And Julie Strain, star of more than 80 films, is the queen of this anarchic realm.

At six foot one in flats—*six foot seven* in her favorite S&M boots—Julie Strain is both a biological force of nature and a true bride of science, her Aryan perfection augmented by various surgeries and implementation. She's real and fake. She was literally *made* for the movies.

But Julie Strain is her own creation, her artificially amplified body a virtual icon of strength and domination. In her films she performs torrid ambi-sexual sex scenes, blasts opponents with heavy ordinance, rips men's guts out or tramples their flagging posts of desire while dressed in enough leather and latex to keep half the fetish industry in business.

She's also an ardent Christian who does softcore with no qualms. She's been called Queen of the B's, but her aim is higher: she wants to be Queen of all Media.

It wasn't always this way.

Julie comes from lower-income, heartland-America stock. While out riding a horse at the age of 11, she was kicked in the head by a stray mare. The result was total amnesia.

After many years spent reconstructing her identity from scratch, she then spent even more time in a stifling marriage. At the advanced age (by Hollywood standards) of 28, she left her small town life for a vague dream of stardom.

Five years later, Strain had starred in *eighty* films and videos, most of them in the horror, action and sexploitation genres. She has two photo books and several CD-ROMs out. *Premier Magazine* voted Julie "Queen of B Movies." There's even a Julie Strain computer screensaver.

From the depths of formless amnesia and a rural American nowhere, Julie Strain has re-made and remodeled her body and her self. Even her re-interpretation of Christian mythos becomes a personal text that has spiritual room for whip-wielding lesbian dominatrixes, machine-gun-toting cake-girls and foul-tempered vampires. Save a few unpleasant stints in major studio films, Ms. Strain has always done the movies on her own terms.

IG: Do you find you intimidate "powerful" male executives?

JS: I'm sure I intimidate *most* people I meet, although I eventually end up winning them over.

As far as powerful mogul types, I just walk in, slam my hands on their desks and sit on the top of a chair and just go "Hey! What's up?" instead of [little girl voice] "H-h-hi—can I come in and be a victim?" and have them play their power trips on me. I want them to know I'm not someone to tangle with. I am strictly business. I am six one and I *have* an *attitude.*

I took my pick-up and garbage can of clothes and drove to Los Angeles. I ate food out of cans. I was literally starving. I was about 28-29. I went, by *choice,* from riches to rags. I started in this business a bit older than everybody else, and with not much training, so I did every single job that came my way. I did infomercials for a hundred bucks. I would drive my truck anywhere. I would do the nudity they needed me to do. That bit part [as an extra] in *Bugsy,* that was a $35 job! I did whatever it took. A lot of girls end up doing things that are illegal, but I've never been forced into that position. Prostitution, dancing or whatever.

IG: Do you consider those things immoral?

JS: Well, a Christian—a "true" Christian, somebody who was on the judgmental side, know what I mean?—would think they're immoral.

I say the girls gotta do what they gotta do—they're gonna give it away for *free? Free* is fucking Tommy Lee [Jones] and pieces of shit like that. They might as well *charge* Mr. Stallone and get paid for it.

[Laughs] My motto.

IG: About your amnesia, resulting from that horse fall you suffered when you were a kid, did you have to build Julie Strain from scratch, after that?

JS: The amnesia.

I woke up in the hospital and said "Who am I?" I went to school for about a month with retarded people to learn my ABCs and 1-2-3s. Anything that was a trained thing—I won't call it brainwashing—but patterns that someone else tries to set for you, fears they *instill in your head*—they kinda get wiped out. So you have this clean, fresh person.

IG: And from there you created "Julie Strain."

JS: Yeah! I was married at the time to a very controlling man, and at the age of 25, I had to ask if I could have a glass of wine in my own home!

IG: From amnesia victim, to put-upon housewife, to "Pet of the Year."

JS: Yeah! Yeah! I was a "Pet of the Year" *after* the age of thirty! And with the money from the lawsuit from the horse accident, my girlfriends and I went to Las Vegas. At a Sugar Ray Leonard-Duran fight, a gentleman said "Oh! You're great—come to LA—I'll make you a star!"

I definitely *wanted* to do it...but I had no clue as to how. That's how I started. It was about survival—now I'm sitting on top of Mount Everest on my ass, with my hands on the flag and a bottle of champagne in the other hand! I've just *conquered* it!

IG: Did you try hard in the beginning to fit into the Hollywood system? Or did you target B movies right off?

JS: I realized that was where I was comfortable, that any time I had a speaking role in an "A" movie, there was a lot of pressure. So I was happiest being the big fish swimming around the little pond in B pictures. I would do, say, a great job on *Witchcraft IV*, which was one of my first big roles. I did a movie with Jessica Hahn, one with Morton Downey, Jr.

IG: Some of your credits: "Annihilator" in *Beverly Hills Cop III*, "Dominatrix" in *Naked Gun 33 1/3*. Did you get the feeling you were being typecast right off?

JS: I don't mind that. I tell people I'm the only one who can play those parts. After you see my picture book, who else would you choose to play a dominatrix, who else would you choose to play a vampire? I mean, that's the niche *I built for myself*. I found what I was good at and bought those thigh-high leather boots.

IG: Speaking of building yourself, you're pretty up front about implants and such. Do you think actresses are forced by the market to compete, or is it some weird aesthetic?

JS: My motto on all that plastic surgery is: "You don't take a car to the car show without chrome on the bumpers, baby!"

IG: [Clears throat]

JS: *It's a contest!*
      Unless you are some magical Hail Mary comin' from home town with *big* ol' titties and *full* lips and the *perfect* ass—God bless you, there aren't too many of 'em!—then you better come here and get it done, because 500 other people going for the same job have had it done for them.
      It's just a necessary part of the job. It's all—Bigger! Better! Hollywood! It's bigger than life...

IG: I've heard tell of a sort of black market circle of doctors who do most of this implant work. Is this just paranoid science fiction or—

JS: There are *definitely* "B" doctors in LA who specialize in doing boob jobs, who give these strippers these jumbo tits. It's kind of a word-of-mouth business, so whoever you see, and you like their breasts, you go, "Hey, who's your doctor?" Still, I think a person should get psychological counseling before they're allowed to have implants beyond a certain size. I mean—really. Like Pandora Peaks, the girl that's in *Striptease*. Big, *big* boobs. They can be taken out, but gosh! Boobs bigger than your head, how are you going to get groceries?

From an anonymous post on the Internet:

"There's a LOT of body modification in the sex industry; in fact there's still a bizarre Big Tit Mafia operating out of Boston, fronted by a woman named Eleanor; dancers present her with their press kits, and if they pass the audition process, they are fronted the $7K it takes to obtain obscenely large implants, after which they are literally indentured dancers showgirling their way out of debt to Eleanor & Company.

"Strange offshoots of this have included a black market in pre-viously-used implants among dancers, to say nothing of the various heinous physical compromises, including loss of feeling in arms from nerve compression, implants "wandering" off, and of course, the potential that the damned things might burst, which has been rumored to have happened at least once…"

—a very well-informed source, in an e-mail to the author

IG: So what do you like more? Straight drama, sex, or kick-ass ultraviolence?

JS: The love scenes are *not* fun! It's like, "*Oh my God,* I don't believe I have to lay in bed with this person for eight hours!" And it's so *technical*—put your hand here, kiss my shoulder.

      The scenes I like are the ones where I have the most freedom to just *go off.* Like, when I'm strapping a girl to a post in a dominatrix scene. Now *that's* pretty fun! To really smack the *shit* outta somebody! And then get to walk away afterwards!

IG: You don't see any deep psychological aspects to this…

JS: Nope!

IG: It's just fun to kick ass.

JS: Yeah! It's *great* to kick ass, and carry big guns and heavy artillery. I've fired AK-47s and M-16s, and how many people get to do that and get paid for it? I'm havin' *a blast* down here in Hollywood.

IG: Some people might still say *you're* the one being exploited, but it seems *you're* the one exploiting the market.

JS: Yeah! Maybe that's a possibility. I've taken all the rules of what's acceptable and broken them, and started a new wave. A *Penthouse* girl—you'd *never* see them in a movie. Now, all of a sudden, all these girls, all my friends—Shauna O'Brian, Samantha Phillips—they're all doing movies now! I'm kind of a revolution, in that I'm making things happen that never happened before. And the fact I was *30* when I started. I figure, whatever Sharon Stone did, I can do better! I show nothing more than she does, I just do it so much more *erotically*.

IG: Do you find yourself being more private and careful?

JS: My husband and I are very private. I go to bed at nine o'clock. Pretty basic stuff.

Nudity

Via e-mail, I asked author Susan Brownmiller (*Against Our Will: Men, Women, and Rape*) the reason she thought movies favored female over male nudity. Her answer:

"I think you know the answer…it's because nudity is vulnerability, and males do not like to be vulnerable."

The obligatory nude scene as used in major studio films is perhaps the most overtly fetishistic aspect of the movies. It is usually done, as the chart below clearly demonstrates, by women. The nude scenes themselves are often shot separately from the rest of the film, as are other special effects scenes.

With all this skin, it's of note that the unveiling of the Celebrity Phallus was so long in coming (mainly thanks to the ever-game Harvey Keitel). Elderly people (those over 40) are not much in evidence.

NUDE SCENES

Male Actor		Female Actor	
Baldwin Alec	3	Andrews, Julie	3
Beatty, Warren	1	Arquette, Rosanna	9
Brando Marlon	1	Basinger, Kim	3
Bridges Jeff	2	Dunaway, Faye	4
Connery, Sean	1	Ekland, Britt	8
Costner Kevin	3	Fenn, Sherylin	8
Cruise, Tom	3	Fiorentino, Linda	7
Day-Lewis, Daniel	1	Fonda, Bridget	5

Gibson, Mel	4		Foster, Jodie	3
Redford Robert	0		Griffith, Melanie	9
DeNiro Robert	3		Hannah, Daryl	4
Depp, Johnny	1		Hawn, Goldie	5
Douglas, Michael	3		Hunter, Holly	2
Eastwood, Clint	1		Jackson, Glenda	5
Hoffman, Dustin	2		Kidman, Nicole	5
Keitel, Harvey	6		Leigh, Jennifer Jason	13
Lowe, Rob	4		Madonna	4
Malkovich, John	1		Moore, Demi	8
Newman, Paul	1		Pfeiffer, Michelle	1
Nicholson, Jack	3		Redgrave, Vanessa	6
Penn, Sean	1		Russell, Theresa	7
Reeves, Keanu	2		Ryan, Meg	3
Rourke, Mickey	1		Sarandon, Susan	8
Russell, Kurt	2		Shue, Elizebeth	5
Slater, Christian	3		Stone, Sharon	13
Spader, James	2		Strain, Julie	13
Stallone, Sylvester	3		Scacchi, Greta	11
Schwarzenegger, A.	3		Weaver, Sigourney	4
Woods, James	2		Young, Sean	9
	___			___

TOTAL:
58 performers.
Male nude scenes: 100   Female nude scenes   221

So: no nude scenes for older people, no frontals for males (again, save for Harvey Keitel). Ratio of female-to-male nudity: more than two-to-one. And the men mainly show off their butts.

The Life-Affirming Qualities of Extreme Gore

"The Texas Chainsaw Massacre *seems to be one of those movies that horror enthusiasts either love or hate. I loved it; for a 'Generation X'er,* Chainsaw *was the best kind of junk food...*

The scene I remember is where the main protagonist [a woman, trapped by a "family" of cannibals] is tied to a chair. What I remember is that the chair was partly made of human bone and that the table is littered with what looks like rotting meat. She screams, and they all scream with her, the truly creepy bad guys, their grainy skin wet with a faint gloss of slime.

For that extended dinner table scene, I was transfixed; the camera steadily closing in on her face as they try to bash her head in with a sledgehammer as the old man keeps dropping it into the metal tub via her skull. It seemed to go on for hours. The lens of the camera finally rests across her rolling eyes, so close that each tiny vein is huge, that I actually feel her panic.

Anyway, she breaks free pretty soon after that, and...you see her begin to lose her sanity as her own blood runs down her face and the camera closes in...

That entire film had a horribly sweaty feel to it, as if that dead landscape and the fashion and the type of film all came together exactly, so as to be terribly uncomfortable to watch...Pretty hardcore directing, you ask me."

—Danelle Perry, horror author

The gruesome depiction of violence—that is, *gore*—was first highlighted in films produced by the British independent studio, Hammer Films. Up until then, onscreen deaths were either depicted offscreen or by an actor clutching some wounded area and falling down. At most, a tiny droplet of blood was discreetly shed. In 1958, Hammer's *Horror of Dracula* changed all that. Although thought of as exploitive at the time, Hammer films actually presented violence with an eye towards artistry and a sense of the consequences of violence. Wounds bled, bodies decomposed, and death was often an agonizingly *slow* process. Based on box office tallies, audiences loved it.

Pro trend spotters such as producer William Castle quickly followed Hammer's example, adding gruesome bits to films like *The Tingler* (1958), although explicit depictions of violence wouldn't hit "respectable" films until many decades later.

As suggested by Ms. Perry's spirited take on *Texas Chainsaw Massacre*, extreme violence and its gruesome results invoke an unexpectedly invigorating aspect of movies: the depiction of extreme gore as an art in itself. It is also an art in the process of being corrupted and co-opted into meaninglessness by modern Hollywood, its viewers anesthetized by a lack of narrative context and consequence as the location of a "gore aesthetic" moves from horror to "action" films.

Stephen King has suggested that our interest in gore is based upon an "urge to stop and view the remains." While this is a part of it, an even more integral appeal of filmic gore is that it is a vicarious rehearsal for, and way of dealing with, mortality. Gore is—among other things—the *physical representation* of the scariest thing in town: death.

And so the gorier the better, if only as in *The Fly II*, where a cop's head gets too intimate with a hydraulic press (splat), yet we are given the slight assurance that, jeez, at least we won't end up like *that*. Or as the Marquis deSade put it in *The 120 Days of Sodom*: "It is in the sight of he…who suffers, that comes the charm of being able to say to one's self 'I am therefore happier than he.'"

The very presence of gore admits that violence not only *hurts*, but that its perpetration has *consequences* (the gruesome scene). Gore is life-affirming because it is, by definition, the literalization of everything *not* life-affirming. Sometimes, one needs a scalpel to find the cancer buried within.

This is not something limited to horror films: *Patton* (1970) communicates the lunacy of the titular general (and so makes complex his other attributes) by sticking our faces in the spilled entrails of battle. *Bonnie & Clyde* (1967), with its slow-motion end sequence showing the protagonists' bodies twitching, flailing and spouting blood from a seemingly endless hail of gunfire, is still nearly unbearable to watch. With this scene, the film graphically portrayed what forty years of gangster epics stringently denied. Death, in *Bonnie & Clyde,* was without glamour or any reassurances.

According to critic R.H.W. Dillard, (*Focus on the Horror Film*) gruesome movies function "in a decidedly 'instructive' fashion, much like a medieval morality play...to cope and even prevail over the evil of life." Fellow critic Robin Wood (*Film Comment 14*) echoes the sentiment by saying such fare allows us to deal with unconscious or symbolic fears "in more radical ways than our consciousness can countenance."

So we have what one could call the psychotherapeutic/instructive mode of gore (figuring out how to deal with our conscious recognition that we are mortal). There is also great cathartic value in seeing unconscious or symbolic fears blown—in the movies—to grotesque smithereens. If that was all there was to it, then gore would be a fine thing.

But there's even more:

Another enthusiast, writer/publisher Tim Lucas (editor, *Video Watchdog Magazine*) elaborates for us that—

> It isn't the quantity of gore, or the quality of the special makeup effects behind them, that makes a violent scene memorable—it's presentation, the context.
>
> One gore scene that I find particularly instructive is the spearing of Claudio Volante in Mario Bava's *A Bay of Blood* a.k.a. *Twitch of the Death Nerve.* He is speared to the wall by Luigi Pistilli, who covets his property, and there's the usual spurting, twisting, oozing and moaning. The scene is extremely violent, but by this point in the film, we have become inured to extreme violence. The scene doesn't make the viewer sit bolt upright until Volante surprises his murderer by vomiting blood onto his hand. All at once, the scene resonates with accusation and guilt, and we're reminded that murder is a dirty business, that shed blood runs hot, and that violence is an ugly, degrading thing.
>
> And then, in an inspired moment of contrast, the scene ends with the camera slowly tracking away from Volante as he dies pinned to the

wall, bathed in an almost holy light, the awful percussion of murder replaced by romantic, elegiac piano on the soundtrack. Before our eyes, this nasty character is relieved of his human burden, perhaps even forgiven his sins. In movies like this and the pioneering gore film *Blood and Black Lace*, Mario Bava took special care to imbue his most violent scenes with a spiritual quality that remains unique. No matter how mangled the body, he always took care to show the angel in the wreckage.

Mario Bava was a filmmaker possessed of a singular (if macabre) brilliance that was honed after years of working in various capacities for Frederico Fellini. As Lucas notes, it was Bava's unfettered artistry and his "care to show the angel in the wreckage" that not only justified, but made the on-display gore an integral part of the filmmaker's art. And Bava operated with *no corporate or studio supervision* of any kind once filming started. As poet/filmmaker Jean Cocteau wrote, "When I write, I disturb. When I show a film, I disturb…I have a knack for disturbing. I will be disturbing after my death."

Even the most gruesome or disgusting image can not only be a thing of beauty (if beauty of a very morbid kind) but also an integral part of a coherent work of art, an act of vision when created by an artist, as opposed to that of a hack. See the works of Goya, Hogarth, Rubens, Fuseli and Francis Bacon for examples of this in the "fine" arts.

Still, no matter the medium, it all depends on presentation and context— *and who controls and profits from that presentation and context.*

And here we hit a real-world mystery.

From 1970 until 1989 or so, the horror film was one of the single most commercially viable genres around. Yet, in true Agatha Christie fashion, the entire genre just up and disappeared somewhere near the twilight of the Reagan/Bush years.

Before we look at the strange lurch between the 1970s–'80s Horror Boom—in 1985 alone, there were 48 horror films released *theatrically*—and the rechanneling of horror energy and techniques into the new action film, here's a list of films that artistically explore sexual, psychological and political topics, are classics of their genre, and constitute what I classify as "Good Gore."

GOOD GORE HIGHLIGHTS

Film	Gore Highlight

Dawn of the Dead (1979) Pretty much nonstop gore of every imaginable sort, including flesh-eating zombies being stabbed, gutted and otherwise messily dispatched while trying to shop post-death in a huge mall.

Scanners (1981) One of a group of powerful telepaths (the creation of a decades-spanning pharmaceutical corporation's secret drugging of females to create such telepaths) proves his powers by blowing up another telepath's head. Scenes where people are simply shot with guns are not shown, because, as director David Cronenberg put it: "We all know what getting shot looks like." (*Cronenberg on Cronenberg*)

I Spit on Your Grave (1983) Woman is raped by several loutish males. Woman kills rapists, including graphic castration.

Driller Killer (1979) City life drives an urban painter mad, as he begins killing the neighborhood's elderly male bums, surrogates for what he fears he may become. With an unforgettable scene of the deranged painter discovering a new use for his power drill on an old wino seen through the glass of a bus stop.

Serpent and the Rainbow (1988) An anthropologist travels to Haiti to investigate possible cases of voodoo. Directed by Wes Craven, the film has several of his trademark "nightmare" scenes, but attains its gore highlight when (film takes place during the fall of dictator Duvalier) a good guy is tortured by the Ton-ton Macout (secret police), ending with what looks like the Macout smashing a nail through the good guy's balls.

So, we have men and women (or rather, "zombies") eating each other at the mall, someone's head blowing up, a woman castrating a rapist, a guy power-drilling bums, and nails through the scrotum. Taken that way, *as a list of simulated atrocities*, (which is always the way the MPAA, the Christian Coalition and other censorious groups do it), well, it doesn't seem either too life-affirming or too artistic.

On closer examination, one notes:

1) Each film was created by individual artists whose grim visions hit the screen uncut.

2) Each film presents the viewer with many horrid tableaux, but presents them within a context: an active reaction to rape in *I Spit on Your Grave*, and a comment on consumer society in *Dawn of the Dead*.

3) Each of these films shows the consequences of these acts. In *Scanners*, this special power leads to individual isolation and co-opting by insidious government agencies, while *Serpent* shows that because of the atrocities, the Haitians were galvanized to overthrow a two-bit dictator's real reign of horror.

All this artistic, visionary, *contextually-intractable* gore just fell off the map around 1990.

I must say that I don't believe in coincidences.

Horror (and gore) is in the business of pinching various psychic pressure points for its shocks. Among these pressure points are sex, identity, social mores, morality and, most importantly, *consequences and responsibility* arising from any dramatic presentation involving these topics. In this light, Ingmar Bergman's *The Virgin Spring,* with its themes of class warfare and sexual politics being turned into a "gore film" by Wes Craven in *Last House on the Left* isn't so confusing—Craven just updated it and took away the subtitles. Bruce F. Kawin, writing for *Film Quarterly* in 1981, remarked that the work of artists like Craven "often present us with images that are painful, grotesque, awful—horrible to look at—but they regularly imply that these images somehow need to be looked at, that they will show us something we might be more comfortable not to see but ought to see nonetheless."

Somewhere near the end of the '80s, those "things we ought to see" and the films that most matter-of-factly showed them petered out as horror energy was transferred to the new "action film" or summer blockbuster. The most visible turning point for this was with Paul Verhoeven's $90 million, sci-fi/action film, *Total Recall* (1990, presented in 70mm, Dolby SurroundSound™)

Verhoeven displays an impressive loathing for the human species in this story of a dim blue-collar guy (Arnold Schwarzenegger) who is implanted with the memories of a spy. Battling mysterious enemies at every turn, Arnold must then go to Mars for various contrived (and self-cancelling and therefore contextually empty) reasons, where he can slaughter even more enemies.

For Verhoeven, going to Mars is a regular laugh riot, as it allows Arnold to both bed *and* kill Sharon Stone ("Let's consider this a divorce!" quips Arnold), *and* to shoot, garrote and impale literally hundreds of extras. Arms are chopped off, guts ripped open, and—last, but certainly not least—Verhoeven treats us to the spectacle of watching a triple-breasted mutant prostitute get sprayed with gunfire.

"So what's the problem?" one might ask, considering my enthusiasm for this sort of thing.

In the case of *Total Recall*, much of "the problem" has to do with gore that is all empty sound and fury. The director's hatred and scorn of his fellow bipeds is *assumed* to be something we all share, and therefore, without context. I vividly recall walking away from the theater after seeing *Total Recall* feeling both pumped up (as if on cheap stimulants), enervated (as if coming down from said stimulants' ersatz "high"), and, in general, vaguely sullied. Bearing the film's title in mind, it was remarkable how little of what I'd seen stayed with me.

So it seems there is also a *non*-life-affirming version of on-screen mayhem (exemplified by *Total Recall*), a very corporate-friendly variety—what I'll call "Bad Gore."

The gore in modern action movies like *Total Recall* isn't gratuitous, it's most often the entire point. Like a porn film, graphic bloodletting is the modern action movie's "cum shot." Which is fine for porn, where the function is to inspire the viewer to masturbate—but with that in mind, what does *Total Recall* aspire to? Whatever the answer, it's worth mentioning that *Recall* batters its audience into the aforementioned excited/numbed-out state while simultaneously featuring a constant profusion of blatant on-screen "ads" for *USA Today,* Pepsi™ and other fine products.

BAD GORE HIGHLIGHTS

Film	Gore Highlight
Die Hard 2 (1990)	A smart, competent and foreign agent is dispatched via an icicle to eye. Seen in not one, not two, but three close-ups. Another highlight has another bad guy sucked into a jet's turbine, with predictably messy results. Both killings are committed by a dumb, loutish, but very American, Bruce Willis.
The Last Boy Scout (1991)	Private eye Bruce Willis teams up with his foul-mouthed daughter (she's around 11) and the two have a field day killing in assorted, high-tech gruesome ways (no particular highlight) a bisexual Bad Guy and his creepy buddies, all shot by ex-ad man Tony Scott in a sexy, smoky style that evokes more than anything, an Obsession™ perfume commercial gone terribly wrong.
Under Siege (1992)	Highlight of this Steven Seagal vehicle has Seagal and his love-interest (a feisty "cake-girl" with inhumanly large breasts) shoot cross-dressing bad guy Gary Busey with a redundant number of bullets. Said bullet redundancy also applies to the scores of other faceless bad guys offed with orgiastic abandon.
The Specialist (1994)	The main Bad Guy, a well-dressed, erudite and sweaty (read: gay) fellow is dispatched by semi-simian Sly Stallone in a hail of body-bouncing bullets.
Braveheart (1995)	Two of the king's men—a pair of bickering gays—exit film via fall from multistory window for no apparent reason. Splat. Female lead raped and killed in first reel. A Mel Gibson film. Academy Award Winner: Best Film.

From our Bad Gore table we see that the recipient of the action-gore violence is: non-white, smart, gay or female; all the Bad Gore films received an R from the MPAA with nary a frame cut; and all were, without exception, the product of major studios, who, by 1989 or so became the entertainment arms of larger media conglomerates.

Every "Good Gore" film was an independent production (with the exception of *Serpent and the Rainbow*, where Craven enjoyed a certain latitude with Universal Studios due to his massive success with *Nightmare on Elm Street*).

Each film dealt with ideas—radical politics, disrespect of corporate/consumer culture, rape, screwed-up families—that were troublesome enough *without* gore, but with it, ended up either unrated or slapped with the dreaded X or NC-17.

At this point, it makes sense to look at the social environment that led to the displacement of gore into context-free, consequence-free, corporate-designed "action" films.

Among other things, Reagan and his corporation-friendly administration "enabled the nation to revert to infancy, turn its back on the complicated reality of grown-ups in favor of the back-to-basics, black-and-white...fantasy lives of children..." (Peter Birskin, *Seeing through Movies*). And children have no understanding of things like consequences—it's something they learn.

I'm no expert, but I *was* alive in the '80s, and I saw the fallout of the Reagan administration—the effects of deregulation, the trumped-up anti-Commie fervor, the exclusion of minorities from anything that paid a decent wage, the purposeful ignoring of AIDS, the destruction of the middle class while the myth of family values were used as a blunt ideological hammer by members of both parties. So I don't think it entirely coincidental that, at the same time a good portion of the country was taking a serious economic and ideological pounding from the upper seventh percentile of the population, this virtual flood of gruesome entertainments appeared. Between the years 1970 and 1989, there were approximately *five hundred and thirty five* films released labeled as "horror."

This unprecedented trend was a sort of collective letting off of steam, an unconscious group recognition that things were sucking in new and scary ways. An accidental window of opportunity was opened as a side effect of the ready availablity of incredible amounts of free venture capital created by the Reagan administration's deregulation of Savings and Loans' lending practices. Many a fine gore film was then the product of limited partnerships, investors from myriad countries, and adjacent tax shelter scams often designed to get these movies into theaters (not yet "vertically integrated" into megacorporate controlled monopolies) or video stores (the same).

Slowly, the tax shelters dried up, foreign investors realized that "net gross" was Hollywoodian for "piss off" and finally, video swallowed the market for theatrically released movies that made less than, say, *Batman*'s $251 million.

At the same time the grisly *Total Recall* hit the screens, the gore-intensive horror movie virtually fell off the map, and the *new* action film appeared.

A classic action film such as Robert Aldrich's *The Dirty Dozen* (1967) builds suspense via the director's vision and strong characterization. We care what happens when things blow up because we care about *who* might be blown up. One barely cares, let alone recalls, what happens to the nominal characters in corporate products such as *Demolition Man* (1994), *Virtuosity* (1995) or the *Lethal Weapon* series. The violence in such films is truly mindless, a cheap filler between corporate-dictated plot machinations and product placement. The artistic, contextual gore of mainstream films like *Bonnie and Clyde*, and horror films like *Scanners*, was then transferred piecemeal to the new, seemingly apolitical, context-free, post-MTV action movie.

A quick look at Bruce Willis, Arnold, Stallone, Steven Seagal, etc. shows them to, indeed, be modular action figures—imminently interchangeable. Their non-vocabularies come replete with tie-in merchandise-friendly catchphrases ("Hasta la vista, baby!").

Most importantly, these action heroes *cannot die* (bad for sequels, to say nothing of the matter of heroes dying and thus bringing up the undesirable, thought-provoking *idea* of death). Inventive and gory deaths of the designated villain are still omnipresent, and include total body shredding (*Die Hard 2* 1990), death by jet exhaust (*True Lies* 1994), exploding bodies (*Timecop* 1995) and various close-up body-part penetrations (you name the film).

Clearly our mass appetite for gruesome mayhem hadn't died, it had just switched genres.

So what we really have here is yet another case of all roads leading to Viacom (or its corporate mirror images). We now have corporate-mediated mass catharsis. The endless "debates" about violence and gore in media (owned by the same corporations who make the movies) are a red herring, just another piece of the information pie to be used in strict accordance with the corporate agenda du jour. As to what's on that corporate agenda, a screening of *The*

Relic (1997, Universal/Paramount Pictures) is very instructive. With cutting so fast an on-site ophthalmologist is needed, the entire job of *The Relic's* struggling female scientist (a vague Penelope Ann Miller) and blue-collar cop (a cipher-esque Tom Sizemore) is to make sure the mayor and his coterie of rich, corporate and government friends survive the attack of a Chicago museum by a digitally-rendered, *Alien*-like monster. The creature's origins are explained in a scene showing some dank Third World jungle, with dark-skinned, grass-skirt-wearing "natives" summoning the beast.

Once in Chicago, the monster rips the heads off people and sucks their hypothalamus. This is shown with a lingering attention to visceral detail. The only characters who die in such a dreadful fashion are lower class and/or black people. The one wealthy white person who dies does so in tasteful semi-darkness. This scene is played for deep tragedy, as is Mel Gibson's character's plight in *Ransom* (1996).

In this action film, Gibson plays an obscenely wealthy, generally reprehensible corporate head whose child is kidnapped. The film ends with a extremely bloody, mano-a-mano battle with a lower class/union organizer-abductor. One doesn't have to be a dyed-in-the-wool Marxist to see there's a rather rotten-spirited sort of class fable here amidst the car crashes and explosions. There's the absurdity of a rich guy like this doing his own dirty work—in real life he'd hire an army of detectives or a hit man. It's an unsettling experience to root for a corporate millionaire kicking the ass of a person who, in terms of what he does (a worker), is much like the audience itself. Both *The Relic* and *Ransom* breezed by the MPAA uncut, and were rewarded with R ratings.

Racism and classism aside, the only "entertainment" value *The Relic* or *Ransom* offers is much like that offered by *Total Recall*: a cheap-jack "catharsis" transmitted at lightning pace, sudden and senseless gore, and the satisfaction gleaned from the monster (and the movie) coming to a loud and bloody end.

After seeing the only interesting horror film in some time, Wes Craven's *Scream* (all gore scenes trimmed by MPAA decree), it's clear that the issue of gore is in how it's presented. Craven's kind of gore becomes a symbol for everything that is anathema to the by-committee, by-the-numbers filmmaking of corporate Hollywood, leaving the field clear for ruthlessly corporate-accommodating directors such as Renny Harlin (*Cutthroat Island* 1995), Tony Scott (*Top Gun* 1986) and Peter Hyams (director of *The Relic* and also innumerable modern action films).

Violence has Consequences: Director Wes Craven

PARTIAL FILMOGRAPHY

Together (assistant producer)	1971
Last House on the Left (director, screenwriter)	1972
The Hills Have Eyes (director, screenwriter, editor)	1977
Deadly Blessing (director, screenwriter)	1981
Swamp Thing (director, screenwriter)	1982
A Nightmare on Elm Street (director, screenwriter)	1984
The Hills Have Eyes Part II (director, screenwriter)	1985
Deadly Friend (director)	1986
Flowers in the Attic (screenwriter)	1987
A Nightmare on Elm Street 3: Dream Warriors (executive producer, screenwriter, story)	1987
The Serpent and the Rainbow (director)	1988
Shocker (performer, director, executive producer, screenwriter)	1989
The People Under the Stairs (screenplay, director, executive producer)	1991
Wes Craven's New Nightmare (screenplay, director, actor)	1994
Vampire In Brooklyn (director)	1995
Scream (director)	1996
Scream Again (in production as of this writing)	1997

"One woman retreated after the screening to the corner of the room, where she began sobbing quietly. 'I don't understand these things,' she said to me later. 'I'm only a housewife!'

By the end of the quarter, however, she had written me that The Hills Have Eyes *was indeed her favorite film…*"

—Charles Derry, Ph.D., reporting events
during a seminar on horror films in *American Horrors*

With 23 theatrical and television film credits to his name, Wes Craven has gone from being a doctorate professor of the humanities at Johns Hopkins University to America's premier chronicler of familial horror. It is then perhaps no surprise that every one of his theatrical films, each suffused with a sense of consequence and morality absent from most Hollywood product regardless of genre, has been cut to ribbons by the MPAA.

IG: I was doing this video review book and the editor saw *People Under the Stairs*. She calls me, voice shaking, and says, "Jesus, what was that?" She was freaked. And she couldn't explain *why* she was so upset, as *everything* about the film had upset her. I said that was why I gave it a good review. Her reply was "Yeah, but why in the world would people want to see such a thing?"

    I got to thinking that, with films so dramatically neutered for so long, her reaction made sense.

    What I think really upset her was the sheer amount of *ideas* and *content* and their matter-of-fact presentation. I mean, it wasn't the violence—she has no problem with "action movies." But in your work, violence has *consequences*.

    So [gathers breath, all worked up] did I read this right—is violence and its terrible human consequences part of what you're doing?

WC: [A small trouble-maker smile, a pause]

    Yes. [Like the interview is now over, then laughs]

    Violence—I think I write in the exact opposite direction of what most people think violence is for. I just started dating this person and she just saw *Scream* and said, "Wow—that's a total disconnect—I can't connect *that* with *you*."

    I write more from the idea of the *sickness* of violence. I'm somebody who, in his initial impressions of the world, was very afraid. My father was kind of scary—I have few memories of him because he died when I was young—but, I knew he was a frightening, big man, and angry.

    I grew up in scary neighborhoods [in Cleveland] and we grew up during World War II. So my feeling was of a world out there that the adults don't want to talk about, but will, given the chance, come and get you.

    In fact, when we were older, this information didn't seem to be terribly wrong: with Vietnam, the assassinations of presidents, Martin Luther King—there was just this dark evil out there that was kind of waiting, and really moved history more than anybody realized or wanted to deal with.

    The first time, it was not even an artistic notion, somebody said, "We have an opportunity to make a film. These guys in Boston want a scary movie for their theater chain."

That was Sean Cunningham [producer, *Friday the 13th*, 1980, producer/director, *Soul Man,* 1986] and he basically said, "Go on—pull out *all* the skeletons from the closet!"

So I wrote the script for *Last House on the Left* which I still think is the most harrowing thing I've ever done, and it's completely uncensored.

And *that* ends up with the parents turning into just as horrible killers as the film's killers themselves. It was the stance I took through a lot of my films. *Nightmare on Elm Street* was very much about how do you stop some violence that's coming against you and not meet it with more violence, but to somehow turn your back on it.

IG: Yes—but the feeling of your films—the violence and horror—is presented as being claustrophobic. And it's not from outside, it's "from within." Child abuse, incest; a generalized dysfunction of every family aspect.

WC: At a certain point, instinctively, I did this film about a family and these kids who abduct her daughter. *The Hills Have Eyes* was about two "mirror" families [one low-class cannibals, the other middle-class tourists who turn out to be much more unpleasant than the mutant cannibals]. I did a film called *Deadly Friend* after that [with no family component], but somebody else wrote it, and it didn't seem to have the same, well, *power* as my first two films.

I just found myself going back to family situations for real dramatic strengths. It's a great paradigm—the earliest social situation is the dynamic between mother, father and any siblings.

And all the initial truths—what goes on behind doors, what happens in the bathroom, what's up in the attic or down in the basement—those sort of things occur in those first five or six years. There was a resonance with the audience for those early films that was uncanny.

IG: You're probably tired of this story, and maybe it's apocryphal, but, about your run-in with the MPAA—

WC: [Laughs] It happened on *Scream* too!

IG: Well, wasn't it *Shocker,* where you kept turning in edited versions, cutting out all the gore, and—

WC: —and it *still* wasn't acceptable—

IG: —and they said it was too disturbing, and you kinda lost it saying "I make horror movies—they're supposed to be disturbing!"

WC: Oh—that was *Last House on the Left.*

We submitted it—I hadn't the foggiest notion who they [the MPAA] were. So Sean says, "We've gotta send it to The Coast and get a rating."

They just savaged the film repeatedly. The upshot is that we ended up taking the R rating logo from a documentary film a friend was making and stuck it on our film! So [*Last House on the Left*] came out with an R rating. [Chuckles]

IG: That's *so* cool. Is that on the video, this fake R rating?

WC: Probably! Probably is!

But the "too intense" thing happened on *Shocker* and it happened again on *Scream*; just the whole kitchen scene—it's just too intense! [*Scream*'s finale involves two killers who keep stabbing each other, dying slowly and painfully, while terrifying various victims at the same time they discuss, among other things, horror films.]

They said—"We don't even know where to begin to tell you to start cutting your film."

[A rueful tone enters Craven's voice] At first, it was an NC-17. They said, "It's a wonderful film. [Voice curdles with sarcasm] It's a perfect example of what a 'quality' NC-17 film is."

IG: I'm sure you were *real* grateful!

WC: [Sarcastic] Yeah, very much that. By this time I was just baffled and didn't know what to say.

IG: [Trying out some cockamamie idea] Well, I've been thinking —Is "gore" censored because it's a function of death, which is tied in with sex—and keeping this analogy going, extreme gore would suggest an even more extreme sort of sex?

WC: [Amused] You might be pushing the linkage.

IG: [Oh well] But, I was thinking about all these HBO movies that have all this dumb sex and nudity—I mean, it's just there to titillate on the most imbecilic level—but then a film like Cronenberg's *Crash* comes out, and there's half the nudity, hardly any violence or gore, and it gets a NC-17.

WC: They give NC-17 for *content*. Content is anything that is upsetting to those people. That's what it is.

It's protracted suffering, flowing blood, moving intestines. Those are the simple ones. You can't have them.

In *Scream*, that character's intestines just slid to the ground after he was cut. And the girl hanging on the tree—

IG: Excuse me—you mean it's okay to *show* intestines, but they can't *move*?

WC: Yes.

Anyway, when Drew [Barrymore] is hanging from the tree dead, there's steam coming up from her body. [Because it's cold in this scene and Drew is freshly-killed and still warm.]

Someone said, "Well, we've had flies buzzing around bodies, but this steam..." [makes a clucking sound] They finally allowed us to have it, but cut in half and we had to print it twice as fast.

And the guy whose throat is cut: there's this great moment when he looks at his killer and looks sad, like "Why did you do this to me?" A wonderful end to that character.

Cut. Lost.

The kitchen scene: They said they hated the perverse mixture of humor and violence. [*Scream* was finally granted an R rating.]

IG: Uh—from the people who said okay to *The Long Kiss Goodnight?*

WC: It's frightening.

IG: Is it because they have a major studio, Geena Davis, Renny Harlin, while when you do it—

WC: I saw that film. My God, there's so much violence in it! That little girl trapped in the truck while all these explosions are going off...

Or how about the new version of *Romeo and Juliet?* [The 1997 MTV-esque take on Shakespeare with Leonardo DiCaprio] See, the thing they say about the violence in my film is it's "imitable." [Eyes roll]. In *Romeo and Juliet*, every kid has a gun. They make it extremely glamorous.

IG: So are you a whipping boy—an example-to-be-made—by the industry?

WC: I think I'm one of them, probably.

IG: Do they pick out somebody arbitrarily to make an "object lesson" out of?

WC: It's either that, or I just make that kind of film.

Because my films have a sense of reality: the violence is very real. You believe it could happen. People get stabbed, and then they bleed and they hurt as they're dying and it goes on.

IG: Exactly! Real violence has consequences—it isn't just a quick splat!—it's ugly and it goes on and is messy.

WC: Definitely.

And it's one of the reasons I'm getting out of the genre. I just can't do my best work here. Because I do my best work and it's always the thing they single out and demand to be cut.

IG: I keep quoting this to people—it's so eerie in its terseness. John Schlesinger said that *Midnight Cowboy* not only would not be made today, it would not be *allowed* to be made.

Would you say the same thing about *Last House on the Left* or *The Hills Have Eyes*, films now granted as "classics" of their genre?

WC: Absolutely.

I think the scene in the trailer in *Hills Have Eyes* where the elder mother is shot, and the baby—it was very real.

They want people to get shot and Bang! they're done. Like they're just disappearing.

IG: Your films frequently feature blacks as main protagonists and sexually active women who don't get "punished" for being sexual. Does this come as a problem when getting financing? Do they go—"Aw, get some white guy and Uma Thurman" or something?

WC: Aww...no. I've never had problems getting things financed. I'm commissioned, or sometimes I direct something already written, as in *Scream*.

Shocker had two main black characters. [as did *People Under the Stairs*]

[Amused] I was actually criticized by one of the New York papers for not having any blacks in *Scream*!

IG: An executive of a "major media network" told me the job of movies and media in general, with all the pop song clutter, hyper-editing, sub-sonics and unrelated images was to keep the audience in a state of "perpetual dissonance," to make you a better subject for selling you things via product placement and such.

WC: Certainly very early on in production, somebody comes along and says, "I've found eight places where we can put songs."

And then it becomes a struggle for the director—*Vampire in Brooklyn* was rejected because nobody could find "space."

See, what they do is when you're finished they start soliciting record companies. They want to make the record deal—here's the movie—we want, say, eight songs. Then they'll look at a scene and it'll only be fifteen seconds and they'll say, "Well, that's not long enough," so it's not worth our while—we want you to sell our songs."

It means a lot of money to certain people. A record deal is a lot of money—the studios kind of rely on it.

IG: So with *Vampire in Brooklyn* you hadn't shot enough film for there to be enough pop songs to make the film worthy of a record deal?

WC: [Smiles] We kept having scenes where people were talking.

So we didn't get a record deal.

IG: A TV production executive I spoke with said they recently had the cast of *Scream* on VH-1. The actors were then asked to pick their fave vids. They were only allowed to pick from a list approved by VH-1. So it seems it's not so much a plug for *Scream*, as the cast of *Scream* (and their constituencies) being utilized as a stamp of approval on VH-1's playlist, which is controlled by Viacom, which owns Blockbuster and Showtime where *Scream*, one assumes, will eventually show up (perhaps edited to suit Blockbuster's aims). Isn't this more scary?

WC: Yeah. That's one of the reasons an NC-17 is such a big deal: Blockbuster won't carry them.

IG: And they'll cut it. Unless you're, say Renny Harlin with some huge major studio movie and—

WC: —they get around it.

IG: Well, how do you deal in such an environment?

WC: It's difficult.

The films are just so much better without those cuts. Much better. There's more humanity to them.

IG: You've said in articles that horror allows us to confront our fears and thus deal with them. But again, with all our fears dumbed-down to an *Independence Day* level, and with the easy answer of some Father saving our asses, where do we go to get this special sort of catharsis?

WC: Well…I don't know. It's one of the reasons why this film was a hit. I had a lot of people say to me: "It's so…hard. It gets to you."

But I think part of that is because things have been so dumbed-down and so *numbed-down* that my film had an authenticity to it. I can't think of any film out that has anything like that kitchen scene. Two killers arguing and the girl—

IG: And the whole homoerotic aspect—

WC: Yes! It's there.

That kind of *density*, that complexity that you feel in that moment, is, in it's own way, like Shakespeare, where there's terrible violence but within this *context*. As opposed to this surface violence that the MPAA… [trails off]

IG: But it's that "surface violence" that numbs you out—

WC: It does!

I did an article on censorship, and I said the only up-side I could see was the more censorship there is, the more an audience will respond to the film that gets through it. Or—just ignore it, which you can sometimes do when you're first starting out.

But the MPAA is really hung up on this idea that if you see imitation violence, you'll want to imitate it. Or *something* like that.

If it's fantastic—if you fly a Harrier jet into a building—okay, but if you cut someone with a kitchen knife, they figure you can do that. [Shrugs in a "go figure" manner]

I just don't feel it's going to happen. But they say they do. And then they mention—I forget the name of the film—where this guy laid down in the road and cars drove near his head, and then in real life, some kids supposedly did this. [Craven is speaking of *The Program*, 1993, a James Caan movie which contained a scene where several college football players lay down on the center divider of a busy street. Real-life students supposedly aped this scene.]

I think most evidence for this sort of thing is very hard to come by. In the middle of a discussion I gave, somebody goes "Hey—somebody in Boston cut his sister with home-made claws! What do you think of that?!" [Referring to Freddy Kruger's trademarked claw-hand.]

Turned out to be a fake, a total fake. And you're at the mercy...even if this had happened, it's just so *bizarre* the kid would have probably killed his sister one way or the other, if he had an original impulse to do it.

IG: I understood you were going to remake *The Haunting*.

WC: It's in turnaround with Miramax now. [It's dead, until further notice.]

IG: What was your take going to be on it?

WC: Make it a little more erotic, more adult. It would have been nice, but they never felt it had enough "teeth."

But after the next movie, a genre film, I'm doing a pure art film.

It's based on a documentary called *Small Wonder* that we bought feature rights to. It's about this New York school teacher, who teaches classical violin to grade school kids in Harlem. But then, the State cuts the program, and she and her husband have to keep it going with their own savings.

[Warms up to the story—excited] So it's her racing around like a maniac in this old, battered-up car keeping these kids studying. And it ends up with them playing the National Anthem at Yankee Stadium! The kids realize—it's the kicker—they realize they can perform! And then Carnegie Hall...fantastic!

It's a movie I know won't be cut!

IG: How much were other films cut?

WC: Hmmm...*Shocker* was cut in 13 different places. In *Deadly Friend*, when Anne Ramsey gets decapitated [by a basketball flung by a cybernetically-enhanced 12-year-old dead girl, yet] they didn't want that shot in there *at all*.

And I went—Ah, come on! So I went out and did a compilation film of all these other movies that had decapitations, *Scanners*, all this stuff and they wouldn't even look at it!

The MPAA goes "No—there's nothing in the past that affects us today. It's all based on *today's* standards."

So there's no jurisprudence. It's just how they feel about your film.

IG: Others I've spoken with in The Industry defend the MPAA with the claim that it's made up of people who are there to guard filmmakers from the Don Wildmons of the earth. [Wildmon is president of the religious right organization the "Christian Coalition."]

WC: That's wrong.

They are a very separate entity made up of PTA people, school teachers, and activists that want to protect children from violence; they're all very heavily slanted against kids being exposed to violence.

IG: Uh huh. But Geena Davis in *The Long Kiss Goodnight* can have a kid—as a joke yet—inside a gas tank that's going to blow up while a hundred bad guys get shot to ribbons, with every bullet maybe blowing this kid to smithereens. That's okay though.

WC: Right. That's okay, and that really disturbed me. It was so violent, and yet so little was made of the violence.

IG: What about Tarantino's *Reservoir Dogs*—I mean, that's basically 90 minutes of people bleeding.

WC: I was at a screening of it. It wasn't that it was too gory—what I was offended by was this glibness about it. I felt like it wasn't the character enjoying the violence [the scene where Michael Madsen cuts off a bound cop's ears to pop musical accompaniment], but the filmmaker was.

I think what did it for me was having that smart '70s music, and I just felt like this filmmaker thinks this is just really *cute,* the guy's dancing around. I felt Tarantino's presence even though I knew virtually nothing about him at the time. And I walk out and Tarantino is there and he [Craven makes a helium-pitched, hyper voice] *"Hey! I made a movie too intense for Wes Craven. I'm so happy!"*

But it was just the filmmaker thinking it was so cool, not talking about being cruel. It was being cruel without being aware. And at another point, I was just, "I'm out of here, I don't want to watch this."

IG: I'd heard that Cronenberg, back when it looked like Turner was going to block the release of *Crash* and Blockbuster was making weasly noises about carrying the film—Cronenberg said he was purposefully going to badly edit any scenes they wanted extricated. [Finally, *Crash's* distributor New Line, and its president Robert Shayne, exercised a contractual option that gave them final say over a film's content, and *Crash* was released.]

WC: Well, Sean Cunningham on *Last House on the Left*—every time they made a cut, he had me put in some white leader for exactly the length of the cut! So when we sent it back to them, they'd have to put up with watching the screen go blank for that period of time! [Says this with some relish] After a while, there were these huge stretches of white leader! [The same film that sports the bogus MPAA "R"]

Who was it—Brecht? Used to put signs in his plays? [Laughs]

IG: In both *New Nightmare* and *Scream*, you play with our perceptions as an audience viewing a film. You address the entire relationship; in *New Nightmare* you play filmmaker Wes Craven, and the film itself is about your film company trying to make a new Freddy film, while *Scream* practically talks to its audience via all the video clips, characters making references to your and other people's films and so on. Are you consciously playing with aspects of both "high" and "low" art?

WC: Sure! Always!

My intellectual upbringing—say from teaching college—was fine arts. I was teaching humanities, the Greeks, that's what I really immersed myself in.

I come from a working class family—nothing artistic really—so when I was exposed to it...[it inspired me to go] to New York with some foggy notion of doing "art" films like Goddard.

When I got a chance for something that was clearly for drive-in theaters, I knew I couldn't do a Goddard film, but...*Last House* is based on Bergman's *Virgin Spring*. It's possible to make a film that has that same sort of structure and sense to it, with this type of audience in mind. At the same time, I'm reading deeply about levels of consciousness—

IG: So who is Freddy Krueger, really?

WC: Death. The impulse to sleep being seen as death.

IG: I thought he was the ultimate Bad Dad from Hell.

WC: He's that too. But the step beyond the Bad Daddy is sleep, so it becomes: "Who will be the most conscious, and insist on staying awake—and that person will survive."

IG: I love the scene where Heather Langenkamp [in *Nightmare on Elm Street*], this teenager, looks in the mirror and goes: "My God! I look 20!"

WC: [laughs] It was a line I heard my daughter say!

My daughter also cast Johnny Depp!

She was 13. We had the role down to four guys, very handsome, all these muscular leading-man types, and there was this wan, chain-smoking guy, and I asked her, "What do you think?" And she goes, "Johnny Depp, Dad! Johnny Depp!"

IG: So your daughter discovered Johnny Depp! [Chuckles at fate]

I was looking at your filmography, and it hit me that really, a lot of your films are like cautionary and very instructive fables. That they are perfect films for children to see. I mean, were I to have kids, I'd show them these films, but not action movies like *True Lies* which screw up their heads about violence, men's and women's roles, cause and effect, responsibility—the whole nine yards.

People Under the Stairs shows there's really bad people, but it also shows kids using their brains and communities to triumph over these evils. I mean, to me, you're the family filmmaker!

WC: [A hearty laugh] Thank you very much!

That's funny though—I was raised in a very moral background. Baptist, Fundamentalist. I walked out of all that, but some of those values have stuck.

IG: Not a Christian thing, just common sense.

WC: Yes.

And a lot of the stories of my films come from finding these true, super stories that intrigue me.

People Under the Stairs was based on a story that happened in Santa Monica. There was this couple of upstanding citizens but were away at work and the police came to find the place broken into and found a place in the house that was barricaded. They broke down the doors and discovered these three kids who'd never been outside. Dressed in rags, they couldn't speak English.

IG: So can movies still scare you?

WC: Oh yeah. But I haven't seen a good scary movie in a long time.

The American Soul: Director Ulli Lommel

PARTIAL FILMOGRAPHY

The Tenderness of Wolves	(1973)
Second Spring	(1975)
Adolf and Marlena	(1976)
Blank Generation	(1978)
Cocaine Cowboys	(1979)
The Boogeyman	(1980)
Olivia	(1981)
Boogeyman 2	(1982)
Brainwaves	(1982)
The Devonsville Terror	(1983)
Cold Heat	(1990)
Overkill	(1986)
Warbirds	(1988)
Before Sunrise	(1997)
Holy Joan of Balboa	(1998)
The Nothing Generation	(in production)

"The movie we made was about this man who worked for the police as an informer, but he uses his position to get to the kids he's interested in: boys between 12 and 15 or so. Runaways, kids who hang around train stations. He'd take them home, take care of them, be really nice.

"Then he would kill them and have sex with them (dead and alive) and cut them into pieces. But everybody likes him. This guy kills people, eats them, but everyone else lives in denial, saying: He's such a nice guy!"

The above plot is from *The Tenderness of Wolves* (1973), the person telling it to me is the film's director, Ulli Lommel.

Laconic and soft-spoken, Ulli Lommel *could* be interpreted as a man who has battled the machine and, if one goes by multiplex visibility, lost. But even after almost three decades of filmmaking on two continents, and manifold censorship and distribution battles, Lommel still has the bubbling-under enthusiasm of a young boy who has just discovered something wonderfully *bad*.

Starting as an actor and compatriot with the brilliantly eccentric German filmmaker Rainer Werner Fassbinder, and followed by a stint with Andy Warhol and his Factory alumni, the German-born Lommel finally, in the late '70s, moved to Hollywood to make what *he* thought were art films but were branded and sold as "horror." With this sort of background, it's safe to say Lommel has lived his life on fringes most people don't know exist.

But between the massive success of his meta-slasher film *The Boogeyman* (1980) and the re-release of his first and most disturbing work, *The Tenderness of Wolves* (1973), Lommel has been operating below the public waterline, churning out bill-paying direct-to-video action films while waiting for the zeitgeist to turn. Unlike, say, Renny Harlin (*Die Hard 2*, *Cliffhanger*), who ditched his Euro-roots and aesthetics for some corporate instant gratification, Lommel proves an inspiration for holding on to his vision, as grotesque and disturbing as it often is.

IG: Some people might say that with movies like *Tenderness of Wolves*, you're just going for shock appeal, and nothing more. Which is fine, but—

UL: It's not graphic, but it's, ah...pretty strong.
    It opened at the Berlin Film Festival, and when the first murder took place, half the theater emptied! What they were most upset about was that we created *sympathy* for a character who suddenly does these *unspeakable* things. Instead of this separation in society—this pointing the finger at others—we wanted to say that this is in *all of us*, that it can't be separated. Of course, some people don't want to see things this way. Even though it goes pretty far in what it shows, it's not exploitative. It's more like a rather melancholic poem.

IG: What happened when you brought this film to America?

UL: It was never released! It was shown at a festival in New York. We got a good review from Vincent Canby. Rex Reed was *appalled* [laughs].

      I showed it to theater owners in San Francisco...they were very impressed, but scared to show it. It's just impossible to do something like this in America, because the kids are around 12 to 15 in the film. In Europe, this played in serious theaters, but then, things are different than they are here.

Just how different things are, both in terms of movies and morality, between America and Europe, is something Lommel returns to often: in a way, this is Lommel's theme. To get a sense of his history in American film, I ask about his debut in cinematic America, the punk semi-documentary *Blank Generation* (1978).

UL: I'd just moved to New York [in the late '70s] and I approached Andy Warhol to make this movie. I was hanging out at CBGBs, staying at the Chelsea Hotel. I was in the middle of this whole scene, and out of this scene came *Blank Generation*. Richard Hell saw himself as this punk-rock poet, and he was really excited about the movie. Shooting was difficult because he was, most of the time, on heroin.

IG: What was your involvement with Warhol?

UL: He had seen *Tenderness* and really loved it, and I became one of the guys he sort of took around.

      You know, breakfast with Jackie Kennedy, lunch with Margaret Trudeau and dinner with Truman Capote. I enjoyed the scene for a while, then he wanted to do what would be *Cocaine Cowboys* [1979] on his compound out in Montauk. He was in both movies [*Blank Generation* as well]—he usually didn't enjoy that sort of thing, but he really liked this. He played the pivotal role of himself, who takes Polaroids constantly!

IG: What was that scene like?

UL: Oh, that was wonderful! We had this entire place to ourselves! Incredible things took place! One time an actress took home a case full of fake cocaine and a .357 Magnum. The hotel manager called the police, and the police thought the movie was just a cover-up: that we were really smuggling cocaine! [The film is about a rock band that deals coke.] They showed up in helicopters, the DEA, FBI. Local police, unbelievable! Then they realized the "coke" was sugar!

After *Cocaine Cowboys*, I did *Boogeyman* in LA, and I just didn't want to go back to New York because it was so cold! I checked into the Tropicana Hotel [a now-defunct dive], got two rooms—one to live in, the other to edit in.

IG: Was this the time of people like Tom Waits living there?

UL: Yes. Burroughs was there too, doing his stuff across the hall. Anyway, I edited *Boogeyman* and sold it from the Tropicana. A distributor came into the Tropicana and it was great when we ordered the editing equipment. They were used to studios, not hotel deliveries! The Tropicana was pretty wild then. Anyway, the movie came out on Labor Day and it was huge!

IG: That's the movie that people claim you sold out on (I guess because it made so much money). Do you see any difference between that and your earlier work?

UL: I don't know. Maybe *Boogeyman* has more levels to it. Some people thought it was just cheap exploitation, others thought it was a great horror film. [makes a *"whatever"* sort of sound]

Fassbinder always wanted to go to Hollywood, but thought he was just so Teutonic! His approach, everything, belonged to Germany in the '70s, and if he went to Hollywood it would just be a disaster.

He had mixed feelings when I came here, because on the one hand, he would have loved to be here too, on the other he realized it wasn't his thing to do. When you live in Europe and you move here, it's like you've landed on the moon—it's that different! It was like I was reincarnated.

Deep down, the things that *really* matter [in America] are very different.

IG: What do you feel those essential differences are?

UL: Americans are caught up in this American Dream, yet at the same time, in order to service that dream, they have to constantly deny what people are really like, what they really want. And so it leads to all these double standards and all these double lives. I've never seen a place that lives in such denial, where everything is fine and wonderful, and deep down, there's this violence and horror going on.

It's double standards. The American Soul: You really like to do something but you don't tell anybody because you hate yourself so much for doing it so you have to persecute everybody for doing what you are doing. That's the sort of scene that permeates daily life in America.

IG: And maybe why people find your films disturbing.

UL: Maybe.

I ask about one of Lommel's latest films, *Death Before Sunrise*. He gets so excited I'm not sure exactly what the film is about, but it definitely has something to do with "a woman killing an abusive man with a dildo," various forms of necrophilia, and a butler. With a sardonic laugh, Lommel assures me "it all ends with a happy death on the electric chair," and is a return to that sort of artful/horrific aesthetic of his early work.

After we both share a hearty laugh, I ask him what it's like getting funding for such projects.

UL: [Sounding as if this is the *last* thing he likes to talk about] Sometimes I do it through pre-sales to countries like Japan or Korea who are willing to take risks with edgy kind of stuff. I piece it together with pre-sales and various crazy sorts of people.

IG: [Moving right along] One of the things I liked in *Boogeyman II* was the shot of you reading *Hollywood Babylon*—

UL: [Laughs]

IG: —the whole movie seems like a slap in the face of America and the movie industry. Did you mean it that way?

UL: Yes, yes! But few people looked at it that way. Very few people saw—they just thought it was a rip-off of the first one—which was on *purpose*.
   A whole bunch of distributors—including Paramount—saw *Boogeyman* and wanted a sequel. And I felt awful about this and just wanted to move on [Lommel hates sequels with a passion].
   So somebody came along and I finally said, "Okay, just let me do whatever I want. We'll just call *whatever* I do *Boogeyman II*." I shot it in ten days, in and around my house.
   [Laughs] When the investors saw the movie, there was this complete silence. After a while they just left, and...well, the next day, they just sort of went crazy.

IG: You've spoken before in print about how you hate modern computer special effects, saying they call attention to themselves and destroy the film's mood. And your films are so much *about* mood. Do you think modern studios want this disruption, and want to make sure there's so much razzledazzle the audience never really gets involved with anything of substance?

UL: I think the reason the studios love these effects is because you can do it in *post-production*, you need less and less a director with *vision*, and you— the studio executives—can make the picture yourself. The studio executive can just have some computer freaks sitting there, and tell them what *he* wants. Most of it has [nothing to do with] making movies—it's more like Universal City: The Ride or something.

IG: So it is a control thing.

UL: *Exactly.*

The studios detested writers because they cannot duplicate what they do. They need talent, not just money. Now it seems, if you mix the MTV style of photography—which you can just order—mix that with some effects, then you're already 90% there. So it gives a lot of power to the studios, but at the same time, the alternative movies also have a chance to be a *real* alternative, because you just get tired of these one-sided movies.

As an example of the early stirring of corporate control over not only content, but, perhaps even more importantly, over where that content is seen—that is, the number of available screens—Lommel recalls the friction created when *Boogeyman* started eating up screens usually reserved for "major" productions.

UL: When *Boogeyman* opened on Labor Day [1980], the studios were booked for *three weeks*—just for this little film!—and some of the major product couldn't get in.

The theater owners said: "Well, this movie is doing so well, you'll have to come in next week."

At first the major studios thought this was a joke, because this was a small, independent movie. How could it possibly jeopardize them? And I think it was at that time when they all kind of got together and said "Look—movies like this do well, why don't *we* make them? Just put in a little more money, big stars, and then they're *finished!* Then, let's give them an X rating so that the independents can't get released and take play dates from us." I talked with Bill Lustig [director, *Maniac Cop*] and he thought they [the MPAA] weren't that devious, but I think they are. They may not do it on purpose, but it's just like the Right Wing in America: they may not do these things intellectually, but because this is what their whole emotional makeup is about, it's what they do.

IG: Major studios put out a *Friday the 13th* with just as much gore and disgusting stuff—

UL: —and these major films are so much less campy and fun because they take themselves so seriously! Whereas, in '80s exploitation, everybody knew what they were making, and they had fun doing it, and you had this spirit of people having a good time. Whereas these big studio pictures are nothing but *exhausting*...

And sequels give even more power to the studios because they have a proven commercial property. In Europe, well, if a film is planned as, say a trilogy, like [director Krysztof Kieslowski's] *Blue, White* and *Red,* well okay, but sequel-wise, I don't know.

I think you find more producers there [in Europe] who really enjoy, really *love* projects. I think 90% of people who make movies in Hollywood really hate movies. I mean have *hate,* or disregard, or indifference let's say. Sometimes not hate, just indifference, to making movies.

[Getting worked up] How can it be in Hollywood that the people in the '20s and '30s who *made* this industry live on the streets, are ignored, live in poverty, totally forgotten? If you forget your past, you have no future! Most of the people who run Hollywood don't care about Hollywood's past, or think to make films that honor older actors, or take care of them. Nobody thinks that way.

IG: You've used both John Carradine and Donald Pleasance—both fine actors who took to hammy performances in their later careers—and got fine performances from them.

UL: Thank you. They were a bunch of guys who enjoyed making a movie, who loved what they were doing, and that makes a difference to them.

IG: I recall the scene in *Boogeyman II* with the priest doing the old horror movie thing with his cross and not coming out of it too well...[The cross ends up in his eye.]

UL: Well—the *next* movie is called *Holy Joan of Balboa.* It's about a devout Catholic woman who begins to think she's like Joan of Arc, but her confessions lead to nothing. So she discovers this other church—The Church of Balboa—in Manhattan, and the priest is a woman who is a dominatrix who does S&M.

At first Joan is a bit skeptical, but then she realizes the *true* church, the true healing takes place at The Church of Balboa. So it's a movie about those double standards I was taking about earlier—the double standards, the pointing fingers. I wanted to make a movie showing that real healing can take place in a joint like this, while the regular *church—nothing* takes place.

IG: So you'll be making lots of friends with this one too.

UL: Oh yeah!

IG: For lack of a better word, do you think you've been in some way "punished"—given X ratings, bad distribution, studio-edited prints—for trying to inject "art film" elements into what seem like exploitation—by tackling difficult subjects and doing them artfully, thoughtfully?

UL: I know what you mean, but I just need to keep making these kind of movies, but make them even better. And even more controversial and subversive. Sometimes I'm still too "soft."

[Laughs] I want to be like [Luis] Buñuel: "The older I get, the more dangerous the movies I want to make."

IG: In American films—sex is usually for titillation, But in your plots it's just part of being human.

UL: You also find in Europe a different tradition with sex—whether it's Catherine Deneuve or Bridget Bardot or whomever—if the movie is about something that involves sex or nudity, it's not even a consideration. But in America, again there's this thing about sex, and I think people don't want to deal with sex because it reminds them of so many unresolved issues. They're afraid of this, or ignore that. I think the whole sex issue in America is such a monstrosity that it's difficult for people to deal with, so the minute they see sex or nudity on the screen perhaps it reminds them of their own sex lives which may be in a shambles...one thing I find fantastic. In Europe, never do I hear about "professionalism" as opposed to "amateurs" as I do here. The interesting thing is that the word "amateur" comes from "amator" which means "lover." In other words, amateurs are people who love what they're doing, while professionals are the ones who have succumbed to a routine, and after a while, it becomes just that: a routine. So ultimately, you can just turn this around: the amateurs are the ones who really make things happen, while the professionals just churn out sequels.

IG: Like Romero's *Night of the Living Dead*, which was derided as amateur because of it's low budget, but is now seen as a classic.

UL: The energy you have in *Night of the Living Dead* with all these amateurs, and the whole amateurish approach—that's true professionalism! That is great! You add $50 million and movie stars and that film would lose everything it had.

Director James Toback and "Warren Beatty"

Ivy League grad, director, compulsive womanizer/gambler, professional "friend of Warren Beatty" and all-around creepy fat guy James Toback was interested in some "new" music for his next feature, resulting in this author, then a composer, being called for an audience with the director in his apartment in New York City's Upper West Side.

Among Mr. Toback's film credits are some with revealingly twisted titles like *Fingers* (1978, the strange tale of pianist manqué/murderous loan shark Harvey Keitel); *Exposed* (1983, wherein Rudolf Nureyev and Harvey Keitel pursue professional strange person Natassia Kinski for unclear reasons) and *The Pick-Up Artist* (1987, self-explanatory and, supposedly, autobiographical. Keitel is absent from this one, and who can blame him?) His most recent credit was scripting Warren Beatty's opus of crime and womanizing: *Bugsy*.

But Toback's real role in life is that of being Warren Beatty's Really Smart Pal. Which casts some light on what Mr. Beatty perceives as intelligence.

Anyway, I arrived at Mr. Toback's residence at around ten at night—Spring of '86, I believe. I knocked on the door with one hand, the other clutching a bag filled with some sample tapes and scores.

Toback didn't answer the door, but a drop-dead gorgeous, glazed-eyed girl with a name not unlike "Brittany" did. "Brittany" said something like "Wow," and then wandered off, leaving me alone in this place that looked like it belonged to a demented professor with severe cash management problems. There were books and magazines everywhere, along with literal *piles* of greenbacks of high denominations strewn atop the stereo, the microwave, whatever. Brittany was wearing a very nice towel. Besides the books and obscenely naked cash, the stench of cigar smoke was ubiquitous.

I moved some cash from a deco couch and seated myself. The glassy-eyed towel girl (at least 19) reappeared in some black clingy couture and then uttered the rather cryptic line:

"Keep your eye on the phone." Beat. "Warren."

I construed this to mean she thought my name was Warren, and was about to correct her when she abruptly giggled and left the place.

Suddenly, a male of impressive girth, wearing a terry cloth robe, emerged from a gloomy bedroom.

"My man!" he shouted upon seeing me.

"Um—"

"Just a sec." A phone was clutched in one clubby hand from which a voice made insect sounds. To the phone: "Right, Warren. Yeah, some girl. *The one on Sunset? The one on fuckin' Sunset?!*"

He burst into gelatinous laughter, as did the insect on the phone, who apparently was in Los Angeles, hence the reference to Sunset, as in Boulevard.

"Oh Christ, no. I mean, yeah, she was here. Yeah—she likes my new car. Broads, right? Christ."

He then lapsed into a speed-freak recitation of horse racing data, none of which I understood, although large sums were mentioned. James hung up with "Warren," and, without missing a beat, said to me, "You like pasta? I'm cooking pasta. Have some."

He then wobbled over to a ramshackle kitchen, threw a stack of hundreds out of the way, found some pasta, and started cooking.

"Pussy, right?" he yelled from the range.

"Excuse me?"

Finally, he reappeared with a huge tureen of steaming pasta, poured two portions onto nice-looking china. His was larger.

"See, the thing about pussy…ah shit."

He ran over, turned on what looked like a radio. Suddenly I heard a voice reciting racing results. He listened for a second, frowned, then burst into laughter.

"Ha! Six hundred!" He snapped his fingers. "Gone! I gotta tell Warren."

He got back on the phone. Putting the puzzle of the conversation together, I believed "Warren" was again asking about some girl. James said, "Forget her" and hung up.

"Pussy, right? See, pussy is *easy*. I belong to this club, I smoke cigars, I make movies, wear good clothes. A woman sees all that, *forget it*. They climb over each other to get some. And that's all there is. It's in my new script." He beamed pleasure. "Look, there's this broad; I met her in LA. Just driving, right, but driving the right car. Listen man, I see this chick—she's okay, no big deal, but whatever. I climbed out of my car, right there on Sunset, and"—James snapped his fingers—"I get her number. The hunt, right? Being outrageous. A couple fucks later, I can't get rid of her." The belly chuckle. "Now Warren, fuckin' pussy-hound, he's all worked up because he knows I get the best pussy. He knows I have the knack. So he's nuts about jamming this girl, and listen, let's keep it between ourselves, okay?"

It was at this point that I realized I was trapped with a certifiable lunatic. I nodded, to be on the safe side.

"How's the pasta?"

"It's fine—ah about my—."

"—look; when Warren calls, say I'm out, say you don't know me. Do not say you know anything about this girl, okay?"

"What girl?"

"The one that just left. I told her to leave because another one…" Suddenly, he became immersed in deep thought. "Yeah. Okay. Look, do me a favor? I gotta go down to OTB [Off Track Betting], set some bets. That girl from Sunset—she flew in. She's coming over, it's a long story. Could you just sort of hang around, keep her occupied until I get back?"

I said I could. He left the room, came back dressed in expensive clothes rather haphazardly donned. I saw this was my last chance to get a gig, and a gig's a gig, even if it's with a maniac. I lifted my bag of tapes, and his eyes darted towards it as his hands moved fast.

"Leave it on the couch. I'll get back to you." A rakish smile. "You got six hundred bucks? Ha. Just kidding. Guy like me has plenty of money. Later."

And then he was gone. The phone rang a few minutes later. The person on the other end asked where James was—I said OTB. The voice laughed. Feeling like a complete idiot, I asked if I could take a message. He said sure, tell him Warren Beatty called. More laughs—for some reason this struck the person on the phone as immensely funny.

A few minutes passed and there was a knock on the door. The other girl, blue-blood, blond, but rather bland-looking in her preppy clothes, asked for James. I told her he was at OTB.

"The one on Broadway?"

I didn't, of course, have a clue. I asked if she wanted some pasta. She declined.

"He was at the OTB on Broadway when I got here. I just got in from LA."

And that was it for conversation. I guess she suspected I knew why she was here, and her embarrassment, darting eyes and wringing hands was getting kind of overwhelming.

After an hour, I thought "Fuck this," told the girl I was going home. She suddenly looked all vulnerable, said she was staying at a women's residence, didn't know New York. Asked me if I could stop by the OTB on Broadway and 79th, see if James was there.

Dope that I am, I did. As we prepared to leave, the phone rang, and there was this absurd moment where I stared at it, hoping against hope that it was Toback remembering that he needed music for his film, the girl, her plain Puritan face screwed up, hoping God knew what. "Click," and from the answering machine came the whining voice of the guy who claimed to be Warren Beatty.

I got us out of there and to the Broadway OTB. The place was lit with interrogation-room fluorescents, filled with cigar smoke, and guys that looked either like extras from some bad gangster movie or were one step from detox. Toback was not among them.

I never heard from Toback again, never got my stuff back. I ended up buying the girl some coffee and a donut and got her a cab. She looked miserable.

POSTSCRIPT: 1997

In the February 2 edition of *The Daily News*, reporter Denis Hamill announced that Mr. Toback had joined Gamblers Anonymous. Later in the piece though, Mr. Toback showed his old spunk by saying, in regard to his own prostate problems, that "my doctor has a theory that high testosterone, like mine, can lead to prostate cancer. He says eunuchs never die of prostate cancer, which means half of Hollywood might live forever…"

A Little Dish from the Chef to the Stars: Caterer Donna Hall

In her 44 (very) odd years, Donna Hall has dealt with Old World aristocrats, Lee Iacocca, Jack Nicholson, Sandra Bullock and almost every other kind of famous person in between. She has a double black belt in karate, sports a shaved head, is covered with various Samoan tattoos, is a nonchalantly "out" lesbian and speaks in a voice that is equal parts police procedural and streetwise New Yorker. How she survived almost two decades of Hollywood silliness without inflicting serious wounds is both a mystery and a testimony to her utter professionalism.

Oh, by the way, she's a cook.

Not any cook, mind you; she was a cook for the infamous Chateau Marmont, first opened in 1929 and since then, home and hideaway for many debauched stars and rockers. This is where Jim Morrison, legend has it, passed out—out a window, that is—where John Belushi OD'd, where Harlow slept and Garbo found solitude. And where it was Ms. Hall's unenviable job to feed and tolerate the hungry glitterati of Hollywood.

All this after earning her M.F.A. from Parsons School of Design.

IG: How did you get from being a chef for power-brokers on the East Coast to high life to Hollywood stars?

DH: —because of Eva [Ms. Hall's life partner].

She was in Los Angeles at Smash Box Studios, managing the kitchen. And she had me come to LA to do some big parties. Smash Box is the biggest still photography and video complex in LA. The heirs to the Max Factor fortune own it, so anybody who's anybody in movies or music all have their photo shoots there, and we would cater their lunches and that's how I got introduced into that, ah, group. There was a guy there who'd been hired to revamp Chateau Marmont, and he needed a chef...

IG: Did you work as a private chef for other people?

DH: Yes, [actress] Jamie Gertz, Lou Adler [co-founder of A&M Records] and Michael J. Fox. Fox is a sweetheart, his family is lovely, his wife Tracey [actress Tracey Pollan] is a wonderful person. Couldn't say a bad thing about them, they're the nicest people.

IG: So Michael J. Fox would be the best kind of client you could have?

DH: Yes.

IG: Who would be the most hideous?

DH: [Without hesitation] Faye Dunaway.

IG: Okay. There's been so much hearsay written about Dunaway—that's she unstable, foul-tempered, or just an out-and-out bitch and I just wondered: What's the deal? What's wrong with Faye?

DH: What's wrong with Faye? *I* don't know. When I dealt with her she was the most difficult client I ever had to deal with.

IG: Example?

DH: An example? When she came into Smash Box she refused to leave the dressing room until everyone wearing the colors white and red were removed from the premises. With no calling ahead to inform anybody of this, ah, stricture.

IG: And this was done to Ms. Dunaway's satisfaction?

DH: Yes. And Ms. Dunaway had been given a copy of the menu a day before, but upon arriving and receiving lunch, she refused to eat it and asked us to make her a special meal, which I then proceeded to do, and was told that she was not yet ready to eat, that I was to stay there and keep it warm, to which I replied, "It's here on the counter. Take it when you want it."

IG: How does one usually deal with people like that? Hardcore professionalism?

DH: Definitely. I do my job to the best of my abilities. I don't get into ego-matches with people like that. Outside of Dunaway, the most difficult person I ever dealt with was Dominick Dunne [best-selling hack writer/journalist].

He would call every morning for his fresh blueberry muffin and coffee before he went to the O.J. Simpson trial, and that was fine—

IG: —he was writing about it—

DH: —for *Vanity Fair*, who kept him in a *very* nice suite at Chateau. But they had really bad food at this point and were charging $16-22 for frozen food. I'm serious. Frozen ravioli, chili—pre-fab shit. I came in and introduced home-made and fresh food! I sent Dunne, one night, some home-made turkey chili—he sends it back saying it's the worst thing he ever tasted, he wants the regular canned chili. In a nutshell, that's my opinion of Dominick Dunne.

IG: Any memorable tales of strange dietary requests?

DH: Yes—for k.d. lang, when she stayed at Chateau—she's a vegetarian, so her dietary restrictions are pretty goddamned severe. She can't eat *any* animal products: no dairy, no cheese, no milk. We would have to give her tofu cream cheese! Oh, wait! And Darryl Hannah's favorite food is Cap'n Crunch™!

After some laughter over Ms. Hannah's sugary breakfast preference, we talked about a rising male character actor whose main dietary supplement came from hand-delivered bottles of Jack Daniels. At Ms. Hall's urging to ensure future employment, this person's identity will not be revealed.

IG: Okay! And what was that Sandra Bullock story you told me?

DH: I come off a plane from New York. Get to LA at quarter to eleven. I go directly to Smash Box. One of the assistants for this photo shoot for Sandra Bullock comes up to me and says, "Sandra Bullock would like a cappuccino—can you make it?"

        I go, okay. I make the cappuccino. I take it into the studio, and am told "She's in her dressing room, take it in."

        So I go in with the cappuccino and Sandra Bullock is standing stark naked doing a fitting. So I say, "Sandra, what if I put your coffee here?" And she goes, "No, bring it over and let's chat—I'm just getting fitted."

        So I'm talking about my plane flight, and all that, and she was just really charming and really nice.

IG: Um...you also remarked—

DH: —and I noticed she had no plastic surgery. [Laughs]

IG: —that Sandra's breasts are real—

DH: —yep!—

IG: —the only real item in Hollywood, if I recall you correctly. So what *is* the deal with all these beautiful women going for these surreally huge breasts?

DH: The first party I did at Chateau was this book release party about old Hollywood. Mamie Van Doren and Esther Williams were there well— more plastic surgery than I'd ever seen in my life. Mamie Van Doren's tits are like launching pads—they're up to her fuckin' ears!

IG: Even now? How old is she?

DH: In her sixties, I guess.

IG: And she's *still* having her tits done???

DH: Yep! Lifted and lifted! And Faye Dunaway has had a *shitload* of plastic surgery! Her face is pulled so taut, it's so chemical peeled, her skin is almost translucent.

IG: Well, okay; that's the Eternally Young thing. What I don't get is why already attractive females are making themselves into Virtual Valeries [a CD-ROM programmable sex toy], little RoboGirls...

DH: You know, it's such the trend in Hollywood, because nobody works for their bodies. One of the biggest myths, and any trainer will tell you, is that people in LA are healthier. It's a fuckin' lie. People in New York are much healthier overall because they eat better, they exercise in gyms. People in LA just go to the doctor and go under the knife.

      I personally know people in LA who have tit jobs, and it kind of stunned me.

IG: Did you ask them why?

DH: Yeah. One of them is an actress and said, "It's the movies. If you're flat-chested or sagging, nobody wants to know you." The stuff people do in Hollywood—it's stunning. Just to get work, or what they *think* they need to do to get work.

IG: Okay, I want to ask about the ever-expanding Steven Seagal—about him having this serious *reputation* as a "mystery man," a real "dangerous" sort. You have two black belts, right?

DH: [A tense silence]

IG: So you don't buy Seagal's "mystery man" routine?

DH: No.

IG: Did you work for him?

DH: No. [Conclusively]

IG: But you know stories—

DH: Yes.

Ms. Hall relates some particularly unsavory, detailed stories regarding Mr. Seagal which, out of respect for her place in the tightly knit world of professional martial arts—to say nothing of Hollywood—I must omit here.

One can understand Ms. Hall's reticence. Since Seagal became a reigning action figure in the late '80s, he has surrounded himself with conflicting and sometimes rather scary tales. According to a March 1991 article in *GQ*, appropriately titled "Black Belt, White Lies," he was born variously in Brooklyn, Chicago and California. He left for Japan where he boasted that he dared Yakuza gangsters to fight to prove his mettle concluding, "I will say this, which I shouldn't, that many, many different kinds of people came to discredit me, kick ass or kill me, and it never lasted more than a few seconds. And I'm not the one who got hurt or carried away." He obscurely alludes to having a "CIA Godfather," was an "advisor to several CIA agents in the field…" and did things he was "very, very sorry for."

All that is known for certain is that he was discovered by Michael Ovitz, for whom Seagal worked as a private aikido instructor.

IG: [Clears throat] I hear Van Damme's an okay guy.

DH: He's an okay guy—a really nice guy. He's the real deal, he's not bullshit Seagal—anyone who knows anything about martial arts will say he's fulla shit. Chuck Norris—he's the real deal too. Out of all of them, Norris has the best credentials, he's the only one who is recognized by the Japanese Association.

At this point, Ms. Hall moves from the topic of Seagal to that of an extremely famous pop singer, and the way her rise to fame was mainly predicated on a variety of Mafia-related "deals." Out of a sense of dead-serious concern for both our welfare, she insists the tape recorder be shut off, lest both of us "get whacked."

IG: Well...wow. How about, say, Oliver Stone, then. Any stories you can tell about him?

DH: What, that he bounced a check?

There were three principal actors in *El Salvador*. Two of them have checks that have bounced. James Woods is not one of them. [In an earlier, conversation, Ms. Hall told of how James Belushi—one of those whose Stone-endorsed check bounced—had framed and placed the rubber I.O.U. on his wall].

IG: Why? I mean, this was a major film. Where did the money go? Why would he bounce someone's check?

DH: Your guess is as good as ours. I have to say that after working at Chateau Marmont and seeing the stuff that went on there, Hollywood left a bad taste in my mouth.

A Small Vignette of Unappreciated Drapes: Director Tony Scott

One night early in the '80s, I was sitting next to a somewhat thick-set, though sportily dressed, man at Ports, a popular West Holloway watering hole.

Quite obviously deep in his cups, he stood there muttering to himself, unaware that the young man next to him was a writer with a very good memory.

"Bloody bahs-tard," the thick-set man mumbled. He then squinted, thinking perhaps he'd been recognized but he continued, "Hey, I'm Tony. I'd like to tell you about my brother, the bastard."

I nodded carefully, allowing him to buy me a drink. "So about your brother…"

"My brother! Christ, mate; he couldn't direct himself out of a film can. Makes fuckin' *horror* pictures. Crap. What does he fucking know from art?"

"Art?"

Tony slapped the table, the movement almost throwing him off the chair. "Fuckin-A right. *Art.* I"—his voice waxed sloppy-theatrical—"*I am an artist. My brother is a fookin' hack,* is what he is."

And then I realized this angry Tony was Tony Scott, ex-British TV adman coming off the resounding failure of his lesbian/gothic/horror film *The Hunger*, of which the high point was—to this date—the sole onscreen sexual pairing of Catherine Deneuve and Susan Sarandon. It was also notable for long gauzy shots of stunning drapery.

As *The Hunger* was otherwise really terrible, I could only summon, "I liked the drapes."

Tony nodded vigorously. "See? There you go! The drapes! You know how I had to fight with the bastards for those drapes?"

Seeing little to be gained in mentioning that constant gratuitous drapery shots were part of what made *The Hunger* so interminable, I asked, "Which bastards?"

"The studio! Fuckin' don't know from art."

"Like your brother?"

Tony's face clouded over. "Are you mates with my brother?"

"No."

"He's a right bastard."

I nodded, realizing that the reason I recognized *Tony* Scott was mainly because of his resemblance to his brother, director *Ridley* Scott, fresh off twin triumphs with the classic *Alien,* which had made tons of money, and *Blade Runner,* which had garnered much critical respect.

Tony ordered another drink. "So the bastard makes his monster movies and they think he's hot shit. The bastard."

The bastard who made horror movies and didn't know shit about art would also go on to direct *Thelma and Louise.* Brother Tony would very soon hook up with mega-macho action kingpin producers Don Simpson (now deceased as a result of too much sex, drugs, food and drugs) and Jerry Bruckheimer, with whom he would direct *Top Gun, Beverly Hills Cop* and others. All these films would be noticeably lacking either drapes or allusions of any kind to "art." Apparently Tony Scott had learned his lessons with *The Hunger.*

"Look," Tony slurred, "I don't want you to think I'm a bastard myself, what with all this about my brother."

"Sure."

"He's just been fuckin' *lucky.*" Scott rose unsteadily. "And so will I. Gotta go. I'm feelin' a bit pissed, y'know?"

As of this writing, there is little in the way of photographic evidence showing the two Scott brothers together. In interviews I've read, the two have never even mentioned each other's existence.

POSTSCRIPT:

Judging by the Showtime Network's official web page, a sort of by-default Scott family reunion finally transpired when a cable version of Tony Scott's *The Hunger* played its first installment on July, 1997. Another evocatively titled episode, *The Swords*, is directed by Tony himself, while the series is produced by brother Ridley Scott. Another show is directed by yet another, fraternally un-specified Scott, "video pioneer Jake Scott." Though *The Hunger* is far from a work of great art, Scott still displays a masterful use of drapery.

Indian Giver:
Kevin Costner

In 1984, he wowed 'em as a sexy, determined (if somewhat emotionally limited) Navy man out to find the nasty truth (and bed a fetching Sean Young) in the box office hit *No Way Out*.

In 1987, hearts were set aflutter as he played a tough family man and determined (if somewhat emotionally monotonic) Treasury agent out to nail Al Capone in the Brian DePalma-helmed blockbuster, *The Untouchables*.

But, unbeknownst to an America who'd taken him to heart as a stoic, can-do hunk in the Gary Cooper tradition, Kevin Costner's ambitions went far beyond mere acting and wealth. Not content with mere global adoration, Kevin Costner would show us all that he was also an auteur *par excellence* in what would be his next box office banger, *Dances with Wolves*.

One would think that Costner would thank his lucky stars at being able to escape the sexploitation trajectory of such jiggle-fare as his debut film, *Sizzle Beach, USA* (1974, playing a somewhat dense surf-boy) or 1981's grade-Z slasher flop, *Shadows Run Black* (filmed in 1981, released on video in 1986). One would be wrong.

Costner's *Dances with Wolves* ode to a sensitive white man would be rewarded with not only a $500 million box office tally, around $50 mil in take-home pay and a virtual sweep of the Oscars, but also carte blanche to do whatever the heck he wanted for the rest of his career (see Waterworld, p. 10). His acting range still spanned the gamut from A to A, but hey—he had the strong, silent thing down pat.

Still not content with mega-success, Costner actively sought out and received the blessings of the Lakota Nation, whose land and history he used for his liberal-pleasing film about a disenfranchised Lieutenant Dunbar, who, during the Civil War, decides to go Indian in a big way. After the film's success, Costner co-produced and appeared in a documentary called *500 Nations*, chronicling the plight of Native Americans. Costner was even adopted by a Lakota family and given an eagle feather, the tribe's highest tribute.

But soon Lakota leaders denounced him as *wasicu*, a greedy white man, while another went so far as to speculate that Costner "wasn't a human" (*Esquire,* June 1996).

Kev and brother Dan Costner had already bought and managed a gambling house in Deadwood, South Dakota, called Midnight Star, complete with blackjack tables, authentic Olde Tyme saloon staffed with black-gartered and bustiered waitresses, and lotsa booze. It also featured shrines to Kevin's film successes with memorabilia from his films and a gift shop stocking costumes and props.

Not content with the success of Midnight Star, Kevin and Dan acquired land in the nearby Black Hills, championed as sacred by the Lakota and fought for by generations of Indian Movement activists. The Costners decided to build a $140 million resort, casino and golf course, the largest private project in South Dakota history, and call it Dunbar. Despite an outcry of protest the project is still proceeding.

Lakota activist Madonna Thunder Hawk observed "It's a betrayal. Costner is making millions on our backs." (*Time,* July 1995). Cheyenne River Sioux Tribal Chairman, Gregg Bourland suggested a new role for Costner: George A. Custer. (*LA Times*, May 1995).

Costner, in response to charges from lots of people that he might not be doing an extraordinarily nice thing here, had the unearthly pluck to simper to the *Esquire* reporter, "My intention has never been to hurt anybody. I don't have a mean spirit. But it's hard to back me down, 'cause I like to think my aim is true." He went on to claim he was being picked on because he was famous and moaned, "Please, let's not go into *Waterworld...*"

The Media Sideshow:
Critic David Skal

"We accept you. One of us!"
—cheerful entreaty from freaks in *Freaks*

"Whatever you do…don't sleep! You're next!"
—hysterical entreaty to remaining humans
in the first *Invasion of the Body Snatchers*

"I'm a Pepper, he's a Pepper, wouldn't you like to be a Pepper too?"
—advertisement proclamation

It was in the mid-'70s, while dealing with the usual post-adolescent identity issues (sex, social place, hair) that I first came head-to-head with an old movie called *Freaks* (1931), directed by Tod Browning.

The film (which I viewed at an art theater, now a multiplex) was about a group of traveling sideshow freaks. Among them was a hermaphrodite, a black male "human torso," Siamese twin sisters, and a married pair of midgets. The sideshow also boasted a complement of "normal" humans, most of them vile. One of the "normals," a beautiful blond trapeze artist named Cleopatra, discovers that the male midget has an inheritance, and sets out to seduce and then poison him.

After a hearty meal, the freaks (unaware of Cleopatra's plans) toast her with "We accept you! One of us!" This key freak-phrase—"One of us!"—overrides the audience's inclination of repulsion towards their harrowing difference: that is, their *freakishness*, which is turned around so that they empathize and accept them.

The freaks learn of Cleopatra's deception. A nightmarish scene of retribution follows. The freaks crawl, slither and lurch through a muddy, rain-drenched night to descend upon the horrified woman...

A jump-cut, and we see another sideshow. A barker is hyping to the shills an astounding new atrocity of nature. Then we get the payoff:

It's Cleopatra, her legs cut off, nose broken into a grotesque "beak," eyes staring blindly. Her entire body—what's left of it—is encased in what appears to be a chicken suit. With her pitiful squawking, the film fades to a merciful close.

How the freaks wreaked their vengeance is never shown; our imaginations fill in the grisly blanks. Up until their moment of revenge, the freaks had been creatures we could empathize with, but director Tod Browning turns the table; they are not only freaks, but *monsters*.

To say the least, Browning knew how to get a reaction. Still, *Freaks* tanked at the box office in a hail of protest from Depression Era representatives of the usual suspects (clergy, state censors, etc.). In England, it would be banned for three decades, while Hollywood did all it could to distance itself from this breach of cinematic social etiquette. Then, as now, addressing disturbing psychosexual themes is considered socially acceptable only if one disguises these themes in the form of a made-up creature, you sure as hell don't use The Real Item.

But Browning did, and for decades his movie wandered the land as a road-show attraction, itself becoming a sad, abandoned thing.

Why would a mere horror film raise such a ruckus? And, in a larger sense, what do we even *really* mean when we talk about *Freaks* the movie, and the idea?

In the context of the film and several colloquial uses, I'd say that we are talking about whatever it is that makes us feel we are, in some deep, secretive fashion, *weird*. In *Freaks* we saw that inner weirdness, that sense of being different and frighteningly unique (that is, human), made horrifically visceral. We were also uncomfortably reminded of the disparity between the "haves" (people with normal bodies) and the "have-nots" (freaks). For extra zing, the film also ran a wide gamut of sexual disturbance: a physically trans-gendered person, genital-free people, and a pinhead dressed in drag.

For more insights on *Freaks* and its themes, and how "freak-energy" is channeled into modern culture, I spoke with film historian and media critic David J. Skal.

David J. Skal is a film commentator for several magazines and the author of such critically acclaimed studies of the horror genre as *Hollywood Gothic* (1990) and *The Monster Show* (1993). With Elias Savada, he is co-author of *Dark Carnival: The Secret World of Tod Browning* (1995). He is also the writer of the seminal cyber novel *Antibodies*.

IG: What is the nature of the enduring appeal of *Freaks*?

DS: *Freaks* is the ultimate film about the socially disenfranchised—a category into which more and more people feel themselves slipping, and I think this accounts for its perennial popularity.

It's not a particularly well-made film, but it's full of these primal, riveting images of outsiders; everything we're afraid of becoming ourselves. These images just never leave you, no matter how superior you might feel to the film's technical aspects and terrible acting.

After its disastrous first release in 1932, *Freaks* went underground until it was rediscovered on the midnight movie circuit in the 1960s. Soon after, it became a rallying point for a whole Vietnam-era generation who embraced the designation "freak" as a political badge of honor. Whatever its failures, *Freaks* does manage to convey an intolerable sense of social imbalance and injustice: "big people" versus "little people," obscenely literalized.

Tod Browning was an extremely cynical director for his time, but the popular mood has certainly managed to catch up with him. He'd be perfectly at home in today's media culture, which is the modern equivalent of the freakshows he grew up in.

I emphatically disagree with the liberal/PC estimation of his work, which regards *Freaks* as some kind of compassionate, humanitarian statement. Bull! If *Freaks* is still popular, it's because it resonates so eerily with our own unbalanced world of big people and little people, insiders and outsiders, the obsession with physical beauty, the terror of mutilation and deformity, and so on. It's full of imagery that just won't let go. No one who sees *Freaks* ever forgets it, no matter what they think of it as art.

If Browning had been in any condition to notice the summer before he died, the 1962 Thalidomide disaster would probably have made him cream his pants. He had a cruel, voyeuristic streak, and was an early example of the opportunism and venality that have now completely consumed Hollywood. Browning came out of America's turn-of-the-century carnival culture and never lost the ethos: "us" versus "them," the carnies versus the rubes. [Browning ran away from home at age 16, and joined a traveling sideshow, where he worked as a barker, a clown, an escape-artist and, by burying himself for days, as "The Hypnotic Living Corpse."]

The mere act of watching one of his films somehow turns you into a rube, whether you're viewing one of his literal sideshow films or one of the more metaphorical ones. Renfield, the insect-eating maniac in *Dracula* is a variation on the sideshow geek, for example.

IG: I recall this awful horror film called *The Sentinel*: besides being a crappy movie, it also featured a climactic sequence featuring the demons of hell being played by *real* freaks mixed in with monster-suited actors. Why does this disturb me?

DS: It upsets you for the same reason *Freaks* upset people in 1932.

Using real human anomalies in a fictional context breaks a tacit contract with the audience that they've entered a safe realm of escapist entertainment. It's disorienting and unpleasant. There's usually also an obvious gap between the quality of performances given by professional actors and people hired on the basis of disability and this further breaks the illusion. *Freaks* would have been a much better film if it had been produced as a silent picture, the way Browning originally intended. The freaks themselves simply couldn't handle dialogue, but in a silent film they would have had an imagistic purity and power. Browning was a consummate silent film director, and a silent *Freaks* might have been a true masterpiece instead of just a major cult oddity.

IG: What performers would you say carry the freakshow torch (either by behavior, looks or whatever)?

DS: The media environment today is so voyeuristic and trashy that a better question might be, which performers *aren't* carrying some kind of freakshow torch? Michael Jackson is the obvious, tired example; I made a case in *The Monster Show* for his being a new Lon Chaney [the silent-movie actor, who due to his extraordinary skills as a makeup artist and contortionist, earned the popular nickname, "the Man of a Thousand Faces"], the difference being that he uses surgery instead of makeup.

But you get a whiff of the sideshow any time there's media interest in stars who stray away from average physical stats. The weight reduction struggles of Elizabeth Taylor, Oprah Winfrey and many others strike me as a kind of a mythic public manifestation of a struggle between the archetypes of the fat lady and the human skeleton. It's a show that always draws a crowd. And while there has been plenty of attention given to the "modern primitives," tattoos and piercing, I'm still waiting for someone to do a definitive study on the anthropology of breast enlargement in Hollywood, which seems to be an accepted, central component of female celebrity.

In an age where social and economic mobility is getting tighter and tighter, popular fantasies about personal transformation center more and more on altering the private, isolated body, which is frankly a lot easier to shape and change than the public, communal world. I think there's finally a freakshow aspect to almost any public display of the body in today's midway media culture. After all, isn't saying "Look at me, I'm different, I'm special, I'm unique" just euphemistic ways of saying "I'm a freak—want a peek?" I'm sure Tod Browning would love tabloid TV, the latest repository of the American sideshow that started with P.T. Barnum and never really went away.

Breast enlargement is probably the most socially acceptable form of body modification, but is it really much different than piercings, tattoos, or plated lips? I don't think so. In carnival slang, a self-made oddity is called a "gaffed" freak, and that's exactly what this epidemic of plastic surgery amounts to. We aspire to be a nation of gaffed freaks. Katherine Dunn understood this perfectly in her novel *Geek Love*, about a normal family who deliberately twist their chromosomes to make it big in the freak business. Michael Jackson is the biggest gaffed freak of all time. There's got to be a name for the syndrome—Elephant Man Envy? The cosmetic surgeon's operating room has more in common with the sideshow tent than we want to admit.

IG: Off the topic of *Freaks* for a moment (or maybe not): as films as disparate as *Fargo, Scream* and *Lone Star* prove, there is still an audience happy to accept relatively clever, even smart, entertainment, and yet Hollywood keeps striving for dumbness and planned mediocrity: what is the thinking—if that's the word—behind this?

DS: Of course audiences will respond to original, intelligent fare. They just don't respond in huge numbers. If today's kids—who virtually everything is aimed at—seem to have a taste for crap, it's because they're only fed crap and don't know anything else. It's a self-perpetuating trap. Another reason for all the dumb, homogenous action pictures is that the studios are targeting an international audience, where crashes, explosions and violence require nothing in the way of translation.

IG: Why do you think that Vincent Price's possible gender preferences caused such an Internet ruckus? Are we still that infantile sexually, or do we *choose* to be sexually infantile—and why? [During a six-month period on America Online, a worldwide ruckus was created when somebody revealed that the horror icon might be gay. Even for AOL, the response was absurdly over the top.]

DS: I don't know whether or not Vincent Price was gay; I worked with him professionally once and got the impression that he and his wife, Coral

Browne, were probably bi and had worked out a nice arrangement between themselves.

But who knows? There was an incredibly nasty America Online discussion board on the whole topic, which brought out such name calling and vituperation that lawsuits were threatened between participants and the whole thing got erased by AOL. It did demonstrate one of my pet theories about horror fans—that they focus obsessively on the monsters and horror icons in order to avoid the thing that really scares them, which is sex. In *The Monster Show*, I discuss the way monsters embody adolescent male sexual anxieties, one of which is a fear of homosexuality. Whether Vincent Price was gay or not, he certainly embodied many of the qualities stereotypically associated with gayness: the campy over-refinement, a passion for the arts, cooking, etc. So in a way it's perfect this was all superimposed over a supremely scary screen persona.

IG: Finally, what drives you (and others with similar fascinations) to invest creative energy in exploring *Freaks* and monsters in general?

DS: Before I wrote *Hollywood Gothic* I had been away from monsters for a long time. It had been a consuming obsession for me in elementary and junior high school, but not a steady fixation. I got interested in monsters as a Cold War kid who was terrified of the Bomb; *Dracula* especially provided a fantasy about surviving death. It wasn't until after I finished writing *Hollywood Gothic* that it dawned on me that my sudden adult interest in *Dracula* had arisen at just about the time I could no longer count the number of my friends, acquaintances and coworkers who were dead or dying of AIDS. So the same dynamic was at work. Monsters let us entertain our worst fears without having to face them too directly.

Personality Crisis

I was lying in bed after my parents had a terrible spat. My father had left the house in a huff, my mother was in bed, zonked on tranks (no slur on Mom—this was the early '60s, and Librium was what most shrinks gave to manage "hysterical" women).

This bit of familial strife had an up-side: nobody around to stop me from watching late-night horror movies! Unfortunately, at the time, the movie showing was *Invasion of the Body Snatchers* (1956). A cold fist of terror closed around my nine-year-old heart as, one by one, the occupants of idyllic Santa Mira, a small suburb not unlike the small suburb I lived in, were slowly consumed by seed pods from outer space. Post-consumption, the remains were spit out as emotionless, but human-shaped, Things.

Soon the entire town is possessed by a single alien mind. The last human survivor (Kevin McCarthy) shouts *at the audience* that one only becomes a Pod-Thing *if one falls asleep.*

Taking the film to heart, I stayed awake. When my father came home, I wanted to yell: "Don't go to sleep! You'll become a—"

I resisted this urge, as he was already in a poor mood and probably felt becoming an alien was the least of his problems. Mom, of course, already *was* asleep—not an encouraging sign.

The next day, when I screwed up a test at school and my mother went orbital, I had my proof that movies were just movies and Moms were, well, Moms. The idea of an entire world of blank-brained creatures controlled by one devious hive-mind, however, was sufficiently disturbing to spawn two sequels.

In the 1978 Phillip Kaufman version, the alien-pod threat materialized as

"Me Generation" hipsters in New Age-y San Francisco. More to the point was the 1990 Abel Ferrara version. The title was truncated to a terse *Body Snatchers*, and the action set on a military base, the ultimate corporate paradigm. A superior film, the invigoratingly anti-corporate *Body Snatchers* was barely released.

But whichever *Snatchers* you see, they all share an unexpectedly seductive aspect: while the hero is doing his best to stay awake (and so stay human), a pod person invariably shows up to utter some variation on the following:

"Sleep. Sleep. You'll wake up in a new world. A world without pain, without complication...or love. A serene world. Sleep."

In the '80s, I read the following words from artist/performer David Wojnarowicz (*Witnesses: Against Our Vanishing*), and heard both an echo and a protest against this same basic, scary message:

"Each public disclosure of a private reality...serves as a dismantling tool against the illusion of ONE TRIBE NATION; it lifts the curtains for a brief peek and reveals the possible existence of literally millions of tribes, the term GENERAL PUBLIC disintegrates..."

It seemed like this gay artist who had died from AIDS, and a couple of odd genre movies, were somehow speaking in weird concert. That "One Tribe Nation" and the plans of the pod people (on- and offscreen) were talking about the all-American idea that we're basically the same under various skins. And that this is simply untrue. This idea is also part of the queasy *appeal* of the *Snatcher* films: In theory, it's nice to imagine huddling together with the other masses in an uncomplicated world under one flag, taking orders collectively as a hive or as willing slaves of some Borg over-mind, but the truth is, we're all a bit freakish.

We are all, being individual bio-units, *unique.* Which is scary (safety in numbers!). This was exactly the impulse the *Snatcher* films played upon: our urge to give up our identities, to be part of One Tribe Nation, one face in a crowd.

In another words: incorporated.

So: opposite sides of a scary coin, the coin of *identity.*

With *Freaks,* it was about admitting to inner deformity and then being horrified. In *Body Snatchers*, it was about the denial and destruction of *any* personality or difference. It was the urge to merge, the seductiveness of being Nobody. And the fear of that seduction.

Put more simply: In much the same way *Freaks* both appealed and repelled with its offer of being unique, *Body Snatchers* appealed and repelled with its promise of making us all nothing more than a cell in the body politic. All issues of identity, the way we define ourselves, the essence of what the hell we are, *gone*.

Looking into the reflecting mirror of modern Hollywood product on matters of identity, we see things are getting more terrifying than anything Mr. Browning could dream up in even his grimmest nightmares.

BASIC ARCHETYPES OF THE POST-*STAR WARS* FILM

by Ian Toll, film historian (coauthor of *Movie Trivia Mania* and coeditor of *Movieweek Magazine Online*).

HERO: A Rugged Individualist. Today, the most prevalent archetype is the tough cop who "doesn't play by the rules." Bruce Willis, Eddie Murphy, Steven Seagal, et al. may do things "their way," but they are still essentially upholding the status quo by protecting suburbanites from the dark hordes of foreign-accented drug dealers and suchlike scum. A subtle change, but what can you expect in an age when even stockbrokers and corporate lawyers feel compelled to identify themselves as rebels, when nonconformity can be yours for the price of a pair of jeans?

VILLAIN: The person with a foreign accent, usually English or German, though South Americans are sometimes permitted, and Arabs are always fair game. As movie budgets creep ever northward of the $100 million mark, it behooves the filmmakers to get as many asses on the seats as they can. This means pissing off as little of one's target audience as possible. [Hence the use of anonymously foreign villains]

THE SIDEKICK: The Sidekick is generally chosen in the same way that major political parties choose vice-presidential candidates. It doesn't matter if he and the hero have nothing in common, or even actively dislike each other, as long as he can bring a segment of the audience that wouldn't automatically go to see the hero's films into the theater he's in.

THE GIRL: In unenlightened days, The Girl was little more than an appendage of the hero: the plucky gal Friday, the straitlaced scientist's daughter, the hooker with the heart of gold. Mostly, they cooed in amazement at the hero's macho feats, screamed in the face of danger, and their rescue served as an excuse for a rousing, third-act climax.

Nowadays, an increasing sensitivity to women's issues is helping to overturn these outmoded stereotypes. Today's heroine is likely to be a doctor, a lawyer, or even a scientist herself, like Penelope Ann Miller in *The Relic*—albeit one who mostly coos in amazement at the hero's macho feats, screams in the face of danger, and whose rescue serves as an excuse for a rousing, third-act climax. Which is to say, she's still treated as a bimbo, but at least she's a bimbo with a good résumé.

THE OTHER: Hollywood filmmakers are often being accused of being out of touch with the world around them, of having less than perfect sympathy for or interest in the lives of those less likely to be found outside Beverly Hills. The Solution? Make films with non-white, foreign, or gay characters, even make their concerns central—just make sure they don't overshadow the "real" (i.e. straight, white) heroes.

As this chart demonstrates, America's already shallow pool of cinematic role models has not only gotten even shallower, but has also been segmented into component parts that are downright interchangeable.

In the early days, Hollywood tried to accommodate (as opposed to its current mode of *assimilating*) those who were not part of the "mainstream": even black and Hispanic people, it was reasoned, bought tickets.

As if operating in a parallel universe, studios and independent companies filmed and profited from lavish all-black productions from the '20s until Eisenhower's reign. Below the Mason-Dixon and in urban theaters across America, one could see all-black films like *Marching On* (1943), a boot camp drama about WWII romance and patriotism, *Murder in Harlem* (1935), a detective film dealing with interracial issues, and even a Vincente Minelli-directed, opulent musical, *Cabin in the Sky* (1943). Black auteurs such as Oscar Micheaux carved out new styles in the '30s, while black westerns such as *Harlem Rides the Range* (1939) were commonplace. Meanwhile, as a matter of course, Hollywood filmed Spanish language versions of major productions for both foreign markets and the foreign element within.

So early American film profited from, and *admitted the existence of*, cultures other than WASP culture. Today, we are steadily given fewer and fewer archetypes to emulate, with characters who are as much prefab, form-fitting parts as is anything that clunks down a Detroit assembly line.

The tension between being a "normal" American and being human was once negotiated, in the movies, via a wide array of strange, exotic and even monstrous characters. In films like *Freaks,* we could vicariously explore all the disturbing stuff that lurks inside us.

Freak-energy is now repressed, reshaped and remodeled. Most of all, it has been *assimilated,* bought by a passive audience who can line up at Blockbuster to rent some hyper-promoted video release such as:

Independence Day.

Here, America is all assimilated as hell. You've got Harvey Fierstein as a caricature of a caricatured Mom-loving gay (but he's so cute!), Jeff Goldblum as a Really Smart Jew (what a hunk!), various powerful females who can still look good in high heels (take *that,* Hillary!), and Will Smith as a can-do Negro (good *boy!*).

Q: **What is the most efficient way of taking the power out of "marginalized" groups?**

A: **Assimilate the fuckers.**

That is, make them all nice, pleasant revisions. Why buy a bunch of sheets, burn crosses, invade abortion clinics or do other things that could cost a lot of money, when you can just make everyone an honorary Normal American, install ready-made glass ceilings and watch 'em pony up for the Laserdisc version of *Independence Day?*

Consensus has been reached—all are assimilated. With *Independence Day,* the sexual/social/racial creed hit its apotheosis: we are, it seems, finally a One Tribe Nation.

And guess who profits.

Flatliners

So all of this has been about identity.

Identity is very important in terms of advertising: Know your market.

But in movies today, where making $40 million off a $20 million film is considered a failure, and every film must be a blockbuster right out of the gate, it is essential that there not be anyone in a film who could imaginably offend anyone.

In short: No character must *have* any character.

Cardboard and cartoony is the definition of characterization in major studio films. If you want to make as sure as possible that your product will "open" to at least $15 million on its first weekend, a cast of familiar ciphers is the best bet. And with Disney/CapCities, Time Warner and its corporate brethren controlling all avenues of media and information, an entire generation has been raised and programmed into an advanced state of passivity, delighted ignorance and the ability to watch *Mission Impossible* without going postal on the theater owners.

The medical term for people in this state (also the name of a bad film starring bad actor Kiefer Sutherland) is *Flatliners.* As in no peaks or dips on the EEG. *Dead/Alive* but with an active VISA account; the ultimate rubes.

But what about *Freaks,* and the way it appealed and repelled with its vision of uniqueness? And the anxiety that being unique might also result in us becoming outsiders on the main street of corporate culture?

And what about those eternal *Body Snatcher* fears? How it's scary to be lost in a group, but at the same time, wouldn't it be terrific to *be* one of the group, and never have to hurt, or think, or do anything somebody else didn't tell us to do?

It seems *Body Snatchers* has won out, even though it will probably never be re-made (why would a corporation remake a movie that is, by nature, a critique of itself?).

Somewhere along the line, I think we all fell asleep.

Sitting at a screening of *The Fifth Element* (1997), with its relentless consequence-free violence, tie-in-CD-friendly "industrial" rock soundtrack, non-characters, and recombinant-DNA storyline cobbled from *Blade Runner*, *Stargate* and *Star Wars*, I felt my head begin to vibrate (not entirely unpleasant) from the sub-woofer Dolby™ sonic assault. Clutching a bag of popcorn printed with an ad for some new Will Smith movie, I looked around at an audience staring like stupefied children at the on-screen babble, and, for a brief moment, fantasized about Kevin MacCarthy bursting through the dimensions to scream hysterically one last warning at all of us on the sleepy road to terminal homogeneity:

"You're next!"

Fake Tits and Self-Mutilation: Psychologist Dr. Ruth Ochroch

For a clinician's view of modern self-image problems that permeate the movies and our real lives, I spoke with Doctor Ruth Ochroch.

Dr. Ochroch has a Ph.D. in clinical psychology, among her other degrees and honors, has taught clinical psychology at the graduate level for 36 years at New York University, and is my shrink.

IG: In a non-performing arts context; what is a psychological profile for someone who chooses elective cosmetic surgery?

RO: If the person does not possess anomalous features—a cleft palate or severe scars for example—usually it indicates a narcissistic, infantile inability to find some sense of self-acceptance. Very typical for adolescents, a normal stage.

IG: Many people claim it is societal or pressures of the marketplace that force them into changing their bodies via plastic surgery, extreme bodybuilding and such. But some take it very far. Your opinion?

RO: Yes—I think that's a very important factor [the body as market object idea]. But I think there's a difference between a desire for self-improvement—which is *integrated* into one's life—and an obsession about it, where one must focus their whole life on bodybuilding and self-beautification.

IG: What would you call it when a person goes so far as to have ribs removed to make a slimmer waist? Or hormones injected to create larger muscles?

RO: I would say they're probably having delusional ideas, or they have a very false self-image—it's a thinking disorder. It's an obsession, a delusional system regarding body image.

[It's] a basic lack of self-acceptance. Physical and psychological. I think the struggle to look and be something one is not, is extremely damaging. They usually start with one thing, and before you know it, they're really mutilating themselves.

IG: What is the psychology behind the new wave of utterly immense breast implants acquired by women in certain areas of entertainment [and in the real world]? What do women think they are "gaining"?

RO: Right now they're very dangerous and cancer-provoking.

IG: Why then would a woman with an in-proportion, pleasant-looking body want to make her breasts, for example, a 42DD cup?

RO: This is well beyond societal pressures. If a woman is "flat-chested"— genetically—and feels she'll be attractive to a man by having more pronounced breasts—within limits—that *might* make some sense.

IG: Did you see that *The New York Times* article about women getting implanted just for the fun of it?

RO: That's not fun—that's a psychological disorder. It reflects a false, vacant or empty self-image and it's related to a narcissistic struggle, that says that a 38D as opposed to a 36D will somehow solve their problems.

       And having treated some of these people, one usually picks up a history of competition with a beautiful mother, or older or younger sister, or a sense of themselves instilled by events in their childhood that made them feel inferior to other little girls.

IG: Why would men want to see images of women with totally unrealistic body configurations? What's the psychology of these men?

RO: I think these are men who have perverse sexual fantasies, or need a woman with huge breasts as a way of bolstering their own sense of being unattractive, like their own jewel in the crown, so to speak. They're symbols of their utter masculine desirability. I think there are differences in men's perceptions: there are breasts as the organ by which a woman nurses and breasts as a symbol of female sexuality. Occasionally, if they merge, you have problems. For instance, it is a common practice for a man to want to taste the milk of a nursing woman—it can blend in an erotic way, but by and large, I would think huge breasts are, again, a way for the *male* to enhance his desirability.

       There's always a power dynamic—not power in the sense of domination and control, but in the sense of self-enhancement. But beyond certain parameters, a lot of this stuff becomes pathological—the fact that a man would *need* to choose a 42DD woman is, for example, pathological.

IG: Do you think an automated, machine-oriented culture fosters a belief in its members that the body is also plastic, a *thing* that can be endlessly modified via surgery with no ill effects?

RO: I think that is an indication of such alienation—there's not just a lunatic fringe in politics, there's a lunatic fringe in cultural groups, and this to me is an indication of such alienation and detachment as to really be dangerous to the person who thinks this way. There is a very gray area between sense and no-sense. If you begin believing your own fantasies, your own aberrant thoughts, everybody has them, so what? But when you make a cult out of some driving force to detach from one's body, you're moving into dangerous psychological turf: it's frequently the beginning of schizophrenic withdrawal. Among many young adults there is the feeling that their bodies are out of control, that they are falling apart, and one of the symptoms you find is this detachment from the body, the mechanization of the body, the sense that the body is not living flesh. This kind of post-modern, cybernetic mechanization is a denial of reality, the reality of one's existence.

IG: Audiences see a star appear with suddenly immense breasts, magically disappeared wrinkles, and yet nobody speaks of this. Is there a corollary between this odd silence and the dynamics of the addled patriarch in the popular configuration of the dysfunctional family?

RO: That's an interesting idea.

"My notion of a wife at [age] 40 is that a man should be able to change her, like a bank note, for two 20s."
—Warren Beatty on women in *Marie Claire*, April 1997

• • • • • • •

And between takes:

"Apparently, on the set of *Judge Dredd*, Stallone always picked up the walk-on actresses. There was, one day, this particularly shapely actress and he came on to her, and during a break in the filming, he took her to his trailer.

He did not realize that his remote microphone was still on his body. So the sound guys suddenly hear his, well, sounds, and it was Sly and this extra getting it on, and suddenly they hear Sly going, 'Slap my butt! Slap my butt! Slap it some more!'

The next day, the crew is all wearing t-shirts that say 'Slap My Butt.' I understand he was a bit embarrassed by this."
—related to the author by Jill Stempal of *Sleaze On Line*

• • • • • • •

"Last night I did something completely insane. I have hurt people I loved and embarrassed people I worked with. For both things I am more sorry than I can possibly say."
—Hugh Grant on committing the unheard-of act of receiving fellatio from a prostitute —*People* (7/10/95)

Hugh refers to his felonious fellatio as "disloyal and shabby and goatish."
                                                                —*Time* (7/24/95)

Months later, decides to confide that "I always find love scenes a tremendous turn-on, because you're kissing strangers and it's so naughty."
                                                                —*People* (12/25/95)

•••••••

The very idea of a "sex scandal" (even one as minuscule as the Hugh Grant indiscretion) in an industry based to a great degree on the elements of this book's title is, by definition, an oxymoron. Like the films they star in, the sexual behavior of celebrities operates within very controlled parameters: Paul Reubens' career is damaged when caught jerking off while watching a porno film (imagine), Eddie Murphy's face is splashed on the tabloids because he allegedly gives a transsexual a ride to his/her home, and various possibly gay people—Tony Perkins, Tab Hunter, Vincent Price—are speculated about in the media long after they've passed on. That being gay is a scandal-worthy topic, even posthumously, in a town rife with the traditions of the casting couch, socially-accepted debauches, "trophy" wives and a general *Day of the Locust* rutting-animal ambiance is in itself so utterly perverse that it would take several other books to even address.

As for women and (cinematic) sex and scandal, suffice it to say that being an actress in Hollywood is basically a tacit synonym for "cheap, available slut," so right off, actresses are, in a word, fucked. And if actresses *aren't* fucked with brain-stunning regularity matched only by coverage in the tabloids, the press will either find evidence that the suspect female prefers the company of girls, or is just a close-lipped bitch. And if she *does* fuck, if she has the temerity to copulate outside approved circles, the bitch label will be hard to shake; witness the career slide of sexy/smart/independent-minded actress Ellen Barkin or Sean Young.

Women are perceived and often treated as being guilty before proven innocent (to say nothing of being borderline psychotics). After the end of the movies' brief flirtation with "adult sexuality" in the '70s, we saw such "progress" in women's on-screen roles as:

The Crucible (1996), in which Joan Allen plays an honest but sexually frosty Protestant, while Winona Ryder is a delusional/sexual hysteric/possible witch. In *Romeo is Bleeding* (1994), Lena Olin is not only a femme fatale, but a psychopathic, sexually omnivorous one. In *The Paper* (1994), Glenn Close plays a smart and powerful newspaper editor. The first two films cited end with the heroines dying quite violently or being shipped to parts unknown. Close survives *The Paper*, but only after rogue reporter Michael Keaton beats her to a pulp (she lacked "heart").

Even in the seemingly benign *Forrest Gump* (1994), America's favorite imbecile falls for a girl who becomes a hippie, has lots of sex, becomes a singer surrounded by what one assumes will be further sexual partners and in general, attempts to find her own, however confused, way through life. Her reward is AIDS and death.

So in *Gump*—one of the most popular films in the last 20 years, we have an archetypal American female dying for, in order of sins: enjoying sex, trying to figure life out, and being smart.

From these few examples, one can only surmise, to paraphrase Nietzsche, that when America looks into the abyss, it sees the bedroom.

A List of Basic Sexual Role Models

1. Gays are clever, but usually innately unhinged people with unusually good taste in furnishings and a fondness for lachrymose musicals, who may have a suspect tendency to have a closer-than-usual relationship with Mom. Recent examples in order of cliché: *Frankie & Johnny* (1993), *The Last Boy Scout* (1995) and *Independence Day* (1996).

   What gays are *not* seen doing is having sex, or even kissing with much vigor. And if they dare to show physical or emotional attachment, it's either glossed over (from what is *shown* in *Philadelphia* (1993) one can only surmise that Tom Hanks acquired AIDS via unfortunate choice of film venues), censored (director Tom Kalin's efforts to show two, fully-dressed men kissing in *Swoon* (1992), a film otherwise empty of sex, resulting in the dreaded NC-17) or shown to cause the gay(s) in question to be twisted into violent psychosis because of their gender preferences as in *No Way Out* (1987). Gays also destroy "normal" marriage (*Making Love* (1982)) or, in a moment of metaphorical candor, are shown to be literal, blood-sucking monsters (*Interview with the Vampire* (1994)). Whatever the case, the chance of the screen gay making it to the third reel is an iffy proposition at best.

2. Sex Outside of Marriage is Bad and Leads to Even Worse Things.
    The majority of American films ever made.

3. Black Guys have Extraordinarily Large Dicks.
    New Jack City (1991), *Full Metal Jacket* (1987), movies that star Eddie Murphy or Martin Lawrence.

4. Women Who Actively Seek Sex are Asking for It.
    As evidence of the above, we cite *Body of Evidence* (1993), an admittedly execrable film, in which Madonna *does* get to tussle with boys, girls and S&M, and even grind glass into a game Willem Dafoe. She turns out to be a psycho-killing ballbuster from hell who gets whacked by film's finale, while Willem gets a nice wife.

5. Feminism Leads to Death!
    A concept well-illustrated by the seemingly feminist-friendly *Thelma & Louise*.
    True, Geena Davis gets to leave her simian husband and hit the road with Susan Sarandon after which the two gals punch a rapist's ticket, but while on the road to freedom, Geena Davis has sex with a slinky Brad Pitt.
    The result: Our heroines, after that fatal fuck and some other plot machinations, choose to cliff-dive their way to eternity rather than live in such a sexually fucked up world. A rather radical response, and one we doubt would be approved by studio heads were *Thelma & Louise* about, say, "Roger & Burt."

Homophobia Anyone?

James Woods, in *Esquire* (April 1984) was whining about the "abuse" he'd received in Hollywood (not getting the roles he deserved because of his looks.) He blamed in all on male studio executives who, according to Woods, think: "'Let's get some guy who looks like Robert Redford for our movies.'" Woods goes on to explain, "They didn't realize that every major star—Humphrey Bogart, Spencer Tracy, Robert Mitchum—had offbeat appeal...Women say,

'We don't want some closet fudge-packer who pretends he's a heterosexual being our image of what a man is.'"

• • • • • • •

Mel Gibson on Gays

Heartthrob actor Mel Gibson, when asked by one of Spain's leading newspaper (*El Pais*) what he thinks of homosexuals, replied, "They take it up the ass." To make his point clearer, the handsome actor bent over, and pointing to his posterior, added defiantly "This is only for taking a shit."

He then admitted to being baffled and angered at being, on occasion, thought of as gay because he's an actor. "Do I sound like a homosexual? Do I talk like them? Do I move like them?"

—*Outlines News Service*, Rex Wockner, Jan. 1992

And more Mel

In a fawning piece of puffery entitled "Mel Content" in *People* (November 11, 1996) it was made clear that Mel's past rough 'n tumble lifestyle was simply a result of alcohol abuse, latter nipped in the bud by AA in 1991. The article does note that, despite this, Mel is still seen now and then toting a glass of champagne.

But then, as a fascinating way of showing the kinder, gentler Mel in action, the piece ends with Gibson's unique means of welcoming Julia Roberts onto the set of his film, *Conspiracy Theory*.

Upon entering her dressing room, Ms. Roberts found "a gift-wrapped box done up in pretty bows." Eagerly, the actress tore open her present from Mel. Inside the package was a freeze-dried rat.

• • • • • • •

Sex and Violence

Devoted "sperminator" Charlie Sheen, one of the few males in Hollywood to be named by super-madam Heidi Fleiss as a very regular customer, was in tabloid sex trouble again. On June 6, 1997, he pleaded no contest to a charge that he beat a former lover, 25-year-old Brittany. According to court documents he knocked her unconscious and split her lip, then hid her bloodied dress and threatened to kill her if she told. She did, the next day. He was released on $20,000 bail.

—*People*, June 23, 1997

"Frame Fuckers"

Veteran sound design master Warren Hamilton is a soft-spoken, good-spirited man approaching his retirement years with impressive grace. He has created sound effects for hundreds of films, laboriously layering sometimes thousands of sounds until the acoustic fantasy world of a movie is complete (try watching John Carpenter's 1982 terror classic, *The Thing*—sound courtesy of Mr. Hamilton—with the volume down: not as scary, eh?). But Warren is not one to rest on his laurels, and enjoys keeping up with the latest in sound tech trickery.

So with Mr. Hamilton's kind demeanor and enthusiasm for new stuff a given, I was quite taken aback when, while discussing modern editing systems, he suddenly turned feral with a short, dismissive bark:

"Frame fuckers!"

"Excuse me?" I replied.

After collecting his wits, Hamilton said that "frame fuckers" was the common term for those who use the new generation of electronic editing systems (such as AVID).

AVID allows the director or editor to tinker with a scene endlessly, or at least until they have no choice but to hand in a finished film, which is just one part of the tip of a very disturbing iceberg of problems. But AVID is only a machine, and, as anyone knows, a machine isn't inherently bad.

Mr. Hamilton's outburst led me to wonder if AVID somehow played a part (however limited) in the dumbed-down, mass produced, hyper-paced, really loud, mind-numbing dreck that passes for movie entertainment today.

In short: Who are the *real* Frame Fuckers?

> "The blockbuster embodies the whole idea of BAD because it is empty of human value at the heart and depends entirely on overstatement…instead of adult narrative and acting, it offers comic-strip motivations and an almost exclusive reliance on special effects, gratifying to the uneducated…who have never learned to achieve excitement over anything but technology. As Peter Biskind has said, the object of the blockbuster is to… 'reconstitute the audience as children.'"
>
> —*BAD, or, The Dumbing of America*, Peter Fussell

And the movie that successfully reconstituted audiences as children, and pretty easily amused children at that, was *Star Wars.*

Common gospel has it that *Star Wars* ushered in a new age of wonder and awe, injecting into the movies the magic missing after the (then-considered) dour, disturbingly "personal" films of the '70s, un-sequel-able classics such as *The Long Goodbye* (1973, Robert Altman), *Taxi Driver* (1976, Martin Scorsese) and *Deliverance* (1972, John Boorman).

But *Star Wars*' real legacy was its famous Really, Really Long Spaceship Opening Shot that had audiences oohing and ahhing in the aisles like children, regardless of age. Within a decade, all "event" films (effects-laden blockbusters) would cynically be geared towards a "childlike" mentality.

Richard Edlund, effects wizard most responsible for that famous opening fly-by, has said, "If somebody sat down in the theater and saw this monstrous thing come over the screen and keep coming, and they were awed by that, then we had our audience just where we wanted 'em. But if they laughed, we were dead."

Mr. Edlund angsted unnecessarily. And the claims that the reason for this effect's success—that it reinstilled a "sense of wonder," whether authentic or not—were, to be polite, a crock.

Whether consciously or not, George Lucas and Richard Edlund were banking not on "magic," but something much more dependable: America's adoration of Really Big Things. Things like Cadillacs, malls, guns and, most recently, women with titanically-proportioned, implanted breasts.

So when they opened their film with five minutes of Really Huge model rocketry, they couldn't help but succeed. It's been said that *Star Wars* inaugurated a new age of effects verisimilitude, which is silly: the matte lines are still there, the model is obviously a model, the starfield is just a notch above a Star Trek episode.

But, to belabor a point, it was an *immense* model, against a *70mm* starfield. And after that, Really Big Objects became *de rigueur*, whether the mothership in *Close Encounters* or an immobile but very large (100 feet tall in stocking feet) giant ape model in Dino De Laurentiis' amusingly awful remake of *King Kong* (1976). And it seems hardly a coincidence that at the early stage of Really Big Cinema, a previously near-unemployable Arnold Schwarzenegger would begin his ascendancy as the leader of a grunting pack of none too brainy, but again, Very Large, new breed of hypertrophied "action heroes" whose main function was to be big enough to visually compete with all the big hardware around them.

What, I wonder, are audiences thinking?

Americans labor under an obsessive work ethic drilled into us since birth, a work ethic made even more demanding by an economy making ever more strenuous demands on its exhausted workforce, in a country now "competing" in a global market. It's a work ethic that now requires most families to produce two incomes in order to cope with a faltering economy, along with a tech-driven sea change in the very nature of the workplace and an increasing reliance on goods and services from abroad.

So with all that in mind, how could we *not* admire the complexity of that model, how could we not appreciate how much damned *work* it must have taken to make such a incredible thing, this awesome Lincoln Continental of the spheres. And, as pornographer Dian Hanson has noted, we come from poverty-stricken and often criminal stock: seeing all this spectacle costs some serious money.

How could we *not* be impressed?

•••••••

"Unlike most machines, computers do not work; they direct work. They are…the technology of 'command and control' and have little value without something to control. That is why they are of such importance to bureaucracies."

—*Technopoly,* Neil Postman

"Oh no! We're in the hands of engineers!"
—Terrified character in *Jurassic Park* (1995)

After *Star Wars,* computers entered the picture, and computer programs were soon erasing those nasty, telltale matte lines. Thirteen years later, George Lucas's effects facility, Industrial Light and Magic, would design the first computer-generated alien in *The Abyss* (1989). It was quite an effect, this floating creature made of water.

Then we had *Terminator 2's* (1991) mean morphing robot, T-1000. Cool! cooed audiences across the land.

Then, interestingly, that same effect showed up in *Stargate* (1994), *Sleepwalkers* (1993), *The Shadow* (1994) and endless other features, and the main audience reaction was to squirm with boredom. In *Jurassic Park*, we saw our first "believable" dinosaurs via computer animation (CGI, or Computer Generated Images), but by the time of *Twister* (1996) and its airborne cow, the same effect was worth only a kitschy giggle.

Yet a film like *2001: A Space Odyssey* (whatever one thinks of it as a film per se), still instills a true sense of wonder, a sense of the chilly vastness of space, of really being on the moon and beyond.

2001's main effects technique was to take a still photograph (a nice one) of, say, a spaceship, and just sort of move it across the screen. For shots of people inside huge model moon stations, 8mm films of people were projected onto the model. Computers back then (1968) were still the size of large rooms, so nobody, aside from the military, used them.

One of the more disingenuous things special effects technicians always say is that an effect is working only if it is not noticeable.

The fact is, an effect *works best* when the effect *is* visible. *Seeing* the effect is the whole point! Did people go to *Independence Day* so they *wouldn't* notice those city-sized alien motherships (which again, were nothing more glamorous, tech-wise, than hand-crafted models)?

We know, for example, that a movie like *One Million Years B.C.* (either the 1941 or 1967 version) is going to need dinosaurs, is going to show them, and there's this tension and expectation built between you and the movie, this *hesitation,* where we wonder excitedly: "How the hell are they going to show dinosaurs?"

With films such as *20 Million Miles to Earth* (1957) and *Jason and the Argonauts* (1963), Ray Harryhausen proved himself one of the most brilliant live-action animators of our time. When one of Harryhausen's patently "fake" but utterly marvelous animated creations roars across the screen, we're thrilled and awed by the sheer artistry of the effect, the surreal beauty of it. All this with visible matte lines, mismatching film grains and other technical "problems." These are problems that don't seem to have hampered Jean Cocteau's 1946 *Beauty and the Beast* ("floating" people obviously suspended on wires, a princess putting her hand through a mirror that is plainly just some reflecting water), or the original, 1931 version of *King Kong* (a yak-hair-covered animated puppet). It doesn't stop the most multimedia-savvy Gen-Xer from still being awed by these films. The sheer otherworldliness of these effects served to actually plunge the viewer deeper *into* the story, as opposed to distracting them away from it.

Then again, after *Star Wars,* "story" or even comprehensible sequences of events started their devolution into something more akin to early porn. And, like a porn film whose framing storyline is only an irritating excuse for the next semen-spurting mega-coupling, movies became not much more than a series of connecting links for more and "better" effects.

With that in mind, why do CGIs become the heroin of effects, with the audience needing a bigger, better, more extreme visual hype with every film, while *2001* and its dopey photos and filmstrips continue to amaze?

Well, it's like sex: Seeing your new mate naked for an hour or ten is very exciting; seeing them naked all the time is, well, boring. And if your mate were a computer generated image, you'd get bored even quicker. Trust me. Until extremely sophisticated computer technology becomes more readily accessible to artists and not business school grads, we're in for more of the same.

But whether or not the technology is effective, it comes down to this: If we have the technology, we must use it. Competition is fierce! If one film has a dog morphing into the Empire State Building, then the next film must have the same—even if it's, say, a story about struggling rice farmers in 18th century Guam. The pressure—and temptation—to go ape with effects is too high.

Along with the cost of these effects, which employ non-virtual armies of technicians, major studios hunger for movies that will garner boffo box office every time out, just like the *Star Wars* films. Movies have to be simple enough story-wise to be easily dubbed for limitless profits in non-English-speaking markets (the World). Characters must be made simple enough to cross national borders without anything getting in the way of their efficiency in selling tie-in toys, lunch-pails, t-shirts, whatever.

The new business school grads claim that we need movies big on effects and screw the rest, movies that don't ever really end, but promise sequels with even more and better effects, movies that then reach every consumer every time in every multiplex (probably owned by the company that owns the studio).

Enter computers (such as the AVID computer editing system), which are really good at managing the information needed to make these films (a decid-edly mixed blessing).

Machines are not, by nature, bad things. This book was written on a machine, and I'm very grateful for its help. And in the hands of a gifted film-maker such as Peter Jackson and his visually sumptuous *Heavenly Creatures* (1994), even that tired old horse, morphing, can be hauled out to startling dra-matic effect. Then again, the film was made in New Zealand, not by a thou-sand VPs, lawyers and agents of a big studio.

It's not that computers are bad, they just draw that way. You have a story problem? Stick in some zippy effect. Want to end a conflict with visual verve? Morph the fucker. Story dragging? AVID-edit the thing into hyper-drive!

What happens then is a sort of cross-addiction: The studio's lust for megaprofits via blockbusters creates an audience whose experience is largely that of blockbusters, and so craves the adrenaline rush of even bigger, splashier and louder blockbusters every season.

But wait, there's more.

This mechanical anti-aesthetic, with its interchangeable characters, effects and endings, has, by corporate-controlled design, helped atrophy the imagination of screenwriters. The problem, however, does not lie with any particular machine.

It's simply a case of who the end user is. And in post-corporate Hollywood, that end user is nearly always an executive who, via the fast transfer of information new technologies provide, is the one calling the shots to better aid the aims of his corporation.

Basically, there are two systems of editing. The first is the original system of taking film, a simple process of viewing film through a Moviola (a small projector), and then cutting and gluing together strips of film via a "flatbed" editing machine. These strips, or sequences, are then glued together by hand until a finished "work print" of the movie is assembled. From there, it is usually up to the editor or director to fine-tune the work print into a finished movie. The producer can have input, but this method of editing is laborious, and changes take some time to implement. And since film is big and very heavy, it's problematic for people from the front office to dictate changes without flying in to wherever the editing is taking place.

Computer editing, such as that done on the AVID system, consists of having the film scanned and transferred to digitized video, with the resulting data entered into a computer. Basically, it works like a word processor, with images taking the place of text. Unlike a word processor, however, AVID is a highly complex system which requires a very well-trained operator who charges an average of $1500 a week for his or her time.

Virtually limitless versions of any given scene are displayed on a large viewing screen, and, like text on a word processor, are cut and pasted together digitally.

Because the editing data is on video (and soon, on disc), and able to be projected on any other AVID system, and because of the system's large screen and easy replay capabilities, most *anyone* can have *significant input* into the editing process.

The following is excerpted from an interview conducted with Franklin Davis, a spokesperson for AVID, with questions and answers exchanged by e-mail.

Q: In simple, nontechnical terms, please explain what AVID and similar systems do. What do you see as the main advantages of this system over older, "hands-on" film editing systems?

A: Digital nonlinear editing systems enable an editor to use a computer to edit sequences of moving images and sounds, with instant access to any of the media.

Q: In your personal opinion, do you think AVID, because of the nearly limitless options, actually effects the content as well as the "flow" of a film?

A: Absolutely...it's very fast...letting the editor experiment with many more approaches. It can allow an editor to try a cut the director's way and let them both see if it works.

[To say nothing of allowing studio executives to also "see if it works" and add their own "contributions."]

Q: Is the increased speed and ease offered by these systems reflected in the actual general cutting tempo of electronically edited films?

A: I don't think this trend has anything to do with computer-based editing. The trend towards faster pacing started well before non-linear editing, with advertising and music videos being the clearest influences. Audiences today respond to fast tempo...the "fast" in nonlinear editing is the actual pace of making the changes, not necessarily the pace of the material being edited.

Q: In terms of cost, is AVID a viable alternative for the independent/low budget film maker?

A: Yes, if it's used right. Personally I know my sister, who is an independent documentary filmmaker in NY and an editor, much prefers editing on an

AVID over a flatbed. She once said, "The AVID is as fast as my brain. If I'm having a slow day, I know it's me, not the system."

I believe nonlinear editing can be used either to shorten time or to increase flexibility and experimentation. Depending on budget vs. artistic desires, an editor can trade these off.

•••••••

Okay, so that's all well and good.

Electronic editing makes cutting film faster, easier, allows more options, and is relatively inexpensive. AVID, like most computer systems, mainly offers the attributes of speed, the ability to process huge amounts of data, and quick access to that data. In the best of all possible worlds, these would be fine things. But this isn't a Best World.

Right off, here's the first problem with electronic editing, an artistic one, the problem of *limitless choice* running smack-dab into release dates—that is, *deadlines.* That is, a director, armed with AVID, not only spends lots of time cutting, cutting, cutting, but also shooting more film and more set-ups, so he has more to cut and play with. Why? Because, often, he can.

That deadline is still there, and sometimes certain things are lost in the techno-rush—things like: Does this scene make any fucking sense? Rent the James Bond vehicle, *Goldeneye* (1996) for a vivid example of this phenomenon.

Goldeneye's fight scenes are undeniably kinetic and exciting on a basic head rush level, but at no point is it even vaguely clear who is kicking whom, how some character ends up on the ceiling, another in a tree, or just how 007 wins a battle. Everything is over-filmed and hyperactively spliced together to make certain the viewer is breathlessly baffled.

With the same summer's release of *Mission Impossible*, all pretenses of storytelling were dropped entirely. Instead, we were presented with a brainless roller coaster ride, an endless parade of fast-moving people and things that jerk from scene to scene for no apparent reason very quickly until, mercifully, the movie ends. Or rather, stops.

In 1990, Martin Scorsese (along with editor Thelma Schoonmaker) created a masterpiece of flawlessly-paced storytelling in *Goodfellas*. Edited "by hand," *Goodfellas* utilized a single narrator (the articulate Ray Liotta) and featured 23 pop songs that were artfully integrated into the story, thus heightening the film's dramatic impact.

Five years later, on a telecast of *Entertainment Tonight*, I saw Scorsese and Schoonmaker talk excitedly about how, with the help of AVID, they'd created Scorsese's then-latest film. Scorsese explained how he could now cut all he wanted, that now he could have *two* voice-over narrators (in this instance, Robert DeNiro and Joe Pesci, people whose speaking styles demand a great deal of attention even when heard separately). He could also add more than *fifty* pop songs to the soundtrack, no problem.

The resulting film, *Casino* (1995) was, to put it charitably, a mess. The music was senselessly overbearing and seldom had much connection to what was on the screen. The two narrators made the simple plot incomprehensible. Most of all, there were the endless, functionless cuts to and from this, that and the other. There were even bona fide *bad edits*, actual transitional screw-ups where scenes just seem to jump around the screen. And this from the team that won an Oscar for their (non-digital) work on the masterfully cut *Raging Bull* (1980).

We know that when people get new toys, they tend to play around with them a lot before settling down. It's the nature of the design of a machine like AVID to tempt one into excessive mucking-about. Unlimited cutting ability on a deadline leads to an occluded sense of what is important.

What's important, in the eyes of an otherwise movie-illiterate MBA VP working for, say, Touchstone Pictures (a subdivision of Time Warner Entertainment), is that a movie keeps moving. And that movies that make sense, that feature fast *and* slow parts, are to be avoided. And all of these things have to do with *pace*.

Pace is what *Dante's Peak* (1997), for example, does not have. In this by-the-numbers volcano disaster tale, even scenes of people in a small town purchasing groceries are filmed from multiple, often off-kilter angles, and cut with ferocious speed. The scenes of volcanoes erupting are also shot and cut in a similar manner. Based upon the way they're presented, acts of consumption and acts of nature literally have no dramatic differences between them.

So there is no pace in this *Dante's Peak*, as pace might make one pause to reflect upon what a cookie-cutter, crappy film it is. An actual "slow" scene might cause the viewer to pause in anger that they had just paid good money to see an onscreen character plug *Money Magazine* for minutes on end. That viewer might not find the irony here all that amusing, so quickly, the film cuts to some thing else. Meanwhile, the theater rumbles with extraneous SDDS™/Dolby™ Stereo sound, helping to keep the viewer in a special-effected stupor. AVID's Franklin Davis claims that MTV and the general hyped-up tempo of modern life necessitate this sort of high-velocity filmmaking. Maybe. It also puts an audience in the advertiser's dream profile of what an ideal consumer should be: malleable, semi-insensate, unquestioning...

> "The film I'm working on is intentionally slow-paced. We had a research preview. They brought 250 strangers off the street, everyone said they thought it was slow, but after thinking about it, they thought, well, maybe it needs to be slow. But the thing is we are being dictated to by MTV—just the visual bombardment..."
>
> —Lisa Churgin, film editor, *Bob Roberts* and *Dead Man Walking*
> (both directed by Tim Robbins), the latter of which contains
> the credit "This film was edited on old-fashioned machines."

Which brings me back to the idea of *hesitation,* and why corporations don't want any of that in the films they finance, distribute and control. Because hesitation is what happens when one thinks—you can see the conflict of interest, perhaps.

Semiotician Tzvetan Todorov, speaking about "the fantastic" (i.e. horror, sci-fi, fantasy) in films (*Genres in Discourse*), repeatedly goes back to the fundamental idea that when, for example, via a substitute mechanical doll, Linda Blair's head abruptly does its first 360° spin in *The Exorcist* (1973), the viewer experiences a moment of hesitation. That is, they know something unusual has appeared in the frame, and they spend a millisecond of time deciding to either accept or reject this "unreal" intrusion/effect.

Since all advertisements are, by nature, unreal intrusions, especially when placed in the middle of a movie via "product placement," one can see why this hesitation bit—this thinking business—is something your average corporate studio wants to avoid like several plagues. And why movies are cut in such a way as to suggest the editor is on amphetamines, making it so one can only gawk attentively at the relentless image assault.

And one can see why movies are often not much more these days than Frankenstein-like cut-and-paste jobs of what critic Theodor Adorno called "part interchangeability." Most obviously, this is seen in, but not limited to, action films, where plots and "action hero" personae are cobbled together from basic elements used in already proven successes. And so the prison setting, "wronged" ex-con hero and "escape plot" of *The Rock* (1996) are merely a repeat of the same used in *No Escape* (1994), *Escape from Alcatraz* (1979) and so on.

Most irritating to the modern studio VP is the fact that money and technology cannot make a wretched script any less wretched. Money and technology didn't stop *The Abyss* from sinking into same at the box office because, after a half hour, audiences were bored silly with its by-the-numbers plot.

So it really isn't the fault of AVID or any other machine. They are only the tools of an industry, run mainly for its own blue sky greed and domination, which seems intent on controlling all avenues, forms and outlets of expression.

Perhaps we're getting much closer to who the real "frame fuckers" are.

The Indie Sell

For reasons having to do with desirable shooting locations, easy travel from LA via the red-eye, and the availability of numerous students (free labor) attending New York University's famed film program, the locus of "independent" filmmaking is Manhattan. Ironically, the main point of purchase for these films is Robert Redford's Sundance Festival, located in Aspen, Colorado, making Aspen a literal halfway house to Hollywood.

What *kind* of film plays Sundance is another story altogether. Presently, the phrase "independent film" is the "hook" of an incredibly cynical ad campaign used by corporate Hollywood to appeal to what is perceived to be a "Gen X" demographic: young, white, middle-class, and hungry for easily purchased sounds and images of youthful rebellion.

In this way, a major corporation such as Time Warner may foster the illusion of being "small" and speak to the needs of young consumers via ersatz hipness in the same way R.J. Reynolds—the second largest tobacco concern in the world—used the cartoon character Joe Camel and his be-bop friends to lend a "with-it," personal touch to ads selling Camel cigarettes.

Outside of gore and exploitation films, and unlike other countries and times, America has never seen any artistic consensus on independent film. There were films that played "art" houses and midnight shows. These were mainly foreign imports or the occasional "experimental" film. John Cassevetes, for example, made low-budget movies that were self-financed, looked very "rough," and dealt with racism and aberrant male behavior. They were not, however, called independent.

The real origin of independent film is in another locale—Seattle, and another medium—rock music.

During the mid-'80s, a clutch of bands in and around Seattle started releasing self-financed CDs. These bands had little in common except the urge to create interesting music outside the corporate sphere. One of them was Nirvana, whose first album, *Bleach,* cost $606.17 (paid for by the band's producer). The (at the time) very small distributor, SubPop, released it, creating considerable word-of-mouth success. Nirvana was signed to David Geffen Records and sold 1.25 million copies.

Seeing platinum in the general Northwest region, other corporations quickly focused on a small aspect of Nirvana's sound, some distantly-related bands' "look," and declared Seattle the nexus of all this music, and the term for the entire thing "independent rock." A nice, easy-to-recall ad slogan. The fact that there was a real boom in self-financed rock all over the country was taken in stride by the music industry as a new, all-encompassing "genre" was born— a genre which had nothing to do with music, but everything to do with corporate America wanting to reach an affluent segment of the population.

At the same time, the bands that filled the now-corporate-dictated parameters of "indie rock" became a sort of "farm team" as new groups test-marketed themselves via their own self-financed efforts. In this way, major labels circumvented expensive market research. A similar phenomenon occurred in films.

Hollywood noticed that people, no matter where they got the money, still made movies. More importantly, some of these movies made money. As funding from the National Endowment for the Arts and the private sector dried up towards decade's end, Hollywood bought into low-budget film producers and distributors like Miramax and New Line. "Independent film" became the advertising catch-all for low-budget films that appealed to a trendy audience, just as "independent rock" had done for music.

The major studios saw that, for example, Quentin Tarantino's self-produced, low-budget *Reservoir Dogs* (1993) had done well at the few remaining "art" houses, and even played a few prized multiplex screens.

Corporate bankrolling then helped create Tarantino's star-filled *Pulp Fiction* (1995), an amusing pop culture melange that played to its young audience's video store savvy. Tarantino quickly adapted to Hollywood life, churning out retro-junk like *From Dusk 'til Dawn* (1995) and script-doctoring moribund screenplays like *Crimson Tide* (1995) on the sly, for more money.

The parallels with indie rock continued—without dropping a dollar of development money, Hollywood found in Tarantino an auto-icon of "rebellious" youth who was still studio/product-friendly. And, like music, independent film became another very profitable sort of farm team, that is, a cheap means for corporate Hollywood to find talent that was already succeeding and invest in it for further success.

Just how arrogant the studios can get with the "indie" sell is exemplified by the case of the 1996 release, *The Spitfire Grill*.

The film's director, Lee David Zlotoff, was positioned in press releases as a bona fide independent filmmaker. His film was hyped as an intimate portrait of the hardscrabble lives of sundry little people in a nowhere New England township.

In reality, Zlotoff and his film were backed and promoted by the deep pockets of Castle Rock Films, a division of Turner Broadcasting, owned by Time Warner. *The Spitfire Grill* was a well-produced piece of pap that had all the depth of a TV movie of the week. Castle Rock Films went so far as to actually *boast* about Zlotoff's background as the creator of the TV show *MacGyver* and as a regular contributor to *Remington Steele*. The fact that this film was enthusiastically received at Sundance, that nobody had any trouble reconciling a bad film by a TV hack, backed by a major studio, as an example of independent filmmaking says a lot about the state of independent film.

Still, many interesting and vital films are being made, by hook or by crook, by many filmmakers. But it's an uphill battle all the way.

Keith Gordon, director of the extraordinary *A Midnight Clear* (1992), struggled for three years to finance his adaptation of Kurt Vonnegut's novel, *Mother Night*. Eventually, Fine Line (a division of Turner Broadcasting/Time Warner) offered him a deal.

The result of the Fine Line deal: Gordon would not have control over "final cut" but he would be spared the usual test market process of submitting the partially-edited film to preview audiences for decisions on how to edit his film. "It's a perverse, unrealistic way to get reactions," Gordon wrote in *Details* magazine (June 1997). "...when most people see a film, they're not sitting there trying to figure out what's wrong with it. As a result of these test screenings, films are often reedited to please the lowest common denominator."

During this three year process of making the deal, there was a lot of time spent on working out the financial issues, resulting in "endless redefining of 'net profits'." Gordon notes that it's "an odd use of time, since films never have net profits unless they're *Star Wars*, due to the, *ahem,* creative way Hollywood does its accounting." (The italics are Gordon's.)

If a film miraculously makes it on the indie circuit, the filmmaker faces extreme corporate pressure to make follow-up films with as many rough edges sanded off as possible, so as to vie for constantly diminishing screen space, whether at "art houses" or multiplexes. Tempted by the dangling carrot of major studio funding, a filmmaker's artistic intent is constantly compromised by the active results of that funding: market-researched "cuts" and plot resolutions, product tie-ins and placement, and so on.

Urban Independent: Producer Christine Vachon

PARTIAL FILMOGRAPHY

Christine Vachon: as producer/executive producer:

Film	Year	Director
Poison	(1990)	Todd Haynes
Swoon	(1992)	Tom Kalin
Go Fish	(1994)	Rose Troche
Kids	(1994)	Larry Clark
Postcards from America	(1994)	Steve McLean
Safe	(1995)	Todd Haynes
I Shot Andy Warhol	(1996)	Mary Harron
Office Killer	(1997)	Cindy Sherman
Kiss Me, Guido	(1997)	Tony Vitale
Velvet Goldmine	(1998)	Todd Haynes

Although her name is not a household word, Christine Vachon can lay claim to something few mainstream producers can: This completely "out" lesbian woman and producer of seemingly "noncommercial" films has yet to make a single movie that has lost money.

True, her films tend to be targeted to an ambisexual, urban, and intelligent audience, and thus do not have to make the obscene amounts necessary to raise, say, a *Waterworld* from the celluloid dead. Also true, this is all a matter of scale: a Batman film lurches to the fighting line with an average price tag of $100 million, while a Vachon production usually weighs in at around a sprightly $2 mil or so. [See comparative budgets on pages 188–189].

So for now, and while there are still available screens, Christine Vachon is doing well for herself *and* her directors.

IG: The credit *producer* is always a bit slippery in terms of what it actually means. In your case, what *is* the actual job description?

CV: Generally, I'm on a film from its conception, although not always. I provide, as the script is being written, whatever moral or creative support is necessary for that particular writer/director. I do tend to work with writer/directors. I put together the package—the actors, crew, locations—while at the same time I'm getting the money!

IG: Where's the money come from these days?

CV: It comes from all different places. Each independent film is like reinventing the wheel. The kind of movies I do—I have to be *relentlessly* optimistic. I have to be a one-person cheerleading team.

I then have to transfer this enthusiasm to the investors, the potential participants. I also work with a lot of first time directors, so that's a whole other thing in itself. I enjoy that, there's this sort of serendipity that happens when I work with someone who's doing it for the first time. It makes me remember why it's fun.

IG: I read this interview with a director—conducted some time ago, so the numbers are out of whack—who said if you make a movie below, say, $6 million, it's *your* movie. If you go above about $10 mil, then you're just asking for compromises. Do you ever plan to make that corporate jump?

CV: I don't see it as that simple. I'm sure we've already made compromises, depending on how you define compromise. The way I really define it is: doing something you know isn't good for the movie, because the powers-that-be, the people controlling the purse strings, are insisting on it.

Now, I've never had to do that. I *have* had to entertain other choices, listen to people I was convinced I knew more than—maybe not go with my first choice, but go with a choice I'm still happy with. I don't know the line where the movie stops being yours.

I know exactly what that director was saying, but I think it's hard to define it now. You don't always know who the devil is. I just did the Cindy Sherman film, *Office Killer* [a renowned photographer's first film]. That was an example of a movie that was relatively cheap to make, but it had two very intense executive producers on it, and I had to keep reminding myself, "This is *only* a million dollar film." Even though I'm still running the gamut.

I *have* seen it change since I started making movies. Those under $3 million features still exist, but I do think the demographics of *who* makes them has changed significantly.

When I started out, one would finance a movie partially from—this is *over* now—government funding: the City Council on the Arts, the NEA. And partially from limited partnerships and maybe throwing in a European TV deal. But most of those stations have gone the way of the Council of the Arts. [They died.]

It's really different now. Back then, *Poison* was approximately 50% financed that way. *Swoon* was virtually 100% financed that way, until American Playhouse came in, and that's basically PBS money anyway. At that time you could make a *Poison* or a *Swoon,* even if you didn't happen to be a DuPont. Right?

But *Go Fish* was the real transition film in my career, because that was the movie that three years earlier I would have just said, "Well, girls, you came to the right place!"

I write a *mean grant,* and this was prime grant material because of the subject matter, because they weren't from New York City. They had everything on their side, but by that time it was too late. All those funding sources had dried up. I had to kick around saying "This *will* make money!"

IG: Did it make money?

CV: Oh yeah. Quite a lot of money.

IG: Have all your films made money?

CV: I would prefer to say none of them have *lost* money. Okay? But hey— that's quite a record. [Knocks on wood table] So far.

I feel there's this sentiment around now that says "anyone can make a movie." But I don't believe anybody *can* make a movie. I actually wish that some of these movies would, well, *wane* a little.

[In the mid-'80s]...I got together with Todd [Haynes] and we ended up starting a company together. We did all these short films—at the same time Todd was doing the Karen Carpenter film [about the life of the anorexic pop star played out with Barbie dolls].

Posion started coming together and I got a taste of feature production, and I realized my fate would be very wound up with Todd's. Part of its success was the fact there weren't any gay films—in 1990—you didn't say there is a gay audience.

IG: I recall seeing the line for *Go Fish,* and noticed as many—or more— straights there.

CV: Well—there *was* lesbian chic. And comedies always do better. Especially now. Things are hard. People need to laugh. I say I have to do a "feel good" movie every so often because I do so many "feel bad" movies!

IG: Is the Cindy Sherman film really a horror film?

CV: It really is.

James Shamus had been trying to put together a fund for horror films that would be directed by interesting directors. He wanted to make "art" horror films. Then I went to...Cindy's studio and there were all these dismembered body parts, and I said, "Cindy—you have to do this horror film!" It was still the same dog 'n pony show though, when it came to getting financing. It turned out very well though.

IG: The casting struck me—you've got Molly Ringwald with her John Hughes stigma, Jeanne Tripplehorn [ex-"supermodel" and star of *Waterworld*] with her "sex symbol" thing, and Carol Kane who is just perceived as, well, strange. It seemed like these were three women who wouldn't get leading parts right now. To say nothing of all of them being in the same film.

CV: What happened was Jeanne—who's a huge fan of Cindy's—approached her and said, "I don't know if you know who I am, but I'm a fan." Cindy was like—*Jeanne Tripplehorn? Who?*

We were searching for the right lead—the killer—and Carol was delighted to do it. Molly was suggested by our casting director.

I'd been fearing the worst about Ringwald, because I'd heard "*Agh! She's a nightmare!*" But she couldn't have been more of a professional. Then you think about how young she was when she made all those films [perky '80s John Hughes/Brat Pack films], and I'd sure not want to hear about what I was like at that age! I also think she has an inner serenity, from having gone up so high, and then come down. She's *been* there.

IG: Speaking of horror, I thought *Safe* was the signature horror film of the '90s, dealing, as it did, with the body assaulted by technology, a hostile environment—was that what you were trying to get across?

CV: Oh—absolutely! I always felt that *Safe's* day would come, that it would be recognized as the masterpiece it is. But the climate in which it premiered was really hard. Critics came up to me at Sundance, saying, "I don't know about *this,* Christine." I'd say two or three of those same critics put it on their Best Ten list! It's a movie unlike any other, and it strikes at a place that is so frightening, and its themes resonate intensely, it's hard for people to acknowledge it.

IG: What are those themes?

CV: It's very...organic. I remember Todd saying he'd read about these people who live in these trailers because they're allergic to everything, and they call it *Twentieth Century Disease!* Isn't that *amazing?* And that was it— Boom! The next project.

IG: I like that the characters in your films, like *I Shot Andy Warhol*, are not identified by gender choices—they're people first.

CV: The thing I love about *Go Fish*, was, Wow! This takes place in a post-coming-out space. It's not about, "Ya know, I finally realized what's wrong with me is..."

    You know. I get criticized a lot by the so-called gay and lesbian community—and I say "so-called" because I am loath to refer to people as a community purely because of who they sleep with. But I'm stuck with it. I'm more than happy to be an inspiration to an up-and-coming gay or lesbian producer or director, but I'm also just happy to be an inspiration to anybody who wants to make good films.

IG: You have to be compartmentalized.

CV: That's why "the community" didn't get behind *Safe*. They were like, "Well! Is it about AIDS or not?" To reduce *Safe* to being purely about AIDS is so reductive it's *stupid*.

IG: Did you get shit about it having heterosexual characters?

CV: Oh *yeah*. But Todd's better than me—I get upset at dumb reviews. I do things like being mean to reviewers who pan my films. One reviewer gave a wonderful review of *Safe* but panned *Warhol*—I was so mad I took his invite away from the premiere. I take it personally, you know?

IG: What about run-ins with the MPAA?

CV: Well, yeah. I've had my run-ins. *Swoon* was laughable, which came out at about the same time as *Basic Instinct*. Most people's complaints about *Swoon* were that there was no sex in it whatsoever. There is a spot second where you see two clothed male characters atop each other—how shall I put it—*wriggling*, you know? They have all their clothes on—that was it! They gave it an NC-17 as a result. Finally I decided to just release it unrated.

IG: Did they ask for cuts?

CV: Yeah—cut that out! But we were like, What the hell? Then I saw *Basic Instinct* with the "winking pussy" and thought—there's something wrong with this! I mean, *that* gets an R? And we get an NC-17 for *nothing*?

    Now with *Warhol*, Goldwyn wants us to deliver a TV version and they sent six priceless pages of changes. Like—instead of having someone say "up your ass." They wanted "up your nose." Instead of "why don't you give him a blow job," they wanted "why don't you give him a *foot massage!*" [Breaks into extended laughter]

Film Budgets: A Blockbuster Budget

Story, Rights, Continuity	$ 2,627,100
Producers Unit	$ 1,913,056
Direction	$ 3,847,135
Cast	$ 5,835,141
Travel & Living	$ 204,297
Fringe Benefits	$ 890,675
Total Above-the-Line	**$15,317,404**
Production Staff	$ 663,731
Extra Talent	$ 612,664
Set Design	$ 1,132,937
Set Construction	$ 4,469,155
Set Striking	$ 900,000
Set Operations	$ 1,694,255
Special Effects	$ 2,263,912
Set Dressing	$ 1,378,475
Property	$ 1,616,107
Men's Wardrobe	$ 2,189,328
Women's Wardrobe	$ 1,325,084
Makeup and Hairdressing	$ 3,006,404
Lighting	$ 1,296,139
Camera	$ 838,409
Production Sound	$ 329,589
Transportation	$ 1,503,380
Location	$ 1,195,511
Production Film & Lab	$ 409,923
Process	$ 58,778
Second Unit	$ 1,944,100
Tests	$ 50,000
Facilities	$ 1,286,285
Fringe Benefits	$ 4,956,065
Total Production	**$35,119,531**
Film Editing	$ 1,147,555
Music	$ 500,000
Post Production Sound	$ 623,952
Post Production Film & Lab	$ 154,740
Main & End Titles	$ 50,000
Special Visual Effects	$ 5,389,200
Fringe Benefits	$ 306,075
Total Post Production	**$8,171,522**
Publicity	$ 36,989
Insurance	$ 75,700
General Expenses	$ 608,938
Fringe Benefits	$ 8,906
Total Other	**$730,533**
Total Above-the-Line	**$15,317,404**
Total Below-the-Line	**$44,021,586**
GRAND TOTAL	**$59,338,990**

Film Budgets: An Indie Film Budget:

Story and Rights	$	0
Writing	$	0
Producer and Staff	$	15,600
Director and Staff	$	3,600
Talent	$	77,225
Fringe Benefits	$	18,470
Total Above-the-Line		**$114,895**
Production Staff	$	28,370
Camera	$	24,085
Art Department	$	22,030
Set Construction	$	3,650
Electrical	$	37,660
Set Dressing	$	0
Extra Talent	$	4,510
Wardrobe	$	10,370
Makeup & Hairdressing	$	6,010
Sound (Production)	$	9,540
Locations	$	46,600
Transportation	$	10,770
Film and Lab	$	50,147
Tests	$	0
Total Production		**$253,742**
Editing & Projection	$	64,300
Post Production Lab	$	23,700
Music	$	54,000
Sound (Post Production)	$	88,485
Titles, Opticals, Inserts	$	17,000
Total Post Production		**$247,485**
Bond	$	0
Insurance	$	8,000
Legal	$	0
Contingency	$	0
Total Other		**$8,000**
Total Above-the-Line		**$114,895**
Total Below-the-Line		**$509,227**
GRAND TOTAL		**$624,122**

NYC, The Farm Team: Producer Andrew Fierberg

Andrew Fierberg has produced six independent features. Among them are *Nadja,* on which he collaborated with his partner Amy Hobby in their company, "double a films" (and which was executive produced by David Lynch), *At Sundance*, a documentary on the Sundance film festival, and *Tempête dans un Verre d'Eau (Tempest in a Teapot)* directed by Arnold Barkus, which, with his typically self-deprecating humor, Fierberg describes as "A couple of French guys walking around New York talking about girls—(Pause) it's a comedy." *Sunday,* a film he produced for director Jonathan Nossiter, won the 1997 Grand Jury Prize at the Sundance Film Festival.

IG: With Viacom and a few other monopolies owning most of the chains, where do you *show* independent fare?

AF: The amount of theaters that show independent films? It's become so marginalized. 85-90% of the films playing are Disney or the equivalent and everyone else—the independents, the Europeans, great filmmakers from Latin America, you name it—are chasing that elusive 10%.

The idea is that when there's 125 channels [cable, satellite] there's going to be a clamor for product. Then the question is: are we making films for television or for the theater-going audience? And what happens to the independent filmmaking world when you stop making films for people who actually go to movies? Yeah—theoretically people are looking for product with all this channel space, but, in fact, there's *tons* of *stuff* being made, where there's so few actual film screens available. And distributors make deals with theaters to get their stuff played—it's not even really corrupt—it's just the only way for them to stay in business!

Like with *Nadja,* someone had to fight to displace a Miramax film or another film that's going to generate a continual amount of money or a tax write-off. And every year there's less screen space allotted to smaller films.

They *say*, with the mini-mall market, that screens in the malls will play films that come out of Sundance. But—*The Brothers McMullen*—is that a step forward that it played in 40 or 50 theaters? I mean, it's not like we're talking art film here! We're talking about filmmakers putting their own money on the line and the major studios trolling around and snagging things. New York independent filmmaking is basically acting as a self-financed training ground for the major film companies. Good deal for them.

IG: Like New York has become a sort of farm team for Hollywood?

AF: Yeah. We're the farm team [in New York]. Glorified bottom feeders.

And what's happening is that everyone says "You gotta have someone in New York"—so they set up these little regional offices—"Oh look! We're in the Tribeca Center—close to *Bobby DeNiro!*"

And then they can charge a fortune for rents and Tribeca is turned into Hollywood East—filmmaking and real estate, two speculative industries holding hands downtown.

IG: And the only people who can afford to make movies are—

AF: —it's a rich *man's* sport. A rich *kid's* sport.

Independent filmmaking is not subsidized and the majors are not throwing any money in our direction—I mean, they're just sitting around waiting. The idea of having film development money out there on the street or having any state funding—no—there's no money for people to develop difficult projects.

The fact is: They should support new talent. Unfortunately, they don't and films are getting shittier and shittier. People don't work at becoming good writers, because they want to produce and direct themselves and they think that if they have enough money to direct, they can write! Respect for craft seems to matter very little.

It all comes down to: Who can support themselves for three years while you put together your feature? And take lots of meetings?

IG: Is this how *Sunday* came about?

AF: Jonathan [Nossiter, *Sunday's* director] had an interest in the food business. He basically subsidizes his—I think—trust fund by doing wine stuff, selling it at auction, doing wine lists for restaurants. [shrugs].

Sunday is about two disenfranchised people falling in love in lower-class Queens. The simple tale resulted in a troubled production, a budget that the director ignored and inflated constantly, and multiple credit conflicts. Despite this, Fierberg is sanguine about the experience:

AF: Life is long. It's a good film.

IG: Okay. Looking at this list of other Sundance films, almost all of them look like civics-lesson movies—very uplifting. All this supposedly "PC" stuff seems—so *blah*. So easily *assimilated*, like an independent version of "dumbing-down".

AF: Yes. It's the odd festival that has *any* films outside a certain kind of box. They seem to think that each year has a certain tone to it. This year it was very politically correct...everyone wears a condom. You touch on all the evils, but everyone knows your film is on the "right" side, no matter how hostile or confused it is.

Sundance is just something you *have* to deal with. It's the biggest game in town. It's the Hollywood festival that surprisingly shows mainly New York films because they still don't have a very strong independent filmmaking network out in LA, although it is growing.

But besides that—LA's just too much an industry town, it's a lot like Detroit, so Sundance—

IG: —is a place you take your film to get a distribution deal.

AF: —you take a film there because you are *desperate* to get a deal!

IG: What about a couple people getting a camera and just fuckin' doing it?

AF: The point is—that's the future. To do it with a few people. The film stock is getting better. It's not harder to make a film. What's hard is getting it into a theater!

That's where we're headed: we're not looking to make $2 million films; we're looking to make *better* $600,000 films.

With all this talk of dollar amounts, I think of the promo hype spread by Siskel & Ebert and other media people regarding Robert Rodriguez's *El Mariachi*.

The story told of how Rodriguez, armed only with talent and about $7,000, had made a Spanish-language, subtitled film in Mexico about a guitar-slinging tough guy.

IG: So was it true *El Mariachi* only cost 7 thou? And that Columbia Pictures kicked in a few hundred thousand to make it slick?

AF: It was a joke!

They almost *rebuilt* the film! In order to make it viewable and release it with a new soundtrack, it must have ended up costing at least half a million.

With the successful "test marketing" of *El Mariachi* in the "art-house" circuit, Hollywood commissioned a big-budget remake titled *Desperado* (1995), starring Antonio Banderas. After making the remake, Rodriguez would end up working with Quentin Tarantino on *From Dusk 'til Dawn* (1996).

IG: And now Kevin Smith, who wrote and directed the low-budget *Clerks* and *Chasing Amy*, has written the latest big-budget *Superman* movie for Jon Peters. [Smith's script was later dropped when Tim Burton became attached to the project.]

AF: Go figure.

If anyone could tell me why someone who's made a film for $200-300,000 should know how to handle $10 million or more—they're a little bit loony as far as I'm concerned.

There's a certain thing about *learning your trade*. It's like the whole thing with people's second films: look at [Ed Burns] *Brothers McMullen* and then *She's the One*. It might have made money, but it's a horrible film. There's a curse to having too much money. So you had enough money to make another stupid film, but did you *understand your craft?* It's such a disservice to filmmaking.

The Pope of Trash: Director John Waters

PARTIAL FILMOGRAPHY

Roman Candles	1966
Eat Your Makeup	1967
Mondo Trasho	1969
The Diane Linkletter Story	1969
Multiple Maniacs	1970
Pink Flamingos	1972
Female Trouble	1974
Desperate Living	1977
Polyester	1981
Hairspray	1988
Cry-Baby	1990
Serial Mom	1994

Books:

Shock Value	1985
Trash Trio	1986
Crackpot	1987
Director's Cut	1997

With the air of a dandified (and disreputable) raconteur, and an aesthetic that could be described as Diane Arbus Meets June Cleaver on a Really Low Budget, John Waters has been independently writing and directing films for over 32 years. He has also written several fabulous odes to bad taste, including *Bad Taste* and *Crackpot*.

Until *Hairspray*, Waters' films were purposefully garish and brimming with a tabloid-like sensibility that was equal parts camp and shock tactics. His eccentric casts were usually headed by "the world's most beautiful person," the 300-pound transvestite Divine (who passed on in 1988). Although *Pink Flamingos* remains Waters' best-known film (because of its infamous scene in which Divine ingests a poodle's feces), all of his films offer equally inspired/twisted moments.

In *Female Trouble*, septuagenarian Edith Massey fondles eggs while garbed in tight bondage gear. *Desperate Living* tells of a mental patient and her very fat maid who beat a homicide rap only to wind up in a village ruled by the debauched Queen Carlotta. And watching ex-teen heartthrob Tab Hunter cozy up with Divine in *Polyester* is a vision only Waters could offer.

It's ironic that some in the media accused Waters of "selling out" when he moved on to make his polished and sweet-tempered tribute to cheesy '60s teen musicals, *Hairspray*. Actually, he'd simply tired of a worn-out aesthetic.

What was once considered shocking, what Waters had been vilified for showing in his earlier films, had been assimilated by the mainstream. Unlike his detractors and the culture in general, Waters had grown. His films still subvert any idea of "normal"; he's just found different ways to make his points, often by utilizing the conventions of other genres for his own purposes (the '50s "juvenile delinquent" movie style of *Cry-Baby*, for example).

Waters remains a fascinating director who refuses to endlessly repeat himself.

IG: I understand you're doing a film called *Cecil B. Demented* [a story of teenage terrorism against Hollywood for making crappy movies].

JW: —oh, that's *old news*. Last spring it was a development deal with all this French money that fell through with, oh, the usual casting problems.

[Perks up] I've thought up a whole new movie. I'm real superstitious and never talk about it until it happens.

I learned *a long time ago* that in Hollywood, if it has momentum, it builds and builds, and as soon as it stalls, it's *over*. In one night.

IG: Are there any particular studios you're friendly—

JW: —oh, I deal with *all* of 'em! Every one of 'em up to the biggest Hollywood studios. Yes, I'm involved in *that* world, yes. [laughs sardonically]

IG: In your book *Crackpot*, you had a piece called "How NOT to Make a Movie." Well, how doesn't one make a movie?

JW: I'm not sure if even *I* followed my own advice ten or fifteen years later. You mean how to *not* get a film financed, right?

Well, first of all, have your first film be a *personal* film about your *grandmother!* Then there's: [haughty voice] *"I don't care if my film makes money."* Well, your backer will!

And then, especially, there's the young ones who have lofty, pretentious ideas about the movie business; they're the ones who will be taken the *least* seriously. Because, starting out, you have so little money to make a movie. The only way you can do it is to make a film that *somehow* hasn't been made yet. Something new, a new twist on exploitation. You know, sex and violence. Sex and violence in your first movie is *a must!*

IG: Then you have something like *The Brothers McMullen*——mediocrity defined. Yet the critics go batshit for it. What's *that* about?

JW: Umm...well, I never say anything negative. My specialty is praising movies that most people *dislike*.

But—*The Brothers McMullen*—a little too hetero for me! I guess when I watched it, I was thinking: Do people really *have these problems?* Obviously they do, because it was very well liked, a hit movie.

I mean, *I* don't know people like that. But I've hardly ever been one to claim to know what the mainstream is doing...if I read that script, I would have thought, "Are there *really* 25-year-old virgins?!"

I think that's the one thing that comes with having success in your life—you never have to deal with people like that, *ever.* And that's what comes with any kind of success—you never have to *deal* with these people! [laughs]

To me, that's *far* kinkier than wearing diapers! I don't know any of these virgins, and if I did they wouldn't tell!

IG: With so few screens available for unusual movies, and so many screens taken up by junk like *The Brothers McMullen*, where can an actual individual talent take his new—

JW: —I'll tell ya, the first movie, *Hag in a Black Velvet Jacket*, premiered in a beatnik coffee house in 1964. Then *Roman Candles, Eat Your Make-Up*, '67, and *Mondo Trasho*, '69, premiered in an Episcopal Church because it was the only place we could escape the censor board. They wouldn't *dare* bust a church...1970, *Multiple Maniacs* premiered in The First Unitarian Church...*Polyester* was the first premiere at the Charles [a rundown, though much-loved, bijou in deepest Baltimore].

IG: Has Baltimore fallen prey to the same sort of corporate, mall-shopping sameness afflicting other cities?

JW: Noooo...it's just fallen even more into *emptiness.* Downtown hardly has anyone rushing around and half the city is empty.

IG: Really? White flight, or—

JW: —yes. But not just whites—blacks want to get out too!

[Laughs] The crazy people are left—that's why I like it! They're still here!

It's a very odd mixture of old money and new lunacy! I like both—a good mix! But I have an apartment in New York—the MetroLiner is my A train! I'm a bridge and tunnel person! [Referring to the tendency of Manhattanites to denigrate anyone from Brooklyn, Queens or neighboring New Jersey as subhuman creatures]

I mean, I *like* New Jersey! I think everybody looks good there—they have a look I think is sexy! Just, y'know—they aren't trying to be chic.

And I have trouble with animal rights people when they say, "Well, at least you're against animal experimentation for eye makeup." I say, "Wel-l-l-l...eye makeup has been *very important* in my life, and if a few cute bunnies have to die so one drag queen has a happier life, I'm for it."

IG: There's a holiday in Baltimore for your birthday, right?

JW: The year *Hairspray* opened, the mayor proclaimed it "John Waters Day." The governor proclaimed it "John Waters *Week*" or vice-versa—I can't remember which. I have the proclamations upstairs, which are very similar to the ones The Wizard of Oz gave the Scarecrow at the end. [chuckles] For having brains?

IG: Any topics that are off-limits for satire?

JW: No—but it depends who you are.

I think if you *have* AIDS, you can make AIDS jokes. If you're Jewish, you can make—you know what I mean? I think "No [topic is off limits]" as long as *you are* what you are making fun of.

IG: Right. I have to say, 1994 was a really awful year for movies, and *Serial Mom* was really a bright spot—

JW: [very sincerely] Why, thank you.

IG: Whereas one of the low points was Oliver Stone's *Natural Born Killers*—

JW: —if a movie's good enough to make people think killing is sexy—even though I think that's kinda scary—if that movie made somebody kill somebody—that's a good movie. Any movie that can make somebody do *anything* must be good.

IG: You've said yourself that killers are the last really glamorous stars.

JW: Oh, that to me *is* a little old hat. I used that up in *Female Trouble*. I used to believe that, but that was 20 years ago.

O.J. was the final ruination of ever wanting to go to a murder trial. Because now, *everybody* wants to.

IG: So you don't go to trials anymore?

JW: No...I can't. I tried to go to one locally, but it was so embarrassing; they all recognized me, thought I was trying to make a movie or something! You lose the right to voyeur people's tragedy with any kind of fame. [laughs a while].

IG: Okay—another topic—the whole size queen thing, with Demi Moore, everybody in sight getting big new breasts, guys getting all pumped up—I even heard some utterly scurrilous rumors that Kenneth Branagh had pectoral implants for his role in *Frankenstein* and—

JW: —implants?! *Penile?*—

IG: —ah, no. Pectoral.

JW: [Disappointed] Oh, pectoral.
      You know, with Divine we just used lentils for breasts.

IG: Lentils? Were they cooked?

JW: No, they were inside a bra and they just kind of *move.*
      I always say I wish I could go to the gym and get the body of a junkie! 'Cause that's what *I* like. Like when I was young and quit smoking! I like the heroin chic look. I don't like *heroin*—thank God!—but I think the junkie look is kinda sexy.
      What I *really* don't like is people my age—I'm 50—goin' to the gym all the time. They do look great but I don't want to see 'em nude! They still look 50! So I think you look better *dressed* after 30.
      And let me say that I have a picture of Demi Moore holding a copy of *Crackpot* in the *Enquirer,* so I'm a big fan.

IG: But why isn't Traci Lords a big star? I mean, acting-wise no big dif from Demi. And I think Traci Lords is just so much cooler!

JW: I do too!
      It's not about fairness—it's just that Traci hasn't yet been in a movie that made $80 million like *Ghost* did. As soon as you do a movie like that, you're up there forever.
      Traci hasn't had that kind of hit yet, but as soon as she does, it'll be the same. As soon as you're in a movie that makes $100 million, you never go back to being a nobody. Never. You never go back to [pause] *scale!*

IG: Did *Serial Mom* do well?

JW: Yeah—it did fine. I mean, it didn't by *Hollywood* standards—they only care about making $100 million, you know what I mean? [a terse chuckle]

I'm interested in *modest* success in Hollywood. And that's not something they really try hard for. It's easier—my agent says—to get a movie made that costs either two million or ninety million. In between—it's hard. [sighs]

You know, I've written about every movie I've seen since I was 16 and rated it. I still go to the movies three or four times a week. I never watch videos, and I never watch TV except for *Homicide* [which is shot in Baltimore]. I *read* for four or five hours every night...when I'm writing—I stick to that schedule.

And then I go out on Friday nights like a coalminer with a paycheck!

IG: Looking for—

JW: —depends! Fun! I look for fun, I look for good lines that I can use in my scripts—I go out for input. I can have a terrible time and it'll still be good for my work.

IG: How would you relate the word "stupid" and the way movies are made today?

JW: Some stupid movies are okay. High-minded movies—*those* are the ones I hate. I love sexy stupid movies—mmmm...*Escape from LA*. That was sexy stupid!

IG: What would be not-sexy stupid? What would be a movie that just sucked in a grandly stupid manner?

JW: [Pause] I really don't do that.

The only movie I've always dissed is *Forrest Gump*. I wanted to call the police in the middle of it. Deeply offended. It was too obscene for me!

IG: Because it was this big valentine to a lunkhead?

JW: Well, I don't mind that, even; I didn't like it when he was supposed to be brilliant. I think lunkheads are *perfectly* fine. I *like* lunkheads. But lunkheads who supposedly *teach* me with their *brilliance*—that doesn't happen too much...

But I like having dumb friends—who wants to always talk to someone who's brilliant? You can talk to a person who isn't that smart and they're funny, there's a freedom in it, and I am not laughing *at* them, I'm laughing *with* them!

IG: There's this William Burroughs quote: "John Waters is the pope of trash."

JW: Well—that's certainly nice coming from him! That's like being ordained by the pope! I think it was really sweet that he said that. "The Duke of

Dirt," "The Anal Ambassador"—I've had a lot of titles, but none can top Burroughs.

IG: When you were a kid, what were the movies that gave you the creeps?

JW: The ones I liked.

Obviously, *The Wizard of Oz.* That was the only time I was ever in drag in my life. When I was seven I wanted to be the Witch! I wanted her green skin! And to live with winged monkeys—I never knew why Dorothy wanted to go back and live in black and white with *smelly farm animals.*

I mean—winged monkeys! Magic shoes! And the Witch would have been nice to her if she'd just teamed on either side—Glenda or the Wicked Witch, they both would have been nice! And she coulda had green skin!

And you know, that's what's next, after all these kids are done getting tattooed—it's skin coloring! Michael Jackson started it—youth can finish it! [Imitates girl's voice] "You know Betty! She's purple!" After branding and scarring—that's it!

IG: Designer-colored kids.

JW: Yeah! Artificial skin color.

IG: Do you end up being pals with a lot of your cast members?

JW: Some of them. Patty [Hearst]—it was very odd because I was at her whole trial—I didn't know her then, I was obsessed by her case. [In 1974, Patty Hearst, heir to the newspaper fortune, was abducted by the Symbionese Liberation Army at the age of 19. She then took part in a series of SLA-related crimes and was arrested in 1975 for participating in an SLA bank robbery. Found guilty, Hearst served 22 months in prison before President Jimmy Carter commuted her sentence.]

At the time I wrongly had certain conceptions about her but now that I know her I know I *was* wrong. She always used to say "It's people like you that got me convicted, because you wanted me to be this thing I never, ever was!" And she's right! But she's got a good sense of humor, she's a good actress—I just like her, she's a close friend.

I'm still very close to Ricki Lake...and Johnny Depp, Iggy Pop. Some I keep up with more than others.

IG: Another thing about *Serial Mom*: while watching it with a fairly "normal" audience, there was that scene where you stick the guts right into the camera sort of like *Andy Warhol's Dracula*—

JW: —Well! That was more like *Multiple Maniacs,* actually—we did the gore in that before *Dracula* and *Frankenstein*—as much as I loved it!

[Laughs good-naturedly] Well, Paul Morrisey's [*Dracula's* director] a friend...and in *Maniacs* Divine rips out David Lochary's heart and eats it! And that was in homage to someone who did it before me, which was Herschel Gordon Lewis in *2,000 Maniacs!*

IG: Well, back to that audience. They were laughing. I kept wondering, How *do* you shock people these days?

JW: I've stopped trying to do that—I try to make people *laugh*.

I mean, *everyone* has seen a gore movie by now. When we made *Maniacs,* they hadn't, you know? They were only in drive-ins and stuff.

Now *Hollywood* has gore. So you don't just try to shock—it doesn't work anymore.

I've never *just* tried to shock people. I think "surprise" is a better word. You'd be surprised—there were people in Middle America who thought *Serial Mom* was as horrifying as *Pink Flamingos* was to my peers in 1972. It just depends on how much you can take! Some people were more offended when she sneezed on a baby's face! When we *shot* that, people were like, "Oh, John! That's *terrible!*" [laughs]

But the baby didn't mind—someone just stood off-camera and threw some gook in his face. And the mother was right there—she approved! It wasn't like we kidnapped a baby and threw snot in his face!

Even the kids in the older movies—the kid who was in the refrigerator in *Desperate Living*—I've met him, and he doesn't even remember it. In *Female Trouble*, where Divine has the baby? I know him. All the kids are *fine,* they didn't have any traumas, and they were up Divine's skirt hooked up to a fake umbilical cord made out of prophylactics!

IG: Now that Divine's passed on, who's left to take on these mantles of madness?

JW: Well, there isn't. I said if Divine died, I'd make a movie starring a boy. [Voice drops] What else could I do?

I just try to keep going without trying to do something that's impossible to do. There's a few [actors] from the early days and they're still in my movies. What we're doing now is basically a second-generation Dreamland.

IG: How has your aesthetic changed since you started?

JW: I don't think it has at all. At all. In the beginning I never imagined I would make Hollywood movies, but it was all so gradual. I mean, I made my first movie in 1964—that's 32 years ago. So I've been doing this a long time, and it's been very satisfying to me. I don't have a lot to beef about. I mean, in the old days [to raise money] I had to have lunch with dentists! At least I know they [the studios] have the money when I come in!

IG: And you don't have to hang around with dentists!

JW: [Melodramatic low voice] Well, *sometimes* [clears throat]—no comment. [laughs]

IG: What do you think about franchise movies—all these endless sequels from big hits? I had this vision of you doing, say, a *Die Hard* movie with Jack Wrangler [gay porn star with a remarkably large unit].

JW: Well, if *Serial Mom* had been a bigger hit, I could have done a sequel to that. I love the idea—I just don't make movies that make enough money to have one.

IG: But you have 32 years of filmmaking—you're a brand name, a brand name of a decidedly curious sort, you have a track record—

JW: —and that's why they do let me make 'em. Because I *am* a brand name in each country—various people *will* see my movies—which is good! And why I make as many movies as I do.

But it's *still* not the brand name that lets me make them *easily* and without any *interference*—

IG: Interference? Even now?

JW: *Nobody* who makes a studio movie—whether Hollywood or independent—doesn't. Go ask Todd Haynes! *Everybody.*

Unless you privately raise the money and make the movie before any of them see it, and then just get a distribution deal, and even *then* they'll say "Oh, you gotta cut this, and you gotta cut *this,*" you know?

I could tell you a hundred stories, but there's *no point* in telling stories. You know, you put out any dirty laundry in Hollywood in public and it's an unspoken rule—you don't do it if you want to continue working there.

IG: Even without naming names?

JW: Oh, well—I had plenty of problems with *Serial Mom.* They wanted me to convict her at the end. It's not surprising. I didn't do it, but there were certainly people who wanted me to.

IG: Where do you get the spirit to keep up this sort of grind after 32 years?

JW: Because that's how I make my living. They pay well—that's one main reason!

And secondly, what else am I going to do? I'm not going to suddenly go work for my father's company.

People ask me, "How can you be so self-disciplined?" And I just go, "If I wasn't, I'd have to work for somebody else!"

And I can go to work in my underpants.

Mr. Waters' diversification into other mediums recently included a series of art installations called *My Little Movies*, in which the director "redirects movies the way I think they should be, or be remembered. Each piece is different—maybe just an image or even a detail—like a hole in a junkie's arm in a Hollywood movie." Included is an homage of sorts to Don Knotts. (This will be published by Scalo as a book in 1997 called *Director's Cut*.)

Mr. Waters is, as of this writing, at work on a film called *Pecker*. ("Because it's about a guy who pecks at his food.")

Actress Sean Young

PARTIAL FILMOGRAPHY

Film	Director	Year
Jane Austen in Manhattan	James Ivory	1980
Stripes	Ivan Reitman	1981
Blade Runner	Ridley Scott	1982
Young Doctors in Love	Garry Marshall	1982
Dune	David Lynch	1984
Baby … Secret of the Lost Legend	B.W.L. Norton	1985
Under the Biltmore Clock	Neal Miller	1985
No Way Out	Roger Donaldson	1987
Wall Street	Oliver Stone	1987
Arena Brains	Robert Longo	1988
The Boost	Harold Becker	1988
Cousins	Joel Schumacher	1989
Firebirds	David Greene	1990
A Kiss Before Dying	James Deardon	1991
Love Crimes	Lizzie Borden	1991
Blue Ice	Russell Mulchahy	1992
Hold Me, Thrill Me, Kiss Me	Joel Hershman	1992
Once Upon a Crime …	Eugene Levy	1992
Sketch Artist	Phadon Papamichael	1992
Fatal Instinct	Carl Reiner	1993
Even Cowgirls Get the Blues	Gus Van Sant	1993
Ace Ventura: Pet Detective	Ton Shadyac	1994
Model by Day	Christian Duguay	1994
Witness to the Execution	Tommy Lee Wallace	1994
Dr. Jekyll and Ms. Hyde	David Price	1995
Mirage	Paul Williams	1995
Everything To Gain	Michael Miller	1996
Evil Has a Face	Rob Fresco	1996

The Proprietor	Ismail Merchant	1996
Men	Zoe Clarke-Williams	1997
The Invader	Mark Rosman	1997
Exception To The Rule	David Winning	1997
Everything To Gain	David Miller	1997
Out of Control	Richard Trevor	1998

I've always been a major fan of Ridley Scott's *Blade Runner*, to the point of repeated viewings in the double digits. It's just a great film.

But when the topic of Sean Young—who played the film's tragic love interest—popped up in conversations about the film, I'd inevitably hear remarks like, "Well, yeah, she's beautiful, but what a nutjob!" When I'd ask *why,* people—all sorts of people—would pause as they realized they didn't really know *why,* they just knew.

I knew there'd been a lot of negative press regarding Ms. Young at a certain point in her career—something to do with James Woods and voodoo dolls—but, I mean, so what? Gossip. Tabloid fodder. On the other hand, this is an actress whose career spanned 17 years and 33 films. She's also worked with a lot of highly respected directors, and in terms of skill could easily go from intense drama to agile comedy.

Yet despite this, Young still suffers from the effects of a media smear-campaign resulting in this across-the-board perception that she is crazy, perhaps drug-addled, bitchy, vindictive, stupid, unreliable or worse.

When I actually researched what happened I was surprised to find out none of these things were true. She is neither crazy nor addicted to any substance. Her case highlights the misinformation and abuse by the entertainment media and the double standard to which women actors are subjected. The power of the media is fierce and even after a decade, this manufactured image of "Crazy Sean" lingers.

Her troubles began when she started working on the movie *Wall Street* with Oliver Stone and Charlie Sheen, two men well-known for their difficulties in the female relations department. Sheen surreptitiously placed a sign on

Young's back reading: "I'm the biggest cunt in the world!"

Young would try to shrug off the entire affair saying casually: "The director, Oliver Stone, has great difficulty with women. Charlie Sheen has had great difficulty growing up. Both of them are intimidated by a woman who has an opinion."—*Vogue*, Nov. 1988. Media-wise she was up against Sheen, who comes from a powerful clan of actors and Stone's a respected director, while Young was the new (female) kid on the block. So the die was cast: Sean Young, although talented, was also a crazy-ass bitch from hell.

She was further plagued by media harassment over her lobbying for the role of Catwomon in Tim Burton's *Batman*. Then she was fired from the set of *Dick Tracy* by legendary compulsive womanizer, Warren Beatty.

In 1989, she filmed *The Boost*, a cautionary tale about a go-go '80s type who nearly destroys his wife via his cocaine-induced mania. Starring with Young was James Woods, who had a reputation for being manic, a tireless womanizer ("I got into this business," he once boasted, "just to meet women."— *People*, March 20, 1989), and a difficult egomaniac (none of these traits ever seem to diminish a male actor's reputation). Richard B. Woodward in the August 20, 1989 *New York Times Magazine* wrote, with obvious distaste for the man, "He may be the only actor in America who tells interviewers his S.A.T. scores," then quotes Woods boasting, "I was obviously—I won't even try to be modest about it—I was an incredibly brilliant kid academically." In *Esquire* (April 1984) to journalist Lynn Hirshchberg, after much whining self-pity about his career, he clucks "...everyone in this business is scared to death of me anyway because they're all morons and I'm not."

Woods, divorced from his wife Kathryn Greko, who said of her ex, "He wanted to control me..." was, during the shooting of *The Boost*, engaged to a woman named Sarah Owen.

Still, it was rumored that Young and Woods had embarked on an affair which ended abruptly. Woods left Young, or Young left Woods (who knows, both denied any affair). Instead of the story ending there, the tabloids trumpeted the bizarre aftermath: Woods claimed to have received hate mail reportedly accompanied by photographs of human corpses, mutilated animals, and, as the *pièce de résistance*, the discovery by Woods, one morning, of a voodoo doll at his doorstep. The doll had a slashed throat, with spattered iodine standing in for dolly blood. But something very odd was reported in *People* by Woods's attorney: a day after the appearance of the doll "a note was placed on Woods's doorstep apologizing for the delivery, but indicating that the person who had done so had done it at Ms. Young's instruction and that Young was upset because he had [not hung] it from one of the rafters per specific instruction." Are femme fatale Young's powers so imposing that she could get someone to do a rather grisly and illegal deed but not imposing enough to restrain him from going *back* to the scene of the crime to apologize for her! Excuse me while I stifle a burst of laughter. But there's more: it was widely reported that a mind-bent Ms. Young had also Krazy-Glued Mr. Woods's penis to his thigh.

Woods wasn't laughing when he slapped a $2 million lawsuit on Young alleging "intentional infliction of emotional distress" to himself and his girl-friend, Ms. Owen. The press labeled this as the sequel to *Fatal Attraction*.

The above mentioned author of the *Times* article writes that he had strict instructions not to ask Woods about Sean Young. After Woods gave an oblique threatening speech that seemed in reference to Young the author wrote "It doesn't seem the best time to ask him about a published report that he once threatened Sarah Owen with a gun. (This item, an aside in a cover story on Sean Young in *Premiere*, stated that Owen went to the Los Angeles police with the charge, then dropped it.) Asked about the incident, Woods turns off the tape recorder. He talks angrily about the irresponsibility of the press. Neither con-firming nor denying the report, he says he hasn't read the articles, and he talks about libel suits."

Mr. Woods dropped all charges. Young and her lawyer had presented evi-dence of her innocence and according to Young, firmly showed Woods and Owen to have set her up. The press ignored this awkward plot conclusion to their *Fatal Attraction* scenario.

Years later, journalist Ron Rosenbaum wrote in *Mademoiselle* (May 1992) that Young was victim to "the legion of people in the entertainment industrial complex who joined in near-universal disparagement of this talented, if offbeat actress" and *Entertainment Weekly* (Feb. 7, 1992) quoted Woods responding to Young's accusations that the lawsuit was a setup: "I love and admire Sean and she's actually half right…" Woods had by then divorced Owen.

Young now has her own film production company, Shonderosa Productions, in Sedona, Arizona, where she lives. She produces and oversees every aspect of the filmmaking process, even to the extent of buying the film stock herself. She still appears in Hollywood productions as a way to bankroll her own projects, and because it is important to her to be a *working* actress.

The Sean Young I spoke with turned out to be charming and very intelligent. Her actions and thoughts seem carefully considered, not out of fear, but out of thoughtfulness.

One day, when it looked like she might be twenty minutes late for a phone interview, Ms. Young called me long distance from a pie shop (where I could hear her sister and her kids laughing) to apologize and re-set our interview. I didn't think that was crazy.

SY: When I went to see *Blade Runner*—the original version that came out— the date [on the opening scrawl] came up as "November 20, 2019," and I was just shocked for a minute because that's my birthday! I was like— whoa! of all the dates they could pick, they picked my birthday!

IG: Did Ridley Scott know—

SY: I don't really know. I was very young when we made that movie so my communication skills weren't as good as they are now.

    When I got my license in Arizona—we're supposed to renew them on our birthday and they last until you're 60—when I saw that it expired on September 20, 2019, I looked at it like—this is really odd! Then I thought, I'll be 59 years old and *expire* all of a sudden! The Nexus 7 version! [laughs in reference to *Blade Runner*'s pre-programmed android death-dates]

IG: Is the new cut the actual director's cut? I'd heard—

SY: I think the one that ended up being rereleased *was* Ridley's cut. Actually, it was minus a couple of ideas he had during shooting—he was going to make Harrison Ford a replicant, and then have him have memory flashbacks. It's just as well it came out like it did, because he wanted his flashbacks to be all about this unicorn and I think he was already thinking about *Legend*. Who knows? [*Legend* 1986, was Scott's infantile follow-up to *Blade Runner*. It takes place in a Tolkienesque fantasy world where Tom Cruise wears a loincloth and unicorns roam.]

IG: *Blade Runner* turned into this watermark in terms of design, technique and influence.

SY: I was really surprised it didn't do better when it was released. It did define a whole new layer of science fiction work that came after it.

IG: In an earlier conversation, you expressed an interest in education, or rather, the decay of the American education system.

SY: I compare it to what people *say* it costs to make a movie today. It doesn't cost that much—but if you're *not* organized, it suddenly costs millions and millions of dollars. If there were better communication skills, I think it would be easier to get a lot more done. And there *is* a way to get things done and people *want* them done.

IG: You mentioned this decay in education was creating a new class—

SY: —a malleable class of people.

I look at it like this: when you take the potential for rebellion and turn it into people who just need a six-pack and a remote control—it's going to be real easy to control them. I said to a friend of mine, "Big Brother isn't watching *us,* we're watching *it.*"

[Pause] I mean, I love my country, but I *fear* my government.

It's a bit scary, because I really do believe there are a lot of good people in the world, but in America we can be so good we're just *stupid.* And it's not so hard to figure out ways to control us. We're living in a technological age that's going to get more and more sophisticated, with communications taking less and less time.

IG: Having a child must make all this a lot more personal.

SY: Ahhh...I don't know. I've felt pretty special all along the way in my life— and there's good and bad to that. Being an actress since I was 19 did two things to me: it made me very confident on one level, but it gave me a very unrealistic approach to dealing with people at large. If you have people kissing your ass all your life, and if somebody suddenly doesn't, it's like—hey! What's wrong with them?! You have to mature. So, along with being a privileged person—

IG: —privileged?

SY: Making more money than other people. Even if it isn't as much as a lot of my *comrades* [makes smirky sound], it's still a lot more than most people make. When you can do that and have that, the fear is lessened in terms of what kind of education your son's going to get. Also—I meet a lot of really smart people the average person doesn't get to meet.

IG: Sometimes it almost seems like a lot of people *choose* to be uninformed, to just take what the media gives them and leave it at that.

SY: It's a *program*. And like any program, you adhere to it. If you watch enough commercials about beautiful cars—pretty soon you're going to want one. If you watch enough cosmetic commercials, pretty soon you're going to feel like this little shadow will make you look or feel more attractive.

IG: Kids are not reading now, and their only reference to history—and this is pretty scary—will be an Oliver Stone's *JFK* or *Nixon*. And they think that's what happened!

SY: Yeah—I walked out feeling that's what happened! And I have actually *no idea* what really happened—

IG: Well, neither does Oliver Stone!

SY: Yeah!

IG: It's nice he raises these historic issues via his films, but it's also like Rachel getting her false history implanted from all these old men (in *Blade Runner*).

SY: That's true. And that's going to happen from now until the end of our lives. In a way I feel it doesn't matter on a certain level. If the world goes into a huge earthquake or comet dust covers the Earth and we all die— that's what happens. I'll be dead, and then I have to deal with the next stage. So all of this is really a religious question for me.

When I die, I really don't believe there'll be nothing on the other side. I believe my spirit is going to continue. It's just something I've always had, so it eliminates certain elements of fear. I also feel that worry and fear are magnets.

You just do the best you possibly can in your own life, and you know that if you're really making that sincere effort to become the best person you can be—in ways *I* find important, like meditating every day.

When I first started I'd close my eyes and feel like there wasn't any space there—but now it's like I'm inside a room that's getting larger and larger. And that seems like a valuable thing to do. When I walk into my various different worlds, I bring a much more powerful person with me. And that's me—that's what I can contribute.

A quiet life may not mean much now. I've written in a journal since I was 13 years old. Consistently. But I'm afraid people might read it and say—

whoa, that was one angry bitch! Because I did leave a lot of the anger on the pages so I wouldn't have to carry it with me wherever I went.

IG: Were you angry before—rebellious?

SY: If you have an actor who suddenly goes on a campaign to prove to your peers that you're a crazy bitch, well [laughs—referring to actor James Woods's attempts to do just that], it'll piss a person off! But mostly I've been pissed off by the amount of immaturity in adults from whom you would expect *some* degree of maturity.

IG: Which leads me to ask; after *Blade Runner* and *No Way Out*, things got, um, unpleasant for you.

SY: That was during *The Boost*. That's about 1987.

IG: But if a man had done whatever it is people claimed you did, at the worst he'd be labeled "eccentric." What are the bad things they claimed you did? I reread a *Rolling Stone* article that tried to show you to be nuts, and out-and-out stupid.

SY: So clever. I personally don't understand why anyone wants to be a writer who puts down other people. I mean, there are people who do need a kick in the ass—but *I'm* certainly not significant enough to warrant the attention! So when people do that to me, I'm like—jeez! I'm just sitting here—what's your problem?

IG: Do you think that men have a problem with women who are both beautiful and smart? Especially "powerful" men.

SY: I know that it's very hard being a really beautiful woman in the sense that it's a distraction for people when they're trying to relate to you just as a person.

    Some of the techniques I've used over the years have been to pretend I'm *not* smart to make people more comfortable and then, once they feel comfortable, they can accept it later down the road. What that usually means is being more quiet up front, so they can acclimate themselves. I find people very easy to work with once they're used to you. But, on the first day of location shooting, I have the honor of being The Mean and Crazy Bitch with everybody going "woooooo!" [laughs]

IG: Can you have fun with that, though?

SY: At this point, I can, but it's been hard to prove myself each and every time. I always said, by the end of the '90s, we'll see who's on top!

    I just think that when you do the best you can, some good things can happen. And by the end of the shoot there'll be 90 to 100 people who'd do anything for me!

I find I have a tremendous amount of regard for the people I'm working with, and they have it for me too. And I think that's the better "man" to be. Because I know, for example, someone like Warren Beatty or James Woods, it's just the opposite.

IG: What do you mean?

SY: People go—Oh! I'm going to work with *Warren Beatty!* Then they go through three months of it and [makes tired, grumbling sound]—who wants to do *this* again? I'd rather be someone people regard highly after they work with me.

IG: Well, looking at your filmography, I was amazed to see you'd already done more than 30 movies.

SY: I just feel like the only thing I would really be angry about at this point would to not be able to work. If the Warren Beattys and the James Woodses and whomevers who want to make it their business to make my day rotten—if they want to put energy in that direction I can't stop them. But if those people could have so much power over my life that I couldn't work, that would have a terrible effect on me.

That hasn't been the case because I've outlived people like that.

IG: Unlike Frances Farmer, you didn't just collapse under the pressure—

SY: That's right! Because she wasn't all that healthy—she was drinking up a storm, she was angrier than the devil, and, well, you could feel sorry for someone like Frances Farmer, but she was this terribly unhappy person, and she really didn't know how to make her life a cohesive thing. For me, it's really *not* about making $12 million and opening a bunch of strip clubs around the country, you know? [in reference to Demi Moore]

The buck is not where I spend my time competing. I've tried to improve my own attitude. I've kept the trajectory of my focus very narrow *on purpose*, so that I wouldn't start spiraling into things I think are meaningless, hopeless, and who fucking cares anyway?

IG: You said that the way you dealt with all that media nastiness was "You just out-create them."

SY: That's right!

IG: I thought that was fabulous.

SY: It *is* fabulous! It is, because it's *simple*.

You go to Hollywood, and they've all got their theories about how to get their dicks farther than the next person and you think, Man!

I've gotten to where I really feel sorry for these people because they have really shitty family lives, they don't communicate well with their kids, their loved ones are not loving them and you think: *What kind of life is this?* So you have forty, eighty, a hundred zillion dollars—has that made them peaceful or serene? I look at that and say, what's valuable here?

IG: One of the seven deadly sins: greed.

SY: Yeah! That's right! I don't need to be a millionaire. I need to work every year, take care of my family and live as beneficially as I can. And it's a simple little thing. Yet in its simplicity, it's a lot more sophisticated in a way a lot of people really don't understand. It takes a lot more strength, but in my opinion, it's the way to go.

IG: After *The Boost* and all the media feeding frenzy that followed, what shape were you in? Where do you find the strength to deal with it?

SY: A lot of different places. Reading. Writing. Just *doing* enough things, one after the other. Where you find it—the strength—is in diligence and looking in the right places. I've always been a bit of a rebel that way.

IG: I recall the stories about you trying to get the *Batman* role—

SY: —the *Catwoman* role—

IG: —Whoa. Right. The thing that I thought, with you dressing in the Catwoman suit and all, I just thought this was fun, a playful sort of thing.

SY: It *was*.

IG: So why is that seized by the press as an excuse to fuck you up again? I'm still not clear what happened.

SY: Well, let me remember! What *did* happen?
I had an agent then, and a manager, and ever since I got rid of them, I haven't been able to *stop* working.
It's weird, it's really weird. Since I fired them, the lines of communication between me and the industry have really improved.
I feel like there's a lot of anger out there, from people who are making movies towards these deal-makers who have hiked all the costs up—it's gone from "Let's make movies" to "Let's have a pissing contest."

IG: You made *Mirage* (a Sean Young Production) for what—$800,000?

SY: Eight hundred and fifty.

IG: Oh, well that's just extravagant!

SY: [Laughs] The point is, though, back then I *did* have an agent, and the agent was telling me "They're not interested in you," and I went "Wait a minute. These are the people who put my *body* at *risk*."

I broke my arm because they asked me two days before shooting *Batman* to ride this horse. I *was* cast in the original *Batman* and I rehearsed for two weeks in London with Jack Nicholson and Michael Keaton and I got knocked out of it because I fell off this horse because—ironically—I was afraid to say no and be difficult, because I'm not terribly fond of horses and I'm a little afraid of them and I had this accident. The whole thing with *Batman* was: [I just wanted them] to give me five minutes of their time. And they wouldn't do it. It was after my being fired by Warren Beatty—

IG: Warren Beatty?

SY: I worked on *Dick Tracy* for a while. And basically, was sexually harassed by him.

        This kind of thing wasn't news to anybody—what *was* news was I blew the whistle on it. I talked about it. Basically I was being harassed sexually by Warren Beatty, and boy oh boy! He didn't like *that*—I was very angry at the time, with all these people having so much power over the perception of me that *they* were creating. Just because I wasn't willing to put up with shitty stuff. So it was like, strike three, you're out. So Catwoman ended up being—there's one rule in Hollywood you don't break—you don't tell the truth about people in the press. And I broke that rule, and I paid a very, very big price for it, because people didn't trust me.

IG: Do you think the whole "crazy Sean" rap was put on you as a form of punishment?

SY: *Absolutely.* I certainly do. I know that many of the people we've mentioned still describe me that way: "crazy."

IG: Is the James Woods mess over?

SY: Oh yeah. Over a long time ago.

IG: How did it end legally?

SY: He dropped it. He dropped it because I came up with such incriminating evidence that he went, "Uh, sorry!"

IG: Did he set the whole thing up?

SY: He *positively* did.

        And what was interesting, what finally cinched it, was that his girlfriend at the time we were making *The Boost* was very unstable, and he's not such a well cookie either and together they just created this whirlwind and pointed it at me and then we found out—my lawyers and me—we found out that the woman had been arrested by the Beverly Hills Police Department along with these eighteen other girls when that

Madame Alex [famed Hollywood prostitute supplier] was arrested. I found out about it from a hairdresser who knew she was, well, a prostitute. So, this became our evidence, and it was dropped, and it was all stupid and inane, and very hurtful to my career. Probably his too, come to think of it. But that's the whole thing about trying to deal rationally with irrational people—they all go crazy.

It's all people seem to be interested in, to just keep going over this. I think the reason people are fascinated with it, though, is because it's so rare to encounter anyone who has the courage to address these things in an honest manner. The truth scares the shit out of people.

But still, who ultimately cares? Is this how you get on with things, is this how you develop your spirit?

IG: It seems to me you're a victim of the double standard for women. Concerning your attempts to get the Catwoman role, you read about male stars doing zany shit all the time, and *they're* presented as adorable and wacky.

SY: That's true. I really can't say I have an anti-man thing, but what I find is what I call the Weenie World.

The Weenie World is filled with men so insecure they're relating to people from a position of insecurity. The Weenie World is the corporate Hollywood studio moaning that it can't get a hit.

People operating in the Weenie World really don't know of any other world, so they may be at an advantage today, or next year, but at the hour of their deaths, that ego will crumble, and that experience will not be a very pleasant one. They'll say—

IG: —"I'm a Weenie!"

SY: —that's right! And, "Oh—my God! It wasn't how much money I had— it's how much love I've shared that matters."

So that's okay with me on a very basic level. And no, I don't like it when Weenies can have power over me and make my day a little worse. No, I don't like that. But I also say, life is long, and how much love have I shared? And that's a hard thing because love is an intangible, and you think it should be easy but it isn't.

Hollywood is one of those places I try to avoid because these people don't love themselves, they don't know how to *find* it, they don't know where to go for it...

But that's just one side. I've been very fortunate. I *like* men! I find men nowadays very resilient, very open to wanting to know what's going on with women.

What I find about men and women today—it's like what Jung talked about—the collective unconscious of men is *confusion*. There's a lot of men who are confused about how to relate, but if they knew, they'd be willing to. So there is an unfortunate situation among women, in some cases, where the responsibility to train them, to understand how to relate to them is there, and that can be a bit daunting with a woman who may not even know where *she's* at.

IG: You've worked with an impressive list of directors—Gus Van Sant, James Ivory, Ridley Scott, David Lynch. You don't see filmographies like yours very often because it seems that many careers are market-research driven, with all these "handlers" telling them what to do.

SY: Yes. And that's one of the things I *really* didn't like! I didn't like the philosophies of some of the agents I went through because they were trying to get me to wait for the big 12 million. And I was like—

IG: "I'm an actress—I want to work!"

SY: *Right! Right!* When I'm 60 or 100 years old, I want to be able to look back at my work and say "I've done *this* much, and isn't that great!" So that the people who like what I do have a lot to look at. It's not about the box office. And in 20, 30 years, maybe a movie that isn't appreciated now will be.

   I mean, *Blade Runner* was not a big hit in '82 when it came out. Everybody went—in terms of the people who produced it—"Oh! It's a failure!!!"

   They said it was a failure because it didn't make this *huge* amount of money. But it's not a failure. It's the standard by which we judge things. If you're just looking at things from the perspective of the Weenie World...it's just not effective.

   Like I've said, I'm not into "the big score." I'm into the long-term.

IG: In the films after *The Boost* and ending around *Fatal Instinct*—for example, *Love Crimes*, directed by Lizzie Borden—your work seemed oddly distracted. Had all the media crap effected you, were their other factors, or do you disagree?

SY: I know what you're saying. It's true.

   What I was really struggling with at the time was being really depressed at suddenly going from being pretty well-respected and highly regarded to being an outcast, being told I was crazy and people believing this obviously insane asshole [referring to Mr. Woods]. It took a lot of wind out my sails and I lost a lot of blood. A lot of times I was kind of walking through it. I mean—I wasn't trying to walk through it, but it was really hard to get it up when I was now getting breadcrumbs instead of the meal. And it was very disheartening. But I felt that I hung in there. I feel I'm a hard worker and everybody knew that, and it's okay that I had a flat period.

IG: I wasn't being critical as much as—

SY: —no, I look at it—this is *my* criticism! *Fatal Instinct*—I don't think I'm flat
in that. I felt I really put something in there, but then I had someone like
Carl Reiner, who's a total gentleman and is very generous and was trying
to help me get back to making me feel good about myself again. Then
there's films like *Love Crimes*.

    Ugh! What a piece of shit!

IG: What *was* that?

SY: It was Lizzie Borden's personal masturbation, is what it really ended up
being. It wasn't well thought out and what you ended up seeing on the
screen is way different from the script—they even reedited it after the
fact. One of the major problems with that film was I hadn't met Patrick
Bergin—who I love, a wonderful actor, but we just didn't have the chemistry we needed.

    It just turned into an awful nightmare for me. It is probably the
worst experience...I went to work for weeks, getting more and more
insecure and frightened it would be a piece of shit, which it was and so
that's what happened.

IG: Here's two directors you worked with. I wondered what you learned
from them.

    First, Ridley Scott—

SY: —whom I loved! I adored him. He was so nice to me, and he gave me a
lot of attention when it was my turn. The thing about Ridley is he's just
so artistic—

IG: —but he gets this rap about being more interested in visuals then the
actors and—

SY: People say the same thing about Oliver Stone.

    But Stone gets really good results from actors many times. I mean,
he isn't always personable, but I'd work for him again if he'd have me. He
probably wouldn't, but I think his work is powerful, though he's not bal-
anced, he's got way too much Vietnam energy. I don't discredit him, on
the level of being a talented director—he's *obviously* a talented director...

    [Pause] Anyway.

IG: [Pause] Any memories of David Lynch? [Young was the female lead
in *Dune*.]

SY: Oh yeah! He bit off a lot to chew, but I think he was very playful, very
visual and very into detail. And he likes actors. It was also a big learning experience for him too. He'd done *Eraserhead* and *Elephant Man*, so
this was his crash course in doing big-budget, high-expectation,

Everybody-Down-Your-Throat moviemaking, and that has a bad effect on a lot of filmmakers.

IG: But he dealt with it gracefully?

SY: Yeah. In the sense of his personality he did. The film had trouble coming together in the long run because it was a long, *long* movie. [Seven or so hours] It would have been great as a miniseries—that would have been so ecstatic because you could have seen all that he shot, but as a movie—it wasn't as satisfying as the book. It's just hard to make an *excellent* film. I run in the other direction when people say "You should direct" I go: "Uh-uh! No! I am *not* directing!" I'm already in the DGA because I do second unit work, but still—ugh!

IG: It seems your approach to sex scenes is somewhat different than other actors. You've done a lot of nude scenes like those in *No Way Out* or *Love Crimes*—

SY: The good, the bad and the ugly!

IG: Ha! But my point is that other actors sort of walk through sex scenes, or bits involving nudity. You seem very involved in the drama of these scenes. When you do "nudity" it never seems, for lack of a better word, "pornographic." It seems—

SY: —authentic.

IG: Yeah—it's hard to describe.

SY: My background, when I grew up was, dance. Ballet. So there's a lot of physical training that I've been through, and I think ultimately there's an emotional thing going on too. It's like this movie I'm going to make called *Men*—it's gotten a lot of attention in some ways because—

IG: Is this a Sean Young Production?

SY: Yeah. It's basically a woman's version of sexuality. The title says "Men" and there are a lot of men in it, but it's really about women, it's really about me, my character. The character's sexuality and its being expressed in an authentic female point of view. For example—I won't actually be nude in this movie, but all the men will—which in itself will be like "Whoa!" [laughs]

It won't be any less physical because I'm not naked in it—the point of view is that we want to protect the integrity of the woman through-out the movie, and we're saying we *always* see women's bodies but we never look at men's bodies in movies. There's a lot of shame there with men feeling bad about their bodies. It's like: "Who wants to look at a man's body?" Well—*I do!* I don't know about *you,* but I do!

But ugly old cigar-smoking producers think [adopts a grumpy-old-fart-voice] "Ah, who wantsta see a man's bodies—arrgghh!" [laughs] Well, yeah, from that point of view, but from a young female audience, maybe they do but you never get a chance.

I think that's one of the reasons people remember the limo scene in *No Way Out* because I look like *I'm* having fun! And if the woman looks like she's having fun, everybody's having fun.

Then there's *Love Crimes*—we did some shooting of the scenes, and I just wasn't connecting with Patrick and I was like [a teary voice] "Patrick! Oh God, I don't know what's wrong!" What was ultimately wrong was the visceral, physical connection I needed to have with him wasn't happening.

I never blamed him for that. I blamed myself. I felt I should be able to relate to anybody, but what I learned is if you're going to do a movie which has a central sexual theme, make sure that chemistry exists first!

I think people's bodies are *great*—but I really don't like seeing movies that have sex without there being an emotional content to it. You know—here's the porn section. Here's your fuck scene.

IG: Assuming that movies are market research-oriented, what's the story behind the Julia Ormonds, Sandra Bullocks, Andie MacDowells and so on? To me, they seem like '90s office girls—bland, interchangeable. You seem capable of evoking a lost tradition of screen charisma reminiscent of Audrey Hepburn and Ingrid Bergman. Those other women, they just look...*blah*. Why would I want *blah* when there's so much *blah* around me in everyday life?

SY: Well, I think it's a reflection. You put it perfectly—that if you're really reporting back to the culture, and the culture is blah, this is what you're going to find...what's happening is you have some very blah people in positions of power who are doing the best they can to make more blah.

It's like that Mamet play, *Speed the Plow.* You've got this character saying "No are you *kidding? That's what thay want!* They *want* shit!" And then you have this female character saying "No, you need this medium to educate people, to do something wonderful." But until these little Weenies wise up, I can't do it. I tried with Catwoman to make a statement, and the result of it was I got criticism.

IG: What was the statement you were trying to make?

SY: It was like "Hey! I deserve this part! And if I don't deserve the part, I at least deserve five minutes! I *did* break my arm for it! We *are* human beings here, aren't we?"

IG: Who didn't give you the five minutes?

SY: Really, I have no idea. I really have no idea.

But the point is, you can't make wise men out of idiots.

And the women you mentioned, I don't really think they're so bad. I think women are becoming more and more powerful. You have centuries of "stay in that role"—stay in that support position. It's going to take some more centuries to get women to grasp the responsibility and concept of being powerful.

Critic Mark Crispin Miller

CEO Sumner Redstone's (61% of voting stock) Viacom owns MTV, UPN, VH1, Showtime, Simon & Schuster, Paramount Communications, Paramount Parks, movie screens in 11 countries, cable systems serving 1.1 million customers, 12 television stations, and Viacom Interactive Media. It also owns Blockbuster. And Blockbuster owns Virgin Interactive Entertainment and happens to be a major investor in Catapult Entertainment.

To this date, there have been no anti-trust actions against Viacom or its subsidiaries by the FCC.

—Public record

Mark Crispin Miller heads the Film Studies Program and is Chairman of Writing Seminars at Johns Hopkins University in Baltimore. He is also the editor of *Seeing Through Movies*, a compilation of critical essays about corporate-controlled cinema, and *Mad Scientists,* a study of US propaganda techniques.

IG: In *The Nation* [June 3, 1996 and March 17, 1997] you referred to Americans being subjects of a "national entertainment state." Could you explain the basic idea behind this?

MCM: It's the state in which our number two export is entertainment—after aircraft.

And it's a state in which two out of the four major—I mean *only*—TV news networks are owned by defense contractors. GE and Westinghouse. Although you should add that Westinghouse has been trying to sell off its defense properties.

IG: The better to just stick to entertainment?

MCM: *Concentrate* on entertainment.

Shortly after Westinghouse bought CBS, they fired 3,000 people here in Maryland from their various factories. So it would be misleading to say Westinghouse is a booming defense contractor and a booming media conglomerate.

The fact is that Westinghouse is virtually part of a "power trust" created decades ago and has built up its defense-related product—while having always kept its interests in some entertainment. Now it's been booming in that regard since the passage of the Telecommunications Act of 1996.

IG: Which was—

MCM: A landmark piece of legislation dictated by the heads of the entertainment industry to a more than compliant Congress with the purpose really of precipitating mergers and eliminating competition. Although the line at the time was "This is going to enhance competition."

They always say that.

IG: How can you enhance competition by wiping it out?

MCM: Good question, but that was the mantra—and they knew it was horseshit, that they were spinning a line of bull. Get behind closed doors...don't let the little fellas into the arena.

Anyway—the national entertainment state is literally one in which defense interests are closely involved with entertainment corporations. It's also one heavily dependent on a world audience for product coming out of Hollywood and New York.

You see it most clearly in publishing: the book-*publishing* as well as the book-*selling* end of things.

You have Rupert Murdoch [owner of nine publishing houses including HarperCollins, more than 200 newspapers worldwide, and massive holdings in all other media] and Si Newhouse [owner of Random House and 21 other publishing houses, Condé Nast, which publishes major magazines such as *Vanity Fair* and *Vogue*, and over 100 newspapers] and Viacom and Time Warner and Hearst dominating *publishing*, and Borders and Barnes & Noble dominating book *selling*. As these stores go head-to-head in city after city, they necessarily drive independent bookstores out of business.

It's a curious business—a cottage industry at its best. One of the curiosities of this business is the practice of the bookstores using returns to pay for books they've sold. Well, returns have been escalating for the last five years. How does this affect small publishers? Well, it's devastating to them.

It hurts Random House, but Newhouse has all that income from the nation's fourth-largest newspaper chain, and his magazines, Conde Nast—those are cash cows. So he [Newhouse] can take a hit from these returns [from Random House] and concentrate ever harder on junk books—you know, trashy fiction, cookbooks, "health" books—that kind of thing.

So what I'm saying is that in publishing, this ever-larger monopoly is driving small presses and academic presses out of business. You get academic presses trying to compete at Borders and Barnes & Noble.

IG: So it's like low-budget films fighting for screens at multiplexes already owned by companies that often fill the same theaters with their product. An effective monopoly.

MCM: Yes...all the houses alike are struggling to meet a mass audience, while academic houses search out trendy subjects. And more rarefied subjects—they just won't do 'em anymore.

IG: Going back to what you said earlier about defense companies running entertainment companies: the way things are today, isn't *information* the same thing as *defense?*

Isn't the new cold war a war of data—who knows what, when?

MCM: Yes. Especially when you consider the important role information plays in propaganda. State propaganda. I mean, you don't want to take this so far that you're envisioning a conscious conspiracy. [But] there *is* definitely an ideological bias in both Houses [of Congress] that comes from the top. You know, for years now certain books have been killed—put out of trace by the CIA. They're published...but you never hear of them. The press is intimidated.

IG: The same with films.

MCM: Yes, but I keep returning to book publishing because historically, it was the most likely of all the cultures to honor the Bill of Rights, precisely because publishing was *not* a mass medium.

You didn't worry as much about offending large numbers of people and you weren't dependent on advertising. Newspapers, magazines, movies, TV and radio have always been fairly timid, because they've always been commercial.

Book publishing *was* different—you could imagine disseminating certain new ideas, gradually, through a subculture of readers. It's harder to do that now. Some titles have been "killed", books that have been—let's say *blunted* by, ah, *interference* of some kind...And of late, it's been happening more and more to books *on* the media, as these huge media conglomerates absorb the publishing companies.

Marc Elliot wrote *Hollywood's Dark Prince* about Walt Disney. Bantam killed it, on the basis of notes the author had sent them! They said this was of unpublishable quality.

Then he found out Bantam had a deal to do the Disney Library in supermarkets! This is before Disney started their own publishing arm, Hyperion.

So there's no mystery why Disney killed it.

IG: So how does "disinformation" work in entertainment, in film? Does this manifest itself in making everything released so content-lite, that it becomes, in essence, a platform for whatever ad or agenda one wants to push?

MCM: I'd say these things work together...the fact is that they rely on market censorship to assure the elimination of any kind of film or book that might trouble people too much.

IG: So it's more of an ambient thing: people smell the weather and just go along with it.

MCM: Right. And don't forget that if you're an employee for one of these companies, you have to develop an instinct for picking winners.

Which doesn't *just* mean things that will sell, but also things that won't piss off your boss!

IG: Yeah, but it's such a precarious way to run things. To put all your eggs in one basket.

MCM: It's like the way General Mills will come out with six cereals, and those six cereals will be competing with each other for shelf space! [An example of how corporations create the illusion of competition] They just don't want Post [a competing cereal brand] to get any space. [laughs]

And—there *is* a limit to how far this can go, it seems to me. Because, the fact is, several of these industries are in big trouble. The publishing houses are *hemorrhaging* money; it's only a matter of time before these big guys start selling them off.

Hollywood has been doing very poorly—both critically and financially. A movie like *Mission Impossible* will often open very big, but end up losing a bundle, because they're spending $30 to $40 million on publicity alone, on top of these obscene salaries they're paying the stars and that sort of thing.

Only one of the big action films last year made any money: *Independence Day.* The rest were all duds.

So it's striking that the Oscar committee only found fit to give one Best Picture nomination to only one major studio release this year. It's amazing.

And the same with popular music—sales are seriously down. The industry is in the doldrums. And finally, TV news—the rate of viewing has declined by something like 10% over the last two years. Now...the people who are not buying new CDs, [or] going to see new "blockbusters" are a lot of people getting bored by stuff that's made by the numbers, according to safe formulas.

The problem is that these people who generate this garbage are like *robots!* They obey a certain kind of market imperative, that pushes them in the direction of ever-larger projects. They will not takes risks. Ever. It's alien to them. The market is risk-adverse.

IG: An executive I spoke with lives in mortal terror of that fateful summer when there's *nothing* but a slate of *Independence Days* and they *all* bomb. Um—not to get all millennial or anything, but is that what it will take for there to be some sort of turnaround in all this crap?

MCM: You mean a big Crash?

IG: Yeah—a Crash of '29, Hollywood-style.

MCM: Well—yes, but the only real change will take place when such economic failure helps to inspire antitrust movements.

IG: So why, in a business environment where production, reportage, distribution—the whole ball of wax—is basically done "in-house", why the hell haven't there been any antitrust actions?

MCM: Both political parties are heavily dependent on these companies. For a certain kind of "coverage," and for campaign contributions.

IG: And the FCC—

MCM: [Incredulous at the very idea] The *FCC?* It's a *joke!*

It was formed as part of the Communications Act of 1934, the purpose of which was to certify the commercial nature of broadcasting.

There was a big struggle between '27 and '34. On the one hand, you had the broadcast industry, on the other, labor groups, religious groups—a rather diverse movement *against* broadcasting being deemed commercial.

By now we accept that as being as natural as the birds and the bees, but it doesn't have to be commercial. They lost that battle, and you could say they lost the war when that Communications Act was passed in '34. And the FCC acts as a sort of umpire between competing large interests. There's no way—

Wait. Listen. I'll tell you a story:

That chart that came out in *The Nation* got some press before its publication. [A chart of Viacom, Sony, Time Warner, etc. and the multiple entertainment/information companies they own, [see pages 230-231]

When Frank Rich did a column for *The New York Times*, I met him at the Media and Democracy Conference in San Francisco. And I was passing out copies of the chart. Well, I got a lot of phone calls from that. I got one from the FCC!

This guy in their Policies and Rules Division called and was struck by what he read. He said he'd been talking to some of the economists here [at the FCC] and "realized that we don't really trace this sort of thing like you have!" Do you *believe* that?!

The FCC asked *me* for that information!!! That was a sobering moment for me. Nobody's watching out for the public interest. *Nobody.*

Historically, antitrust has only happened when there has been a certain amount of popular pressure. So the Justice Department will do nothing unless and until the left *and* right work together, because both of them have a beef with the media, they just go after different problems. The right's worried about "smut" and violence and stuff like that, while the left's worried about corporate censorship and racial stereotypes.

IG: So they're arguing themselves into the margins while the entertainment monopolies just go right ahead with business as planned.

MCM: Oh yeah.

IG: Divide and conquer.

MCM: So they do *The People vs. Larry Flynt* to show how much they believe in free expression by characterizing anyone who didn't like Larry Flynt as being a kind of fanatic or buffoon.

But the real threats to free expression don't come from Bible thumpers—they don't even come from schoolboards, prudes and prigs. They come from very *hip,* well-paid media executives and the whole system which is *geared away* from certain kinds of content.

IG: So that film is really just a self-serving red herring.

MCM: Oh, absolutely! That film was disgusting. A bullshit red herring. Self—congratulatory—as if tits and ass were the most important thing in the world.

IG: Many major studio execs justify the hyper-pace, special effects–driven blockbuster as a simple reaction to the "needs" of the marketplace. But since these same executives work for corporations who *define* the marketplace itself, isn't this defense a bit ingenuous, to say the least?

MCM: Yes. They always act as if they've had no hand in shaping the culture that they're in.

What they have in mind is: One [pause] Enormous [pause] Audience. Of youngish people. And they pitch everything at that audience.

IG: But isn't there an audience for films that have pace, story and characters?

MCM: Yes, yes. The fact is, you can use indirection and narrative devices [such as in *Sling Blade*, a very popular film] and people always act terribly surprised it's been done!...But the main point is that all the studios are interested in are those huge films, pitched as they are to that semi-fictitious "majority" or "plurality" of viewers. The films become ever less coherent, and less riveting. They struggle so hard to keep the adrenaline flowing—

IG: Speaking of adrenaline—there seems to be almost an addiction to this sensory spectacle. Have audiences grown so used to relentless sound levels, ultra-fast, bewildering editing and such, that their ability to engage in less overloaded fare has atrophied?

MCM: It's interesting you should ask me that, because I teach film—I'm teaching Kubrick right now. And I always tell my students at the start that after this you'll be incapable of seeing a lot of the stuff playing at the multiplex. And I'm delighted to say, for most of them, that's what happens.

It's just a matter of *re-learning* how to concentrate in a certain way. So you *can* actually so gripped and interested by [a filmmaker like Kubrick], that the *pleasure* of that is greater than the cruder pleasure of just watching effects and bullets shooting.

IG: Well, there's plenty of bullets flying in Kubrick's films—like that exploding elevator of blood in *The Shining*. But I think it's a matter of context and artistry.

MCM: Yeah—the flash cut of those butchered children. But its effects are *uncanny*, as opposed to simply grotesque.

IG: Yeah, well—in action movies, it's all just the cum-shot aesthetic.

MCM: [Laughs] The point is, people are going to be numbed by *any* sort of mindless, repeated assault.

IG: Which is what I meant by "addicted." Addicted to movies that just numb you out.

MCM: I think so.

There's a phrase of James Agee's I always quote: "That special nirvana of boredom." And he's writing in the 1940s!

Of course, he had *no idea* what was coming...

CORPORATE STRUCTURE

VIACOM

*CEO Sumner Redstone controls
61% of voting stock*

Movies:
Paramount Pictures

Movie Theater Chains:
Cinamerica (50% with Time
Warner), Famous Players, Canada
(50% with MCA), Films
Paramount, Europe

Home Video:
Blockbuster Video,
Paramount Home Video

Cable:
Comedy Central (50% with
Time Warner), MTV, M2: Music
Television, Nickelodeon, Nick at
Night, Paramount Channel (UK
part owner), Sci-Fi Channel
(50% with Seagrams), Showtime,
Sundance Channel (45% with
Seagrams and Robert Redford),
USA Network (50% with
Seagrams), VH-1

Publishers:
Aquilar, Archway, Fireside, Folger
Shakespeare Library, Libros en
Espanol, Lisa Drew Books,
Martin Kessler Books, Minstrel
Books, MTV Books, Pocket
Books, Pocket Star Books,
Scribner, Simon & Schuster
(largest educational publisher in
the US–1995 sales over $1 bil-
lion), The Free Press, Touchstone,
Washington Square Press

Television:
Paramount Television, Spelling
Entertainment, UPN Network
(50%, includes 152 affiliates), TV
stations: 11

Radio Stations: 10

Theme Parks:
Canada's Wonderland,
Carowinds, Great America, Kings
Dominion, Kings Island

TIME WARNER

*Ted Turner owns 10% of stock, TCI chair John Malone and Seagrams
each own 9%, and LA investment firm The Capital Group has 7.5%*

Movies:
Warner Brothers, Warner
Brothers Animated

Home Video:
Time-Life Video, HBO, Warner
Home Video

Cable:
Cinemax, CNN/SI (sports net-
work being formed with Turner
Broadcasting), Comedy Central
(50% with Viacom), Court TV
(General Electric owns 33%), E!
(Owns 49% with others), HBO,
Sega Channel

TV Programming:
Warner Brothers Television, Witt
Thomas Productions

Book Publishing:
Book-of-the-Month Club, Little,
Brown & Co., Oxmoor House,
Sunset Books, Time-Life Books,
Warner Books

Magazines:
*American Lawyer, Asia Week,
Baby Talk, Cooking Light, Dancyu,*
DC Comics (50%), *Entertainment
Weekly, Fortune, Health,
Hippocrates, In Style, Life, Martha
Stewart Living, Money, Parenting,
People, President, Southern Living,
Sports Illustrated, Sports Illustrated
for Kids, Sunset, Time, Vibe, Who*

Music:
Columbia House (50%), Elektra
Entertainment Group, SubPop
(50%), The Atlantic Group,
TimeWarner Audio Books,
Warner Brothers Records,
Warner Music, Alternative
Distribution Alliance

Turner Broadcasting:
CNN, CNN interactive
(internet), Turner Home
Entertainment, Turner Home
Satellite, Turner New Media
(CD-ROM), Turner Publishing,
Turner Retail Group, Castle
Rock Cinema, New Line
Cinema, Fine Line Cinema,
Turner Entertainment (RKO,
MGM and pre-1950 Warner
Bros. Films), Turner Pictures,
World Championship Wrestling

Misc. Turner:
Atlanta Braves, Atlanta Hawks,
Goodwill Games

Misc. Time Warner Holdings:
HBO (25%), Houston Industries,
Seagrams (14.5%), Six Flags
Theme Parks, Time Warner
Entertainment

Various Cable Franchises:
11.7 million subscribers

SOURCE: *The Nation*, June 3, 1996 and March 17, 1997.

CORPORATE STRUCTURE

NEWS CORPORATION	DISNEY/ CAP CITIES	SONY CORP. OF AMERICA

CEO Rupert Murdoch controls about 30% of stock

Sid R. Bass et al (crude petroleum and natural gas production, 6.02% owners before merger) Berkshire Hathaway Inc. (insurance; Warren Buffet, CEO, 12% owners prior to merger)

Movies:
Fox 2000, Fox Family Films, Fox Searchlight Pictures, Fox Studios Australia, Twentieth Century Fox

Television:
22 stations, Fox Network, Twentieth Century Fox Television

Newspapers:
London Times, more than 200 papers in Australia, Fiji, New Guinea, New Zealand, inserts for 622 US papers, *New York Post*, *The Sun*

Magazines:
40% of 18 magazines in Australia, Europe and New Zealand, *Pacific Islands Monthly*, *The Weekly Standard*, *TV Guide*

Cable and Satellite
TV: BSkyB, British Satellite TV (40%), DF1, German Satellite TV (49%), Fox Kids Worldwide (50%), Fox News Channel (50%), Fox Sports International, Fox Sports Net, FOXTEL (Australia) (50%), JSkyJ, Japan Satellite TV (50%), STAR TV (satellite TV, reaches Africa, China, India, Southeast Asia), Various cable stations in Latin America

Publishing:
HarperCollins, Basic Books, Harper Business, Harper Perennial, Harper Prism, Harper Reference, Harper San Francisco, Regan Books, Westview Press

Multimedia:
20 Web sites, CD-ROM publishing, iGuide

Misc.:
Sheep farming, paper production, Australian Airlines (50%)

Movies:
Buena Vista Pictures, Hollywood Pictures, Miramax Film Corp., Touchstone Pictures, Walt Disney Pictures

Home Video: Buena Vista

Multimedia:
ABC Online (with AOL), Americast, Disney Interactive, Disney.com

TV and Cable:
A&E (co-owned with Hearst and GE), Buena Vista Television, Disney Channel, Disney Television, ESPN (80%), ESPN 2 (80%), Lifetime Network, Touchstone Television

Theme Parks and Resorts:
Celebration (a planned community near Orlando, FL), Disney Cruiseline, Disney Institute, Disney Vacation Club, Disneyland, Disneyland Paris, Tokyo Disneyland, Walt Disney World Resort, WCO Vacationland Resorts

ABC:
ABC Radio (21 stations), TV stations in 10 major markets, plus 14% interest in Young Broadcasting, with 8 stations, ABC Network News (including PrimeTime Live, Good Morning America, 20/20, Nightline, and World News Tonight)

Magazines:
Chilton Publications (trade), Fairchild Publications (trade), *LA Magazine*, Institutional Investor, Disney Publications

Newspapers:
11 secondary market dailies, including *Ft. Worth Star-Telegram*, *Kansas City Star*

Book Publishing:
Hyperion, Miramax Books, an unnamed ESPN imprint

Misc.:
California Angels (25%), Mighty Ducks, State Farm Insurance (6%)

Movies:
Castle Rock (distribution), Columbia Pictures, Mandalay Entertainment (distribution), Sony Pictures Classics, Sony Pictures Entertainment, TriStar Pictures, Triumph Films (releasing), Sony Pictures Imageworks (digital effects), SDDS (theater sound system), Sony Studios/Culver City Studios

Television:
Sony Television Entertainment, Columbia/TriStar Television, Columbia/TriStar Television Distribution, Columbia/TriStar International Television, Television library includes: 35,000 television episodes, 270 television series, more than 40,000 episodes of game show programming

Music:
57 Records, 550 Music, Columbia, Epic, Epic Soundtrax, Relativity Recordings, Shotput Records, Sony Classical, Sony Music International, Sony Wonder, The WORK Group, TriStar Music

Music Publishing:
Sony/ATV Music Publishing (which owns and/or administers music copyrights of Michael Jackson, The Beatles, Elvis Presley and more)

Personal and Home Audio-Visual:
Sony Electronics, Inc. product line includes Handycam camcorders, Walkman, Discman, MiniDisc, Trinitron televisions, Sony brand Digital Satellite System (DSS), Sony WebTV Internet Terminal

Bibliography

Angeli, Michael, "Sean Young: Out There Where the Trains Don't Run," *Esquire,* November, 1991.

Angell, Marcia, *Science on Trial: The Clash of Medical Evidence and the Law in the Breast Implant Case* (New York: W. W. Norton & Co., 1996).

Arbus, Diane, *Untitled* (Millerton: Aperture, 1995).

Author Unknown, "Battery Charge," *People,* June 23, 1997.

Baudrillard, Jean, *The Transparency of Evil: Essays on Extreme Phenomena* (London, New York: Verso, 1993).

Bellafante, Ginia, "Broken Peace," [on Kevin Costner] *Time,* July 31, 1995.

Berger, John, *Ways of Seeing* (London: Penguin Books, 1972).

Bernard, Jami, *First Films: Illustrious, Obscure and Embarrassing Film Debuts* (New York: Citadel Press, 1993).

Biskind, Peter, "The Last Crusade," in *Seeing Through Movies*, Mark Crispin Miller, ed. (New York: Pantheon Books, 1990).

Brownmiller, Susan, *Against Our Will: Men, Women and Rape* (New York: Simon & Schuster, 1975).

Cawelti, John G., *Adventure, Mystery and Romance: Formula Stories as Art and Popular Culture* (Chicago: University of Chicago Press, 1976).

Cerio, Gregory, et al, "Mel Content," *People,* November 11, 1996.

Clover, Carol J, *Men, Women and Chainsaws: Gender in the Modern Horror Film* (Princeton: Princeton University Press, 1992).

Cocteau, Jean, *Diary of an Unknown* (New York: Paragon House, 1988).

Corliss, Richard, "Hugh and Cry," *Time,* August 24, 1995.

Donald, James, ed., *Fantasy and the Cinema* (London: British Film Institute, 1989).

Dunn, Katherine, *Geek Love* (New York: Alfred A. Knopf, 1983).

Editorial profile, "Elizabeth Hurley," *People,* December 25, 1995.

Editorial, "Top 10 Movies: Critically Scorned Dr. Moreau Beats Bradys" *New York Daily News,* August 26, 1996.

Edwards, Henry, "Young Times," *Vogue,* November 11, 1988.

Eisner, Lotte H., *The Haunted Screen: Expressionism in the German Cinema* (Berkeley: University of California Press, 1973).

Eliade, Mircea, *Images and Symbols* (Princeton: Princeton University Press, 1991).

Farber, Stephen and Green, Marc, *Outrageous Conduct: Art, Ego and the Twilight Zone* Case (New York: Ivy Books, 1988).

Ferrante, Anthony, "Postproduction Hell," *Fangoria,* April, 1996.

Fleming, Charles, "That Sinking Feeling," *Vanity Fair*, August, 1995.

Fleming, Michael, "Disney, TriStar greenlight top-ticket 'Troopers'," *Variety,* March 25-31, 1996.

Fredericksen, Eric, "Postmark: Seattle, Rock Recession," *New York Press*, June 3, 1997.

Fussell, Paul, *BAD or, The Dumbing of America* (New York: Touchstone Books, 1991).

Gerosa, Melina, "The Agony and Ecstasy of Sean Young," *Entertainment Weekly*, February 7, 1992.

Gordon, Keith, "Hell on Reels," *Details,* June, 1997.

Griffin, Nancy and Masters, Kim, *Hit & Run: How Jon Peters and Peter Guber Took Sony for a Ride in Hollywood* (New York: Simon & Schuster, 1996).

Hamill, Denis, "May the Bettor Man Win," [on James Toback] *The Daily News*, February 2, 1997.

Harlan, Bill, "American Album: Bad Days at Black Hills for Developer Costner," *Los Angeles Times,* May 25, 1995.

Haskell, Molly, *From Reverence to Rape: The Treatment of Women in the Movies* (Chicago: University of Chicago Press, 1987).

Hawkes, Terence, *Structuralism and Semiotics* (Berkeley, Los Angeles: University of California Press, 1977).

Hiaasen, Carl, *Stormy Weather* (New York: Alfred A. Knopf, 1995).

Hiassen, Carl, *Striptease* (New York: Alfred A. Knopf, 1993).

Hirschberg, Lynn, "Introducing Jimmy Woods," *Esquire,* April, 1984.

Hosoda, Craig, *The Bare Facts Video Guide: Fifth Edition* (Santa Clara: The Bare Facts, 1994).

Huss, Roy and Ross, T.J., eds. *Focus on the Horror Film* (Englewood Cliffs: Prentice-Hall, 1972).

Kaplan, E. Ann, ed., *Women in Film Noir* (London: British Film Institute, 1978).

Kawin, Bruce F., "Review of The Funhouse and The Howling," *Film Quarterly*, Fall, 1981.

Kendall, Pamela. *Torn Illusions: One Woman's Tragic Experience with the Silicone Conspiracy.* (New Jersey: New Horizon Press, 1994).

King, Stephen, *Danse Macabre* (New York: Everest House, 1981).

Kuhn, Annette, ed., *Alien Zone: Cultural Theory and Contemporary Science Fiction Cinema* (London, New York: Verso Books, 1990).

Masters, Kim, "Days of Thunder, Nights of Despair," *Vanity Fair,* April, 1996.

McClintick, David, *Indecent Exposure: A True Story of Hollywood and Wall Street* (New York: Dell, 1987).

Miller, Mark Crispin and Jaquet Biden, Janine, "The National Entertainment State," *The Nation*, June 3, 1996.

Miller, Mark Crispin, "The Crushing Power of Big Publishing," *The Nation*, March 17, 1997.

Miller, Mark Crispin, ed. *Seeing through Movies* (New York: Pantheon Books, 1990).

Moravec, Hans, *Mind Children: The Future of Robot and Human Intelligence* (Cambridge, Boston: Harvard Books, 1988).

Mulay, James J., ed., *The Horror Film* (Evanston: Cinebooks, 1989).

Murray, John P. *Kansas City Journal Law & Public Policy*. Kansas City. Vol. 4, 1994

Newman, Kim, *Nightmare Movies* (New York: Harmony Books, 1988).

O'Sullivan, Kevin, "The Sinking of The Island of Doctor Moreau: Incredible behind-the-scenes battle between the stars of the No. 1 movie," *New York Daily News*, September 1, 1996.

Patterson, James and Kim, Peter, *The Day America Told the Truth* (New York: Plume, 1991).

Polanski, Roman, *Roman* (New York: William Morrow and Company, 1984).

Postman, Neil, *Technopoly: The Surrender of Culture to Technology* (New York: Vintage Books, 1993).

Queenan, Joe, *If You're Talking to Me, Your Career Must be in Trouble* (New York: Hyperion, 1994).

Rainer, Peter, ed. *Love & Hisses: The National Society of Film Critics Sound Off on the Hottest Film Controversies* (San Francisco: Mercury House, 1992).

Richman, Alan, "Black Belt, White Lies," *GQ*, March, 1991.

Rodley, Chris, ed., *Cronenberg on Cronenberg* (London: Faber and Faber, Ltd., 1992).

Rosenbaum, Ron, "(Sean)Young Love," *Mademoiselle,* May 1992.

Runstein, Robert E., *Modern Recording Techniques* (Indianapolis: Howard Sams & Co., Inc., 1971).

Salamon, Julie, *The Devil's Candy* (New York: Dell, 1991).

Schiff, Stephen, "The Last Wild Man," *The New Yorker*, August 8, 1994.

Schindehette, Susan, et al, "Fear and Loathing in Hollywood," [on Sean Young] *People*, March 20, 1987.

Schneider, Karen S, "A Night to Remember," *People,* July 1, 1995.

Seminara, George, *Mug Shots: Celebrities Under Arrest* (New York: St. Martins Press, 1996).

Shaw, Andrea, ed. (Grey, Ian, Assistant Editor), *Seen That, Now What?* (New York: Fireside, 1996).

Sherman, Eric, *Directing the Film: Film Directors on their Art* (Los Angeles: American Film Institute, 1976).

Skal, David J. and Savada, Elias, *Dark Carnival: The Secret World of Tod Browning, Hollywood's Master of the Macabre* (New York: Anchor Books, 1995).

Skal, David J., *The Monster Show: A Cultural History of Horror* (New York: W. W. Norton & Company, 1993).

Skal, David J., *Hollywood Gothic: The Tangled Web of Dracula from Novel to Stage to Screen* (New York: W. W. Norton & Company, 1990).

Stott-Kendall, Pamela, *Torn Illusions: Fully Documented, Public Expose of the Worldwide Silicone Implants* (Debcar Publishing, 1996).

Thomas, Gordon, *Journey into Madness: The True Story of Secret CIA Mind Control and Medical Abuses* (New York: Bantam Books, 1989).

Thompson, William Irwin, *Imaginary Landscape: Making Worlds of Myth and Science* (New York: St. Martin's Press, 1989).

Todorov, Tzvetan, *Genres in Discourse* (Cambridge: Cambridge University Press, 1990).

Vollers, Maryanne, "Costner's Last Stand," *Esquire,* June, 1996.

Wojnarowicz, David; Blinderman, Barry, ed. *Tongues of Flame* [*Witnesses: Against Our Vanishing*, Artist's Space, NYC], (Illinois: University Galleries of Illinois State University, 1990).

Waller, Gregory A., ed., *American Horrors* (Illinois: University of Illinois Press, 1987).

Waters, John, *Crackpot: The Obsessions of John Waters* (New York: Vintage, 1987).

Weinraub, Bernard, "Summer's Big Bangs Yield to Thoughts Of Oscars," *New York Times,* September 10, 1996.

Wolcott, James, "*Independence Day,*" [capsule review] *The New Yorker,* July 15, 1996.

Wolcott, James, "Reborn on the Fourth of July: It's America 1, Aliens 0 in *Independence Day,*" *The New Yorker,* July 15, 1996.

Wood, Robin, "Return of the Repressed," *Film Comment #14,* July–August 1978.

Woodward, Richard B, "Fighting His Way to the Top: Brash and Contentious James Woods is Hollywood's Leading Outcast," *New York Times Magazine,* August 20, 1989.

Young, Josh, "Glug, Glug," *The New Republic,* August 14, 1995.

Zierold, Norman, *The Moguls: Hollywood's Merchants of Myth* (Hollywood: Silman-James, 1969).

CATALOG OF AVAILABLE TITLES

Order books directly from us to receive a special mail order discount, or look for them in your favorite bookstore.

Bodies of Subversion
A Secret History of Women and Tattoo
by Margot Mifflin

This book is the first history to uncover the subversive relationship of women and tattoo. It chronicles the rises and falls which parallel women's movements from the 19th century, again surging in the suffragist '20s and resurfacing in the '70s.

Did you know Winston Churchill's mother wore a serpent tattoo on her wrist? Over 180 (many never-before-seen) photos of tattooed women from the last hundred years.

"In this provocative work full of intriguing female characters from tattoo history, Margot Mifflin makes a persuasive case for the tattooed woman as an emblem of female self-expression."–Susan Faludi, Pulitzer Prize-winning author of *Backlash*.

8 ½ x 11, 192 pages, b&w photos. Retail $23.95,　**Mail Order Special $19**.

Dangerous Drawings
Interviews with Comix and Graphix Artists
by Andrea Juno

Fourteen of the most provocative, vital and boundary-breaking artists of today candidly discuss their lives, art and experiences. Featuring: Art Spiegelman (*Maus*), Dan Clowes (*Eightball*), Julie Doucet (*Dirty Plotte*), Chris Ware (*ACME Novelty Library*), G.B. Jones (the lesbian Tom of Finland), Ted Rall, Diane Noomin (*Twisted Sisters*), Emiko "Carol" Shimoda (manga artist), Matt Reid, Chester Brown (*Yummy Fur*), Aline Kominsky-Crumb (*Weirdo*), Eli Langer, Phoebe Gloeckner, Keith Mayerson (*Horror Hospital Unplugged*).

"Comics are a warm, friendly medium. You can deal with the most hateful issues and yet it still comes across as being palatable or even cheerful."–Dan Clowes

8 ½ x 11, 224 pages, hundreds of b&w illustrations. Retail $24.99,
Mail Order Special $19.

Concrete Jungle

A Pop Media Investigation of Death and Survival in Urban Ecosystems
Edited by Mark Dion and Alexis Rockman

"The next time you throw a dinner party, bring this provocative, compelling and amusing volume to the table."–*Time Out NY*

This book explores what happens when urban and human environments intersect with nature.

"*Concrete Jungle* displays a nice millennial desperation, providing for natural history and biology what *Apocalypse Culture* provided for sociology and conspiracy theory."–*Detroit Metro-Times*

7 ½ x 9 ½ 224 pages, b&w photos and illustrations. Retail $24.99,

Mail Order Special $19.

Horror Hospital Unplugged
A Graphic Novel
by Dennis Cooper and Keith Mayerson

Cutting-edge author Dennis Cooper and notorious artist Keith Mayerson team up to bring us this queer psychedelic slacker tale of Trevor Machine: a twentysomething gay-but-sexually-confused lead singer for an LA indie band on its way to fame and fortune.

"Cooper's idiosyncratic morality meets cartoonist Keith Mayerson's manga-like style in this ruthless and rude book. Totally recommended."–*Gay Times*

8 ½ x 11, 256 illustrated pages. Retail $24.95,　　**Mail Order Special $19.**

Angry Women in Rock, Volume 1
by Andrea Juno

"Please note, this book contains a lot of explicit sexual talk, violence and pro-fanity."–*Rockrgrl*

Angry Women in Rock takes up where best-selling *Angry Women* left off–a book that inspired a generation of young women to redefine feminism for themselves. Thirteen female musicians and producers are featured, including Chrissie Hynde, Joan Jett, Kathleen Hanna (Bikini Kill), 7 Year Bitch, Jarboe (Swans), Tribe 8 (the all-dyke punk band), Kendra Smith, Naomi Yang (Galaxie 500), Phranc (the "All-American Jewish Lesbian Folksinger"), Lois, June Millington (of Fanny, '60s hard-rocking, all-female band), and more!

7½ x 9 ½ 224 pages, b&w photos. Retail $19.95,　　**Mail Order Special $15.**

Angry Women

by Andrea Juno

An enduring best-seller since its first printing in 1991, Angry Women equipped a new generation of women with an expanded vision of what feminism could be, influencing Riot Grrrls, college curricula and beyond.

"This is hardly the nurturing, womanist vision espoused in the 1970s. The view here is largely pro-sex, pro-porn and pro-choice."—*The Village Voice*

Including Diamanda Galas, Lydia Lunch, Sapphire, Karen Finley, Annie Sprinkle, Susie Bright, bell hooks, Kathy Acker, and many more!

8 ½ x 11, 240 pages, b&w photos.   **Mail Order $19**.

Incredibly Strange Music, Volume II

"The bible of lounge music is *Incredibly Strange Music*."—*Newsweek*

"Fans of ambient music, acid jazz, ethno-techno, even industrial rock, will find the leap back to these genres an easy one to make."—*Rolling Stone*

Categories include: Brazilian Psychedelic, Outer Space, Exotica-Ploitation, Singing Truck Drivers, Yodeling, Abstract Female Vocals, Religious Ventriloquism, Sitar Rock, Theremin, Harmonica, and much, much more!

8 ½ x 11, 240 pages, b&w photos.   **Mail Order $18**.
                                                    CD available for $13.

Guide to Bodily Fluids

by Paul Spinrad

Bringing bodily functions out of the (water) closet, this book examines everything you ever wanted to know (but were afraid to ask) about bodily functions. Topics include Mucus, Sweat, Vomit, Urine, Earwax, Menstruation, Feces, Saliva, Semen, Toe Cheese, and more!

"The Re/Search Guide to Bodily Fluids is a must buy....Spinrad dips into the river that runs through each and every one of us with the erudition and penetrating insight of one who knows the subtle pleasures of anal retentiveness."—*Bikini*

8 ½ x 11, 148 pages.   **Mail Order $16**.

Qty.	Title	Price ea.	Line total
	Bodies of Subversion	$ 19	
	Dangerous Drawings	$ 19	
	Concrete Jungle	$ 19	
	Horror Hospital Unplugged	$ 19	
	Angry Women in Rock, Volume 1	$ 15	
	Angry Women	$ 19	
	Incredibly Strange Music, Volume II	$ 18	
	Incredibly Strange Music CD	$ 13	
	Guide to Bodily Fluids	$ 16	

Shipping and Handling:

Domestic: Add $4 for the first item, plus $1
    for each additional item.
International: Add $10 for the first item, plus
    $3 for each additional item.

SUBTOTAL	
+ NY Sales Tax	
+ shipping	
TOTAL	

**New York residents please add 8.25% sales tax. Payment in US Dollars only.
Call toll free 1–800–758–5238 to order by Visa or Mastercard**

Mailing address: 180 Varick Street, 10th Floor, New York, NY 10014
Phone: 212-807-7300, Fax: 212-807-7355, Email: junobook@interport.net
Or order from our website at www.junobooks.com
For a complete catalog, send a SASE to the above address.

Name _____

email _____

(Shipping address) Street _____

City _____ State _____ Zip _____

Day phone _____ Night phone (essential) _____

Credit Card (circle one)   Mastercard   Visa

Name as it appears on card: _____

Credit Card Number: _____

Expiration Date: _____